The Noah Man

RANDALL J. BREWER

THE NOAH MAN

CONTENTS

INTRODUCTION

There are seasons in history when the world becomes so loud, so dark, and so rebellious that righteousness looks strange. In those days, compromise becomes common, conviction becomes rare, and men are pressured to bend with the culture instead of stand with God. It was in such a generation that Noah lived. The Bible says the earth was corrupt before God and filled with violence, yet in the middle of that darkness, one man stood out. Noah found grace in the eyes of the Lord. He was a just man. He was perfect in his generations. He walked with God. That is the making of a righteous man.

Noah was not righteous because the world around him made righteousness easy. He was righteous because he chose to walk with God when the world around him was walking away from God. He did not need popular approval to obey divine instruction. He did not wait for the crowd to understand before he began building. He heard God, believed God, feared God, obeyed God, and built what God commanded him to build. While others lived carelessly, Noah lived carefully. While others ignored the warning, Noah moved with reverence. While others laughed, Noah labored. While others refused to prepare, Noah built an ark.

A Noah man is a man who understands that true manhood is not proven by how loudly he talks, how much he owns, or how many people follow him. True manhood is proven by whether he can remain faithful to God in an unfaithful generation. It is proven by whether he can lead his household when the culture is confused. It is proven by whether he can keep building when no rain has fallen yet. It is proven by whether he can trust God enough to obey instructions that other people may not understand.

Every man will face a flood of some kind. It may be a flood of temptation, pressure, ridicule, responsibility, fear, loss, or spiritual attack. The question is not whether the storm will come. The question is whether the man will be prepared before it arrives. Noah's life teaches us that preparation is not panic - it is faith. Obedience is not weakness - it is wisdom. Separation from corruption is not pride - it is devotion. Building what God commanded is not foolish - it is survival.

This book is a call to men who refuse to drift with the current of a corrupt age. It is a call to fathers, husbands, leaders, servants, builders, and warriors of faith. It is a call to men who want more than a reputation - they want righteousness. It is a call to men who are willing to walk with God even when the world walks away. It is a call to become the kind of man God can trust with an assignment, a household, a warning, and a future.

The Noah man does not simply survive the storm. He prepares before the storm. He obeys during the storm. He worships after the storm. And through his faith, his obedience becomes a covering for others. This is not just the story of Noah. This is the making of a righteous man.

| 1 |

"A MAN WHO STANDS OUT"

In every generation there is a dividing line not drawn by culture, popularity, or power, but by the posture of a man's heart toward God. Some choose the safety of blending in, drifting with the current of compromise, silencing conviction to avoid resistance. But others, like Noah, refuse to be shaped by the spirit of their age. In a world saturated with violence and corruption, Noah stood as a contradiction to everything around him. He did not wait for the world to change - he chose to walk with God when no one else would. That is what made him different. Not perfection, but alignment. Not popularity, but obedience. And because of that, Scripture declares that he "found grace in the eyes of the Lord." That same call echoes today. God is still searching for men who will stand out - not in pride, but in righteousness; not in rebellion against people, but in surrender to Him. To stand out for God means you will often stand alone, misunderstood by a world that has chosen darkness over light.

Noah did not live in easy times. He walked with God in a world that had rejected Him, a world where corruption was normal and righteousness was rare. Scripture tells us that Noah found grace in the eyes of the Lord because his heart was set apart. This is the mark of a godly man: he is not shaped by the darkness around him, but by the light within him. When others followed the current of sin, he stood against it. When the world grew louder in rebellion, he grew deeper in obedience showing that a man does not have to mirror the culture he lives in. You can live clean in a dirty world and live upright in a crooked generation. God is not looking for men who fit in - He is looking for men who will stand out. Noah's life reminds us that one man, fully surrendered to God, can become a vessel of purpose and legacy. Your environment may be broken, but your calling is not. Like Noah, you are called to walk with God when it's unpopular, to obey when it's difficult, and to remain faithful when no one else is.

A godly man stands out because he makes a deliberate decision about what will rule his heart. Like Noah in a corrupt generation, he refuses to let the spirit of his environment shape his identity. Darkness may surround him, but it does not seep into him because his life is anchored in God. He understands that righteousness is chosen daily through obedience, conviction, and reverence for the Lord. While others adjust their standards to fit the culture, a godly man holds his ground, knowing that who he is before God matters more than how he is accepted by men. Compromise may be common, but it is never casual for a man of God. He recognizes that small concessions can slowly erode strong character, so he guards his heart with diligence. His strength is not found in isolation from the world, but in transformation within it. He walks through darkness carrying light, proving that purity is still possible, integrity is still powerful, and holiness still sets a man apart.

Genesis 6:9 reveals a powerful truth about what God truly values in a man. When scripture describes Noah as "a just man and perfect in his generations," it is not declaring that he was without flaw, but that he was wholehearted in his devotion. In a world filled with compromise, Noah chose sincerity. In a generation drifting further from God, he anchored his life in righteousness. His "perfection" was not sinlessness - it was spiritual integrity. He was the same man in private as he was in public, faithful when no one else was, and aligned with God when the culture around him was corrupt. This kind of life stands out because it is rare. To "walk with God" means living in step with Him daily. Noah's life had direction because his heart had surrender. He didn't follow the crowd; he followed the voice of God. His obedience was not occasional, it was consistent. His faith was not passive, it was active. And because of that, his life became a vessel for God's purpose in a dark time.

Genesis 6:8 tells us that Noah found grace in the eyes of the Lord, and that moment came before any act of obedience or visible faithfulness. Noah did not become righteous because he built the ark - he built the ark because he had already received grace. What set Noah apart was not first his labor, but his relationship with God. Grace met him before responsibility was given to him. Righteousness always begins where grace is received. No man can stand strong for God without first being strengthened by God. The calling, the obedience, and the endurance all flow from a life that has first encountered divine favor. Just as Noah's obedience was fueled by grace, so every man who desires to walk upright must begin in being dependent on God and not on his own strength. Grace is what empowers a man to stand when others fall, to obey when others resist, and to remain faithful when the world turns away. Before the building, before the battle, and before the burden there must be grace.

When Noah found grace in the eyes of the Lord, it did not lead him into comfort or complacency; it led him into obedience. The same grace that chose him also commissioned him. While the world around him indulged in corruption, Noah responded to grace with reverence, discipline, and action. He built when no one else believed, he listened when no one else cared, and he obeyed when no one else would. Grace did not lower the standard - it lifted him to meet it. A man who has received grace carries a sacred responsibility. Grace strengthens his resolve when obedience is difficult and steadies him when the path is long. The favor of God is not a covering for compromise it is a calling to consecration. When grace touches a man, it teaches him to say no to sin and yes to righteousness. It builds in him a heart that desires to please God above all else. Just as Noah answered grace with steadfast obedience, every man must realize that grace is not an escape from responsibility - it is the strength to fulfill it.

Noah stood out because he chose to believe God when no one else would. In a world that mocked righteousness, his faith anchored him to a different reality - the reality of God's word. While others lived for the moment, Noah lived for what God had spoken. Faith caused him to move when there was no evidence, to obey when there was no applause, and to trust when there was no agreement. He did not need the crowd's approval because he had God's instruction. Faith did more than change what Noah believed - it changed how he lived. It made him prepare for a future no one else could see, building an ark in dry ground under clear skies. Every strike of the hammer was a declaration that God's word is more certain than human opinion. While others laughed, Noah built. While others delayed, Noah obeyed. And when the rain finally came, the man who looked foolish became the man who was ready. Faith will always move a man to build, prepare, and walk in obedience long before the results are visible.

A man who stands out is a man who has settled in his heart that God's voice matters more than the crowd's opinion. In the days of Noah, righteousness was not celebrated - it was mocked. Obedience was not applauded - it was questioned. Yet Noah refused to measure his life by the approval of people. He understood that living for God often means standing alone, building when no one else understands, and moving forward when others stand still. A man who chases approval will eventually compromise, but a man who fears God will remain steady, even when misunderstood. If Noah had listened to the voices around him, the ark would have never been built, and destiny would have been abandoned at the altar of acceptance. But Noah chose obedience over popularity, faith over comfort, and purpose over perception. When a man learns to live for God's approval alone, like Noah he becomes unshakable and his life becomes a testimony that obedience will always outlast opinion.

Standing out for God will often place a man in a position where he is misunderstood by those around him. Like Noah building the ark in obedience while the world mocked, a man who walks with God will not always be applauded - he will often be questioned. People may not understand why you refuse to go along with what is common or comfortable. What they fail to see is that a man who answers to God cannot be shaped by the opinions of men. A man of God must settle deeply within his heart that pleasing the Lord is worth being misunderstood. Even Jesus Christ was rejected and mocked yet He never adjusted His obedience to gain acceptance. There is a quiet strength in a man who remains faithful when misunderstood - a strength that is not driven by applause but by purpose. When you stand firm, you become a testimony that righteousness still lives in a compromised world. You may walk alone at times, but you will never stand alone, for God stands with those who stand for Him.

The life of Noah proves that true righteousness cannot remain hidden; it reveals itself through daily decisions, consistent conduct, and unwavering obedience to God. In a world that was consumed by corruption, Noah's life stood in sharp contrast because he chose to walk with God when no one else would. His righteousness shaped how he led his family, how he responded to God's commands, and how he carried himself in a culture that rejected truth. What was in his heart became evident in his actions. A righteous man does not simply believe differently - he lives differently. True righteousness shows up in the way a man speaks, leads, chooses, and obeys, even when those choices set him apart. Noah did not just agree with God internally; he built the ark, step by step, in faithful obedience, proving that righteousness is something that must be seen as well as believed. God is still looking for men whose character, leadership, and obedience testify to a genuine walk with Him.

A corrupt generation needs righteous men who will stand, speak, and live differently. In the days of Noah, wickedness filled the earth, yet his life proved that darkness never has the final word when one man chooses obedience. When good men become passive, compromise spreads, truth weakens, and sin grows louder. But when a man stands in righteousness, even if he stands alone, he becomes a barrier against corruption and a voice that reminds the world that God still reigns. Noah's life was a visible testimony that God still had a man who would listen, believe, and obey. He did not wait for the culture to change; he chose to be different in the midst of it. His obedience built an ark not only of wood, but of witness declaring that faith still lives on the earth. In every generation, God is looking for men who will not be silent but will stand with conviction, walk in obedience, and carry His truth without compromise. One righteous man, fully yielded to God, can become a turning point in a corrupt world.

A godly man refuses to dissolve into the culture around him just to gain acceptance. Like The Holy Bible declares in Romans 12:2, he is not conformed to this world but transformed by the renewing of his mind. He understands that survival is not his highest calling - faithfulness is. His identity is not shaped by the approval of people but by his alignment with God. He knows that blending in may preserve his reputation among men, but standing apart preserves his integrity before God. This kind of man recognizes that strength is not found in going along with the crowd; it is revealed in the courage to stand against it. Like Noah, who stood righteous in a corrupt generation, a godly man walks a path that may be lonely but is never empty of God's presence. His life becomes a testimony that holiness is still possible, obedience is still powerful, and righteousness still matters. In a world desperate for men who will not bend, he stands as proof that being different for God is not weakness but unshakable strength.

When God extends His grace toward a man, it is an invitation, not a reward. Favor draws him closer, awakening his heart to something higher than the world around him. It is God saying, "Come near." But favor alone is not enough. Faith must rise within that man to believe what God has spoken. Faith reaches beyond what is seen and anchors itself in God's promises. It trusts when there is no evidence, stands when there is pressure, and believes when others doubt. Favor opens the door, but faith walks through it. Yet true righteousness is not proven until obedience takes action. Obedience is where faith becomes visible. It is the evidence that a man's trust in God is not just words, but reality. When a man obeys, especially when it is difficult, inconvenient, or misunderstood, he demonstrates that God's voice matters more than the world's approval. Obedience builds a life that reflects heaven in the middle of earth's chaos. Favor draws him, faith anchors him, and obedience defines him.

Before Noah ever lifted a hammer to build the ark, he learned to walk with God in quiet, unseen places. Genesis 6:9 does not first highlight his assignment it reveals his relationship, "Noah walked with God." In a world consumed with corruption, Noah's distinction came from his daily communion with God. Many men today desire purpose, influence, and visible impact, but overlook the foundation that sustains it. They want the ark without the walk, the calling without the closeness. But God does not entrust public assignments to men who neglect private intimacy. The power to stand when others fall is formed in the hidden places through prayer, obedience, and consistent fellowship with God. When a man learns to walk with God in secret, he develops the strength to stand for God in public. Intimacy is not optional - it is the source. And when the day comes for God to place a calling on a man's life, it will not feel like a burden, but a natural overflow of a life already aligned with Him.

Like Daniel standing in a hostile culture or Joshua stepping into an unknown promise, a man who walks with God learns to stand when others bow to pressure, speak when others remain silent out of fear, and obey when others choose rebellion. His strength is not situational

- it is spiritual. It flows from time spent in prayer, from trust in God's voice, and from a heart that has been shaped by truth rather than trends. This kind of man is not controlled by the crowd because he has already surrendered to God. While others measure their decisions by popularity or acceptance, he measures his life by obedience. He understands that true strength is not found in numbers but in nearness to God. Even if he stands alone, he is never truly alone. The same God who calls him also sustains him, empowers him, and goes before him. His courage becomes a testimony - proof that when a man walks with God, he carries a strength the world cannot imitate and a boldness that cannot be silenced.

God is still searching the earth for men who will stand out for Him in a world that rewards compromise. These are men who understand that faith is lived daily in quiet consistency. They are faithful husbands who love with sacrifice, present fathers who lead with intentional care, honest workers who refuse to cut corners, disciplined leaders who master themselves before trying to lead others, and courageous witnesses who are not ashamed of truth. In a culture that often drifts, these men anchor themselves in God's standard and choose obedience over convenience, conviction over comfort, and purpose over popularity. These are the men who carry righteousness into every space they enter. They bring integrity into their homes, setting a tone of peace and godliness. They strengthen their churches, not as spectators but as pillars. They elevate their workplaces through honesty and diligence, and they impact their communities by living as visible examples of God's transforming power.

Darkness has always tried to define the atmosphere of the age, but God has never measured a generation by its sin - He measures it by the men who will stand against it. When wickedness filled the earth, God was not searching for perfection in the crowd; He was looking for surrender in one man. Noah became that man not because the world was righteous, but because he refused to let the world rewrite his convictions. Righteousness is not the product of a clean environment; it is the result of a consecrated heart that chooses God when everything else chooses compromise. Noah's life declares that one surrendered man can shift the narrative of an entire generation. While others blended into corruption, he walked with God, and that walk became a witness. He did not preach with popularity, but with consistency. He did not influence through approval, but through obedience. And in the middle of judgment, his life stood as proof that God can still find a man who will remain faithful.

Just as Noah "found grace in the eyes of the Lord," so every godly man stands because God has first extended favor toward him. Grace humbles a man and reminds him that without God, he would be no different than the world around him. Therefore, his life becomes set apart not as a badge of honor, but as a reflection of divine mercy working within him. Like Noah, a man who stands out walks with God in the middle of a generation that has lost its way. He listens when God speaks, obeys when it is difficult, and remains faithful when no one else understands. His obedience becomes his testimony, and his life becomes a visible witness of righteousness in a culture of compromise. In a world that drifts further into darkness, his steady walk shines brighter not because he is perfect, but because he is surrendered. May every man choose to walk with God daily, to obey His voice without hesitation, and to stand as a living witness that righteousness is still possible when a man is anchored in God's grace.

| 2 |

"A MAN WHO WALKS WITH GOD"

Genesis 6:9 reveals something powerful about the life of Noah: his strength was not rooted in a favorable environment, but in a faithful relationship. Noah moved in step with the Lord and that personal fellowship became the source of his stability and his unwavering obedience. A man does not become strong by escaping difficulty, but by staying close to God in the middle of it. Noah's life proves that true strength is not produced by surroundings but by connection. He did not rely on human reasoning to navigate a corrupt generation - he relied on divine direction. His walk with God gave him clarity when the world was confused, conviction when others compromised, and endurance when righteousness was costly. When a man walks closely with God, he carries within him a strength that the world cannot give and cannot take away. Like Noah, he becomes a man who stands when others fall, who obeys when others rebel, and who remains faithful because his life is anchored in the presence of the Lord.

A man who truly walks with God learns early that direction is found in the quiet voice of the Lord. His steps are intentional, prayerful, and guided. He understands that pressure will always try to reshape him, fear will always try to silence him, and the spirit of the age will always try to pull him off course. But a man anchored in God refuses to be steered by what is trending or tolerated. Instead, he submits his path to the Lord, trusting that divine direction is better than human acceptance. Even when the road is lonely, he walks it with confidence because he knows who is leading him. The life of Noah stands as a powerful reminder that a man can walk with God in the middle of a generation that has turned away from Him. Noah did not follow the crowd - he followed God, even when it made him stand alone. While the world around him was consumed with corruption and rebellion, Noah remained steady, obedient, and faithful. That kind of walk requires courage, conviction, and daily surrender.

Walking with God is proven by a steady awareness that God is near in every moment. A man who walks with God builds a consistent, daily connection with Him. This kind of walk produces strength that is not dependent on circumstances, because it is rooted in relationship. A man who truly walks with God carries that relationship into every part of his life. God is not confined to a church service or a moment of prayer; He is welcomed into the routine, the responsibility, and the ordinary rhythms of each day. Whether at home, at work, or in moments of decision, this man seeks God's wisdom and direction. He invites the presence of God into his leadership, his conversations, and even his inner thoughts. Over time, this daily fellowship shapes his character, sharpens his discernment, and anchors his life in purpose. Walking with God becomes the quiet foundation beneath everything he does - steady, faithful, and transforming him into a man who reflects God in both the visible and the unseen.

Noah's strength did not begin with the hammer and the ark - it began in the quiet place of fellowship. Genesis 6:9 reveals that Noah walked with God, and that walk became the source of everything he later did. His obedience was not a sudden act of courage; it was the overflow of a steady relationship. Noah didn't rise to the occasion when pressure came; he simply lived out what had already been developed in his daily communion with God. This is the pattern for every man who desires to live faithfully. What a man does when the pressure comes is a reflection of where he has been walking all along. If he has walked closely with God in the quiet, he will stand boldly before men in the storm. Fellowship shapes obedience, and intimacy fuels endurance. The ark was not built by a man trying to impress God - it was built by a man who already knew Him. In the same way, a man's greatest strength will never come from his ability alone, but from his consistent, daily walk with God behind closed doors.

A man cannot lead well if he does not walk closely with the Lord. Before a man can guide others, he must first be guided himself. Leadership without fellowship slowly disconnects a man from the very source of wisdom, discernment, and direction. It may look strong for a season, but it lacks the foundation to endure pressure and responsibility. Strength without surrender becomes dangerous because it operates without restraint, and authority without prayer becomes selfish because it answers only to itself. A man may possess talent, intelligence, and influence, but these gifts are not enough to keep him steady. Without a consistent walk with God, he will begin to trust his own understanding and justify his own desires. But when a man walks closely with the Lord, his leadership is marked by humility, clarity, and purpose. He leads with a heart that has been shaped in private before it is ever seen in public, and his authority becomes a reflection of God's will rather than his own ambition.

Noah was able to hear God because he chose to stay near God. His life teaches that clarity from heaven is cultivated through closeness. The world is loud, demanding attention at every turn, but God often speaks in stillness, in moments that require a heart that is present and attentive. Noah did not just hear God once; he lived in a way that kept him in position to hear God continually. A man who walks with God develops a sensitivity that cannot be manufactured overnight. He begins to recognize the difference between his own thoughts and the prompting of the Spirit. He becomes responsive to correction before it becomes collapse, attentive to instruction before confusion sets in, aware of warning before danger arrives, and open to direction before he loses his way. This kind of spiritual awareness is the fruit of daily fellowship. When a man stays near God, he learns God's ways, and that understanding becomes the guiding force behind every decision, every step, and every season of his life.

Walking with God is not a one-sided conversation; it is a relationship marked by attentiveness and response. A godly man does not rush through prayer just to speak his mind - he lingers long enough to hear God's heart. He opens the Word not just to read, but to be shaped, corrected, and instructed. Through scripture, God speaks with clarity. Through prayer, God speaks with intimacy. And through the quiet conviction of the Holy Spirit, God speaks with precision, putting His finger on attitudes, motives, and decisions that need to change. A man who walks with God develops a listening spirit that is humble enough to receive and strong enough to obey. He recognizes when God is correcting his attitude, redirecting his plans, or calling him higher in character and obedience. Listening means setting aside pride, slowing down, and yielding to God's authority. A man who truly walks with God is not just known for what he says to God, but for how faithfully he listens when God speaks.

Walking with God is measured by what a man does when God speaks. Noah did not prove his fellowship through words, but through obedience that cost him everything. When God gave instruction, Noah did not hesitate, negotiate, or adjust the command to fit his comfort - he surrendered to it. True fellowship is revealed in action. A man who truly walks with God does not simply admire truth; he aligns his life with it. Obedience is the visible evidence that a man's heart is genuinely connected to God. There is no such thing as deep fellowship without surrendered action. When a man walks closely with God, obedience becomes his natural response, not his reluctant duty. Even when the path is difficult, misunderstood, or lonely, he moves forward because he trusts the One who leads him. This is the kind of faith that transforms a man's life - where hearing God's voice leads to immediate response. True closeness with God will always produce a life that says, "Yes, Lord," in daily, consistent obedience.

The path of faith is not always convenient, and it is rarely easy. Day after day, Noah built something no one around him understood, holding onto the word of God when there was no visible evidence to support it. The laughter, the doubt, and the isolation did not move him, because his walk with God was deeper than the opinions of men. When a man is anchored in fellowship with God, he finds the strength to keep going when others would walk away. Walking with God produces a resilience that refuses to quit when the assignment becomes difficult. A man who walks with God understands that obedience is not measured by ease, but by faithfulness. He does not abandon the call when it becomes costly; he leans in closer to God and keeps building. Even when progress feels slow and recognition is absent, he continues knowing that God honors endurance. The man who walks with God is not driven by comfort but by conviction, and because of that, he finishes what God has called him to do.

Daily fellowship with God anchors a man in a stability that the world cannot shake. His strength is drawn from quiet moments with God, where identity is formed, truth is reinforced, and purpose is clarified. In those unseen places of prayer, reflection, and obedience, a man becomes rooted. He stands firm because his life is connected to something eternal. A man who communes daily with God develops an inner steadiness that circumstances cannot erode. He does not abandon his faith when things become difficult because his faith was never built on ease - it was built on relationship. He knows who he is because he knows whose he is. That deep connection gives him clarity when others are confused, courage when others shrink back, and peace when others panic. While the world looks for stability in systems, status, or approval, he finds it in the presence of God. And because he is rooted in that fellowship, he remains unshaken, unwavering, and unmovable no matter what comes against him.

Private fellowship with God is the unseen foundation of a man's visible life. What is built in secret will always reveal itself in public. When he opens the Word daily, truth begins to settle deep within him, shaping not just what he knows, but who he becomes. His convictions grow stronger, his discernment sharper, and his heart more aligned with God's will. Long before anyone sees his actions, God has already been working on his character in private. Public faithfulness is the fruit of a surrendered life behind closed doors. When a man learns to yield to God in secret, he becomes a man who can be trusted with influence in the open. His leadership carries weight because it is backed by obedience no one else witnessed. His decisions reflect wisdom because they were birthed in communion with God. The hidden life feeds the visible life, and when that hidden life is strong, steady, and faithful, it produces a man who stands firm, leads well, and lives in a way that honors God before others.

Noah's walk with God became a covering over his entire household. His wife and children stepped into safety because one man chose obedience over ease and faith over the opinions of his generation. A man who walks with God carries more than his own spiritual life; he carries influence that shapes the direction, protection, and future of those under his care. A man's fellowship with God will always echo beyond himself. When he prays, leads, listens, and obeys, his decisions become guided, his discernment becomes sharper, and his example becomes a living testimony his family can follow. His children learn what it means to trust God not just by instruction, but by observation. His household feels the strength of his covering, the stability of his convictions, and the peace that comes from a life aligned with God. When a man walks with God, he is not only building his own life - he is building a legacy that can carry his family safely through storms they could never navigate on their own.

A man who walks with God becomes a man others can follow because he is guided by the steady hand of the Lord. His decisions are shaped in prayer, his attitude is refined through obedience, and his path is marked by consistency. When a man is truly being led by God, his life begins to reflect order, conviction, and quiet strength that draws others to trust the path he is walking. People are not ultimately looking for perfection; they are looking for authenticity and stability. A man submitted to God becomes a safe place of leadership because his heart is anchored in something greater than himself. Even when others do not fully understand his choices, they can sense the sincerity of his surrender and the integrity of his walk. His life becomes a testimony that leadership is not about control, but about submission that produces clarity, courage, and trustworthiness. When a man follows God closely, he does not need to demand that others follow him; his life invites it.

Walking with God builds a sensitivity in a man's spirit that guards him from compromise. What once seemed small or excusable no longer sits right within him. Sin loses its appeal because the presence of God becomes more valuable than temporary pleasure. Fellowship with God sharpens his discernment, helping him recognize subtle compromises before they take root. He no longer measures his life by what others allow, but by what honors God. The closer he walks with God, the more clearly he sees the difference between what is pure and what is corrupt. A man who stays near to God cannot remain at ease with what grieves Him. Instead of drifting into compromise, he turns quickly, guarding his heart and protecting his calling. Walking with God trains him to value purity over convenience and obedience over ease. In that daily fellowship, he learns not just to avoid sin, but to love righteousness. And in loving what is right, he becomes a man who stands strong, uncorrupted, and aligned with the heart of God.

Noah lived in a generation that was saturated with corruption, violence, and moral decay, yet he refused to let the darkness around him redefine the convictions within him. He did not adopt the mindset that says, Everybody else is doing it," because his walk with the Lord gave him the courage to stand when standing alone was costly. A man who walks with God learns that approval from a corrupt crowd is a poor substitute for the favor of God. When a man is rooted in fellowship with the Lord, he no longer measures his life by popular opinion, shifting values, or cultural trends. Instead, he lives with an audience of One. Noah did not need validation from a wicked generation because he had communion with a holy God. That relationship gave him clarity when others were confused, conviction when others were compromised, and strength when others were weak. In the same way, a man who truly walks with God will stand out, knowing that faithfulness to God is always worth more than acceptance by the world.

Many men can build an appearance of strength through effort, discipline, or reputation, yet remain spiritually fragile within. When pressure comes, what is merely external begins to crack. But the man who has cultivated fellowship with the Lord has a deeper foundation. His strength is not borrowed from circumstance; it flows from communion. In the quiet places of prayer, obedience, and surrender, God forms a resilience that cannot be manufactured by human effort alone. A man who walks closely with God carries a steady, unshaken strength that shows up in how he endures trials, how he responds under pressure, and how he remains anchored when others are shaken. His confidence is not in himself, but in the One he walks with daily. Because he stays near to the Lord, he draws from a source that does not run dry. When storms rise, he does not collapse inwardly, because his life is rooted in something eternal. Quiet strength like this is not loud, but it is powerful and it is the kind of strength that lasts.

Every man must come to a moment of honest examination where he asks, "Am I truly walking with God, or have I become skilled at merely talking about Him?" True fellowship is not measured by what a man says in public, but by how closely he walks with God in private. A man who walks with God listens for His voice, responds with humility, and orders his steps according to God's will rather than his own desires. God is not calling men to wear faith as a label; He is calling them to live it as a lifestyle. Walking with God requires consistency, not convenience. It demands that a man stay near when distractions pull, obey when it is difficult, and remain faithful when it would be easier to drift. This kind of walk produces a steady strength, a quiet integrity, and a life that reflects God's presence without needing to announce it. When a man truly walks with God, his life begins to speak louder than his words, and his faith becomes evident not in what he claims, but in how he lives.

Noah's life stands as a powerful witness that a man who walks with God can remain steady even when everything around him is unstable. While others followed the crowd, Noah followed the voice of the Lord. He may have been outnumbered, misunderstood, and even opposed, but he was never alone. The presence of God was his strength, his confidence, and his direction. Noah's faithfulness in building the ark was simply the outward expression of an inward walk that had already been established. Day after day, before the hammer struck wood, his heart had already bowed before God. That is the secret of enduring faithfulness: a strong private fellowship produces a steady public life. When a man is rooted in God's presence, he does not collapse under pressure, nor does he compromise under opposition. He endures. He stands. And in the end, his life becomes proof that when a man walks with God, God walks with him and that is more than enough to stand in any generation.

| 3 |

"A MAN OF RIGHTEOUS CHARACTER"

A man of righteous character is not first recognized by crowds, titles, applause, or achievements - he is recognized by God. In Ezekiel 14:14, Noah is singled out not because of influence among men, but because of integrity before heaven. While the world around him sank deeper into corruption, violence, and rebellion, Noah walked in quiet obedience. He did not need validation from his generation, because his life was already approved by God. Noah's testimony reminds us that God notices what others overlook. When society drifts, a righteous man stands - not loudly for attention, but firmly in conviction. His life becomes a witness that heaven records even when earth ignores it. A man of righteous character builds his name before God long before it is ever known among men. And when the time comes, it is not applause that preserves him, but the favor of God. In a world desperate for recognition, the greatest honor is to be known by God as a man who walked uprightly when no one else would.

Noah was not remembered because crowds applauded him or because his name was celebrated in the streets. He was remembered because he walked in righteousness when no one else would. While others chased influence, Noah pursued integrity. While the world measured success by popularity, heaven measured Noah by faithfulness. His life reminds us that the applause of men is temporary, but the approval of God is eternal. In a world where many men chase attention, Noah stands as a quiet but powerful rebuke. He teaches us that the greatest reputation a man can have is not what people say about him, but what God sees in him. True manhood is not built on followers, fame, or public validation - it is forged in private obedience, unwavering conviction, and a heart that fears God. When the noise of the world fades, it is righteousness that remains. A man who walks with God may be overlooked by men, but he will never be overlooked by heaven.

True manhood is not proven by applause, attention, or the approval of the crowd - it is revealed in the quiet, consistent formation of character before God. Popularity is fragile; it shifts with opinion, fades with time, and can be gained or lost in a moment. But character is forged slowly, through obedience, integrity, and faithfulness when no one is watching. God is not moved by recognition among men - He is moved by the condition of the heart. On the other hand, a righteous man may walk unnoticed, uncelebrated, and even misunderstood, yet his name carries weight before God. Heaven honors what earth often overlooks. True manhood is built in the hidden places where choices are made in secret, where integrity is tested without witnesses, and where a man chooses what is right over what is easy. In the end, it is not the cheers of people that define a man, but the approval of God. Character is the legacy that endures, and the man who builds it is the man heaven remembers.

God notices integrity when others ignore it. He sees beyond the surface of public recognition and looks directly into the hidden places of a man's life. He sees the moment you choose righteousness when compromise would go unnoticed. He honors the strength it takes to resist temptation in silence, to speak truth when deception would be easier, and to remain faithful when there is no applause. A man of integrity understands that his true audience is God alone. He does not live for approval, but for alignment with heaven. Every private victory builds a foundation that cannot be shaken, because it is established in truth. Though others may overlook it, God records every act of faithfulness, every surrendered desire, and every choice to stand firm. In due time, what was hidden will be revealed - not for the praise of man, but as evidence of a life that honored God when it mattered most. Integrity is never wasted; it is seen, it is valued, and it is rewarded by the One who sees all.

A righteous man is not driven by the need to be seen, but by the need to be true. He does not shape his life around the opinions of others, nor does he adjust his character to maintain an image. While others may strive to appear strong, spiritual, or admirable, the righteous man is concerned with what God sees. He understands that a polished image can deceive people, but it cannot fool God. His goal is not performance, but authenticity before God. He would rather be approved in heaven than applauded on earth. He knows that image may win attention, but integrity wins God's favor. So he walks carefully, speaks truthfully, and lives consistently from a heart that fears the Lord. When no one is watching, he remains the same man, because his standard is the unchanging righteousness of God. This is the kind of man God trusts, the kind of man God uses, and the kind of man whose life leaves a lasting mark - not because he looked godly, but because he truly was.

In the days of Noah, violence filled the earth, and compromise had become the language of the generation. Yet Noah stood as a contradiction to his time. He walked with God when others walked in rebellion. A righteous man is not defined by the environment around him, but by the God within him. Noah's life proves that it is possible to live clean in a polluted world, to stay faithful in a faithless generation, and to remain unmoved when everything around you is shifting. This is the mark of a righteous man: he refuses to let the spirit of the age shape his soul. He does not bend simply because bending has become normal, and he does not compromise just because compromise is common. While others adjust their convictions to fit in, he anchors his life in truth and stands firm. There is strength in that kind of separation, and favor on that kind of life. God sees the man who stands alone and just as Noah found grace in the eyes of the Lord, so will every man who dares to stand when others fall.

Like Noah, a man of righteous character refuses to be shaped by the corruption around him and instead walks in obedience to God. When others bend to fit in, he remains unyielding, anchored in truth. He would rather walk alone with God than be surrounded by people who pull him away from Him. What makes him different is the evidence of a life that has been set apart for a higher standard. He chooses holiness over compromise, knowing that every decision carries eternal weight. He recognizes that blending in with darkness may bring temporary approval, but it will cost him lasting favor with God. Like Daniel in a foreign land, he remains faithful even when it is inconvenient, uncomfortable, or costly. He understands that standing apart is not a loss, but a mark of honor in the eyes of heaven. In the end, he would rather be separated by holiness than accepted through compromise, because he knows that true reward comes not from the applause of people, but from the approval of God.

Righteous character begins with a deep, reverent fear of the Lord - a holy awareness that God sees, knows, and judges with perfect truth. This kind of fear anchors a man's heart in eternity rather than in the shifting approval of people. When a man fears God, he is no longer driven by the need to impress, please, or conform. The opinions of others lose their power because he lives before a higher authority. Even in silence and secrecy, he walks with integrity because he knows he is never unseen. Such a man weighs his choices not by convenience, but by conviction. He considers not what is popular, but what is righteous in the sight of God. Every decision is measured in the presence of the Lord. This produces a steady, unshakable life, because his foundation is not built on human approval but on divine truth. A man who fears the Lord walks with clarity, lives with purpose, and stands with courage, knowing that to be right with God is greater than being accepted by the world.

Noah did not earn God's recognition through a single act of obedience, but through a life consistently aligned with God's will. Day after day he chose righteousness when compromise was easier. In a generation that had turned its back on God, Noah remained anchored in obedience. That is the difference between casual faith and true righteousness - one is occasional, the other is continual. God is not looking for men who shine briefly, but for men who endure faithfully over time. A righteous man is not a flawless man, but he is a faithful one. He is teachable when corrected, repentant when he fails, and submitted when God speaks. His strength is not in perfection, but in his posture toward God. He returns quickly when he stumbles, he listens when instructed, and he yields when led. This is the kind of life God honors—not one without mistakes, but one marked by humility, growth, and obedience. Consistency in walking with God builds a legacy that heaven recognizes, even when earth overlooks it.

Character is what a man is when pressure exposes him. When the weight of life presses in, when temptation intensifies, when circumstances become uncomfortable, a man does not suddenly become something new; he reveals what has already been built within him. What is rooted in the heart will always surface under pressure. In the days of Noah, the world around him was filled with corruption, violence, and moral decay. Yet it was in that darkness that his righteousness became unmistakably clear. He did not become righteous because the world was wicked; he was already walking with God, and the condition of the world simply revealed the depth of his character. While others gave in to the culture around them, Noah stood apart because of what had been formed in him long before the flood ever came. In the same way, when pressure surrounds a man today, it reveals whether he has built his life on truth, obedience, and faithfulness to God.

While others justify disobedience because "everyone is doing it," the righteous man walks a different path. He chooses integrity in private, conviction in public, and faithfulness in every season. His life becomes a powerful declaration that God is still worthy of obedience, even in a generation that has forgotten Him. In the middle of corruption, the righteous man builds. While the world tears down truth, he establishes it in his heart. While chaos spreads, he cultivates peace through obedience. He does not need a holy culture to live a holy life - he carries holiness within him because he carries God's Word. Like a steady pillar in a collapsing structure, he stands firm, unmoved by the shifting winds around him. His life becomes a refuge, a testimony, and a light in dark places. He proves that righteousness is not dependent on surroundings, but on surrender. And in doing so, he honors God not just when it is easy, but when it costs him something because true righteousness is revealed in the midst of resistance.

God is still searching the earth for men marked by truth, integrity, and unwavering devotion. These are men who walk uprightly when compromise is easier, who speak truth when silence would be safer, and who live with a deep awareness that God sees beyond appearances into the heart. They are not driven by the approval of people, but by the desire to be known and approved by God. In a world where standards shift and convictions weaken, these men stand firm, anchored in righteousness. Their lives become a testimony that real strength is not found in power, but in character that refuses to bend. These men may not always be seen or celebrated by the world, but heaven takes notice. God recognizes the man who remains steady, who walks in obedience, and who builds his life on what is right. And when God finds such a man, He entrusts him with purpose, strengthens him in battle, and establishes his life as a lasting witness of what it means to truly be a man of God.

Before Noah ever lifted a hammer to build the ark, he had already built a testimony of obedience, consistency, and reverence before God. His daily walk, his quiet decisions, and his unwavering faith formed a foundation that could support the weight of the assignment God would later give him. The ark was not the beginning of Noah's greatness; it was the evidence of a life that had already been approved in secret. In the same way, a righteous man today must focus first on constructing a life that God can trust. Many seek to build something visible, but God is looking for men who will build something eternal within. When a man is faithful in the hidden places - when he chooses truth over compromise, obedience over convenience, and faith over fear - he is building a name in heaven that no earthly recognition can rival. And when that foundation is secure, anything he builds before men will not only stand, but it will carry the weight of divine favor and purpose.

Many men crave visibility before they've been shaped, influence before they've been refined. They reach for platforms, titles, and recognition, yet neglect the quiet, hidden work of becoming a man God can trust. But God does not anoint ambition - He anoints character. He is forming a man's foundation in the unseen places where motives are tested, where pride is confronted, where obedience costs something. A platform without character is dangerous, because it elevates a man beyond the strength of his integrity. Heaven is not moved by achievements, applause, or influence if the heart behind it is misaligned. A man may gain the attention of the world yet still be lacking in the sight of God. But when a man allows God to shape his heart - when he chooses integrity over image and righteousness over recognition - he becomes a vessel God can truly use. God forms the man before He trusts the man, because what is built in private will determine what can be sustained in public.

Righteous character gives weight to a man's life. It is not loud, but it is undeniable. A man who walks in truth does not need to strive for influence for his life speaks before his mouth ever opens. His words are not empty because they are backed by a life that has been tested, refined, and aligned with truth. When he speaks, there is a quiet authority because heaven recognizes consistency. His life and his words agree, and that agreement produces strength. His leadership becomes trustworthy because there is no division between who he is in private and who he presents in public. He resists what would compromise him, embraces what refines him, and remains faithful when it would be easier to drift. Because of this, people can lean on his leadership without fear, knowing it is anchored in something unshakable. A man of righteous character leads with substance. And over time, that substance builds a legacy that cannot be shaken, because it was forged in truth before it was ever seen by men.

A man of righteous character often walks a lonely road. His decisions don't always make sense to others, his convictions may be misread, and his sacrifices can go unnoticed by the world around him. There will be moments when he is overlooked, misunderstood, or even rejected not because he is wrong, but because righteousness does not always align with popular opinion. Yet his life is not built for applause from men, but for approval from God. Though people may forget his faithfulness, God never does. Every unseen act of integrity, every private battle won, every sacrifice made in obedience is recorded in heaven. The God who sees in secret honors what the world ignores. A righteous man may not leave behind a name celebrated by crowds, but he will leave behind a testimony known by God. And in the end, it is not the opinions of people that matter, but the recognition of heaven. For the man who walks uprightly before God is never truly forgotten - he is remembered where it matters most.

Noah's life is a powerful reminder that righteousness is not measured by how many people follow you, but by how faithfully you follow God. In a generation consumed by corruption and rebellion, Noah stood as a solitary witness of obedience. He did not blend in with the culture, nor did he compromise to gain acceptance. Instead, he walked with God when no one else would. Noah teaches us that a man does not need the approval of the crowd to live right - he only needs the approval of God. Even though Noah did not change the hearts of the entire generation around him, he changed the future of his family and preserved a legacy that would impact the world. His obedience built a testimony that still speaks today. When a man chooses integrity in a corrupt world, he becomes a living witness that God still has men who will stand. And through that stand, generations can be saved, and a legacy of faith can be established that outlives the man himself.

A man God recognizes chooses purity when compromise would be easier, truth when deception would be more convenient, and obedience when no one is watching. While others chase influence, he pursues integrity. While others build platforms, he builds character. Heaven is not moved by a man's reputation among people, but by the condition of his heart. What is celebrated on earth may be forgotten in eternity, but what is formed in righteousness before God will never be overlooked. A man who is remembered by heaven is one who walks faithfully, even when unnoticed. His strength is not in how many know his name, but in the fact that God does. Even if the world overlooks him, God sees every quiet act of obedience and every moment of integrity. In time, what is built in secret becomes a testimony that cannot be shaken. Build the kind of character that heaven records, because a righteous man may be hidden from the eyes of men, but he is always fully seen and honored by God.

| 4 |

"A MAN IN AN EVIL GENERATION"

In Genesis 6:5–6, we see a sobering picture of a generation consumed by evil thoughts, where corruption had become normal and righteousness had nearly vanished. The grief of God over mankind reveals how far the human heart had fallen from its intended design. Yet in the midst of that darkness, one man stood differently. Noah did not allow the moral climate around him to shape his character. While the world drifted deeper into sin, he chose to walk with God. His life proves that even when wickedness multiplies, obedience can still stand, and when society abandons truth, a man can still cling to it with unwavering conviction. In a world where evil can become celebrated and righteousness ignored, God still searches for men who will stand apart. Like Noah, a man can be a light in the midst of corruption, a witness in the middle of rebellion, and a vessel of faith in a faithless age. His life declares that no matter how dark the times become, there is always a way to live right before God.

In the days of Noah, corruption was not occasional - it was constant, widespread, and deeply rooted in the hearts of men. Yet Noah proved that environment does not have to define identity. While others were shaped by sin, he was shaped by obedience. While others blended into darkness, he stood apart in righteousness. A godly man understands that pressure from the outside does not have to produce compromise on the inside. The same truth remains today. A man may live in a broken world without becoming a broken man. He may be surrounded by compromise without surrendering his convictions. The Spirit of God is still able to form a man who walks differently, thinks differently, and lives differently. Like Noah, a man who chooses God over culture becomes a living testimony that righteousness is still possible. Darkness may fill the generation, but it cannot fill the man who has surrendered his life to God.

A man's surroundings may be filled with compromise, but they do not have to control his spirit. Just as Noah lived righteously in a corrupt generation, a man today can walk with God even when everything around him pulls in the opposite direction. The environment may be dark, but darkness only reveals the strength of the light within him. When his heart is anchored in God, he becomes steady in unstable places, pure in polluted environments, and faithful in the midst of faithlessness. A man may work among unbelief and stand among mockers yet still remain unshaken if his devotion belongs to God. Faithfulness is not proven in easy surroundings - it is proven when standing alone would be easier to abandon. When others bend, he stands. When others compromise, he holds the line. His life becomes a testimony that righteousness is still possible, even in a fallen world. And in doing so, he not only preserves his own walk with God, but becomes a light that calls others out of darkness and back to truth.

Many men excuse their weakness by pointing to the world around them. They say the darkness is too deep, the pressure too heavy, and the temptation too constant to stand firm. Yet the life of Noah confronts that mindset with undeniable truth. He lived in a generation consumed by corruption, where wickedness was not only practiced but celebrated. Still, he chose righteousness. He did not allow the culture to shape his convictions; he allowed God to shape his character. When a man walks closely with God, he carries a spirit that remains steady even when everything around him is unstable. A godly man does not wait for easier days to obey God; he obeys in the midst of difficulty. True strength is not proven when conditions are favorable, but when obedience costs something. Noah did not delay his faithfulness until righteousness became popular - he stood when it was rare. In the same way, a man of God must rise above excuses and choose obedience regardless of the times he lives in.

When compromise spreads and truth is rejected, the man who remains faithful does not blend in - he stands out. His obedience is no longer hidden in the crowd; it is highlighted against the backdrop of a fallen world. While others adjust their standards to fit the culture, he anchors himself in God. While others drift, he stands firm. The darker the night becomes, the brighter his life shines because righteousness cannot be concealed in a generation that has abandoned it. A faithful man becomes a living testimony that God still has men who will not bow. His integrity speaks when words are ignored. His consistency preaches when sermons are rejected. Heaven takes notice of the man who refuses to compromise, even when it costs him acceptance, comfort, or opportunity. In a world that grows increasingly dim, his faith becomes proof that holiness is still possible, truth is still worth defending, and God is still at work through those who remain loyal to Him.

Noah's life teaches us that a man does not need a righteous environment to live righteously. In a generation where wickedness was widespread and hearts were continually turned away from God, Noah walked with God when no one else would. He obeyed when obedience made no sense to the culture around him. This reminds every man that righteousness is a personal commitment. A man's obedience is not measured by how many stand with him, but by how closely he walks with God. When compromise is celebrated and conviction is questioned, the pressure to conform can be strong. But Noah proves that one man, fully surrendered to God, is enough for God to work through. When a man chooses obedience without applause, integrity without recognition, and faith without agreement, he becomes a vessel God can trust. Even if no one else stands with him, he stands approved before God and that approval carries more weight than the acceptance of an entire generation.

A man living in an evil generation cannot afford to be careless with his heart. If he is not intentional, his convictions will weaken, and his hunger for God will be replaced with a tolerance for things that once grieved his spirit. This is why a godly man must be watchful over what he allows into his mind, what he entertains with his eyes, and what he agrees with in his spirit. What a man permits around him will eventually begin to shape what lives within him. Conversations, environments, and habits all leave impressions on the soul, and over time those impressions form direction. But a man who walks with God refuses to let the spirit of his generation define him. He draws a line in his heart and chooses holiness even when compromise is common. He renews his mind daily, feeds his spirit with truth, and remains sensitive to conviction. In a world that drifts further from God, the guarded heart becomes a place where His presence still dwells, and from that place, a man stands firm, unshaken, and set apart.

Noah's generation was not only wicked in what they practiced; they were polluted in what they imagined. Genesis reveals that the thoughts of man's heart were continually evil, showing us that sin does not begin with the hand but with the heart. Before a man acts wrong, he often thinks wrong, desires wrong, feeds wrong, and permits wrong things to take root inside him. This is why a godly man must guard his inner life with seriousness. He cannot afford to entertain thoughts that weaken his convictions, stir ungodly desires, or slowly pull his heart away from God. A righteous man understands that what a man allows to grow in his mind will eventually shape his decisions, his character, and his direction. Noah stood apart because he did not let the corruption around him become the corruption within him. In the same way, a man of God must examine what he watches, listens to, and secretly desires. To stay faithful in an evil generation, he must first win the battle within before he can stand strong outwardly.

In ungodly times, one of the greatest dangers a man faces is not open rebellion, but quiet compromise. When sin is everywhere, it slowly loses its shock value. What once grieved the heart can begin to feel normal, and what once stirred conviction can become tolerated. The world may laugh at sin, celebrate rebellion, and excuse what God condemns, but a man of God must stay anchored in truth, remembering that God's standard does not shift with culture, opinion, or popularity. What God calls evil remains evil, no matter how widely accepted it becomes. A faithful man chooses conviction over comfort, truth over trend, and holiness over approval. He does not measure his life by what others are doing, but by what God has spoken. In a generation that redefines everything, he remains steady, unmoved, and clear in his walk. His life becomes a quiet but powerful witness that even in a corrupt world, it is still possible to live in a way that honors God.

Noah's life proves that godliness is not sustained by public approval but by private obedience to God. In a generation that neither understood nor supported him, Noah still built what God commanded, step by step, year after year. His faith was not fueled by the voices around him, but by the voice above him. A man of God must learn that obedience is not validated by the crowd. What God has spoken remains true, even if no one else believes it, supports it, or stands beside him. There will be moments when a man must walk a path that others reject, build what others mock, and believe what others doubt. Noah kept walking in righteousness while the world around him moved in the opposite direction, and because of that, he stood when everything else fell. A man who waits for approval will hesitate, but a man who trusts God will move forward with conviction. True strength is revealed when he continues in obedience without applause, knowing that the only approval that matters is the approval of God.

God has never depended on favorable conditions to raise up faithful men. In the darkest times, His power is often displayed the clearest. He forms conviction when compromise is everywhere, courage when fear dominates, purity when sin is celebrated, and obedience when rebellion is the norm. God is able to shape a man in secret, strengthen him in pressure, and establish him in truth even when everything around him is unstable. In fact, the worsening of the times is often the very reason God raises men up. When sin increases, the contrast of righteousness becomes more visible. When truth is rejected, the voice of a faithful man carries greater weight. God is always looking for men who will stand when others bow, who will remain clean when others compromise, and who will obey when others turn away. The need is greater, the call is clearer, and the opportunity is stronger because in corrupt times, a righteous man does not blend in, he stands out as a testimony of God's power and faithfulness.

A righteous man does more than resist the spirit of his generation - he exposes it. Without speaking a word, his life becomes a testimony that challenges the norms around him. Where others compromise, he stands firm. Where others excuse sin, he disciplines his heart. His choices declare that darkness is not inevitable and that a man is not bound to follow the crowd. In a world that drifts, he walks with purpose. In a culture that bends, he remains anchored. His life becomes living proof that there is another way - a higher way. His faith speaks when others doubt, and his obedience stands when others fall away. He does not need approval to remain faithful, because his conviction is rooted in God, not in culture. His character draws a clear line: corruption may surround him, but it will not shape him. He becomes a quiet but powerful witness that righteousness is still possible, holiness is still attainable, and God is still worthy of complete obedience.

Noah was not called to stand on the sidelines and criticize the corruption around him; he was called to walk with God in the middle of it. While the world around him was filled with violence and wickedness, Noah chose obedience over opinion. Many men today fall into the trap of pointing out everything that is wrong yet never committing themselves to what is right. But God is looking for men who will carry His presence into dark places. It is not enough to recognize evil; a man must resist it within his own heart and remain faithful to God regardless of what surrounds him. A godly man understands that his calling is not to echo the darkness, but to reflect the light. His life becomes a testimony that obedience is still possible, even when it is unpopular. When a man chooses to become what is right instead of just pointing out what is wrong, he positions himself as a vessel God can use. Just as Noah stood as a light in his generation, so can any man who chooses to obey.

The condition of the world should never lull a man into silence or passivity; it should awaken something deeper within him. A prayerful man does not ignore the times; he responds to them by strengthening his connection with heaven. A watchful man discerns what is happening around him and refuses to be caught off guard. The darker the world becomes, the more intentional a man must be about guarding his heart, sharpening his spirit, and staying aligned with God's voice. When many grow cold, a man of God must burn hotter. When compromise becomes common, he must stand firmer. The darkness of the age may press against him, but it must never take residence within him. A man who belongs to God refuses to let the chaos around him extinguish the fire within him. Instead, he becomes a light in the midst of it, standing strong, living right, and proving by his life that righteousness can still prevail even in the most corrupt generation.

In the days of Noah, wickedness covered the earth, yet his life stood as a quiet contrast not because he elevated himself above others, but because he walked closely with God. A man who belongs to God lives by a different standard,. His choices, his conduct, and his convictions reflect a heart that has been set apart, not by pride, but by obedience. A righteous man understands that standing apart does not mean looking down. His difference is carried with humility, not harshness; with reverence, not self-righteousness. He does not boast in his restraint or condemn those still bound in darkness. Instead, his life becomes a steady witness - firm in conviction, yet gentle in spirit. He walks with a holy awareness that everything he is comes from God, and this produces both strength and humility. In a world that drifts further from truth, his quiet faithfulness speaks loudly, showing that it is possible to live clean in a corrupt generation without losing compassion for those still finding their way.

In the days of Genesis, Noah did not just walk with God for his own sake; his obedience created a path of safety for his household. While the world around him was filled with corruption, his steady devotion became a shelter of direction, wisdom, and protection. A man who truly follows God does not live in isolation - his decisions, his discipline, and his reverence for God form a covering that influences everyone under his care. When a man remains godly in a corrupt generation, he becomes more than faithful - he becomes an anchor. His life steadies those who are watching him, whether they realize it or not. His consistency speaks louder than the chaos around him, and his obedience provides clarity in a confused world. Like Noah, he may stand alone in conviction, but he is never alone in impact. His walk with God creates a legacy of protection, guiding his family through darkness and leading them toward righteousness, even when the culture drifts further away from truth.

God is still searching for men who refuse to blend in with the corruption around them - men who choose purity when compromise is easy, steadiness when everything feels uncertain, and obedience when rebellion is celebrated. In a world where right and wrong are constantly being redefined, a godly man does not allow culture to train his conscience or popular opinion to shape his convictions. Instead, he guards his heart, disciplines his thoughts, and lives with a quiet resolve that honors God. His life becomes a testimony that righteousness is still possible, even in the darkest times. When a generation forgets God, it takes courage to remember Him, to seek Him, and to stay close to Him. A man who walks with God becomes a steady light in an unstable world, not because of his own strength, but because he refuses to let go of God. And while the world may overlook him, heaven takes notice, for a man who remains faithful in a faithless generation is a man God can trust.

Be a man God can trust in evil times. Darkness may increase, compromise may spread, and truth may be rejected, but none of that has the power to extinguish a heart that is set on God. A man of God does not drift with the current of sin, nor does he adjust his convictions to fit the crowd. Instead, he guards his spirit knowing that what he allows within will determine how he stands without. Stand as Noah stood, walk as Noah walked, and live as a righteous witness in your generation. Noah did not blend in with the wickedness of his time but stood apart, steady and faithful when the world around him had forgotten God. In the same way, a man today becomes a testimony through consistent obedience and unwavering faith. God is still looking for men who will remain faithful when it would be easier to compromise. And in every corrupt generation, He is still able to raise up righteous men who will carry His light, preserve truth, and walk with Him when others walk away.

| **5** |

"A MAN WHO FINDS GRACE"

Genesis 6:8 declares, "But Noah found grace in the eyes of the Lord." In a world drowning in corruption, where sin had become normal and righteousness was rare, Noah stood as a man marked not by his own strength, but by God's favor. Grace was not a reward for Noah's perfection - it was the foundation that enabled his obedience. While others drifted with the current of rebellion, Noah walked against it, upheld by the unseen hand of God's favor. This same grace is still available today. A man does not stand righteous before God because he is flawless, but because he humbly seeks and receives the grace of God. Grace empowers what discipline alone cannot sustain. It strengthens a man to remain faithful when compromise is easier, to obey when the world resists, and to walk with God when others walk away. Like Noah, a man who finds grace becomes a witness in his generation - a living testimony that even in the darkest times, God's favor can rest upon a life fully yielded to Him.

Grace became the unseen strength beneath Noah's life, sustaining him in a world collapsing under its own corruption. Grace gave him the power to obey when obedience was costly, to remain faithful when faithfulness was rare, and to stand firm when everything around him invited surrender. His life reminds us that true spiritual endurance is not rooted in human willpower, but in divine favor that strengthens a willing heart. This same grace is still the foundation for any man who desires to live rightly before God. It does not remove weakness, but it empowers a man to overcome it. It does not excuse sin, but it provides the strength to resist it. A man who walks in grace understands that his ability to stand is not self-produced - it is God-given. When the favor of God rests on a life, it produces obedience, shapes character and builds a legacy that outlives the man himself. Like Noah, a man becomes unshaken not because he is perfect, but because he is upheld by the grace of God.

True manhood is not built on the fragile foundation of self-confidence, but on the unshakable ground of dependence on God. A man becomes truly strong when he recognizes his weakness and turns to God as his source. It is in surrender, not self-sufficiency, that a man finds real power. When a man leans on the Lord, he is no longer limited by his own understanding; he is guided by divine wisdom, sustained by divine strength, and upheld by a power greater than himself. Dependence on God is not a sign of weakness - it is the mark of spiritual maturity. It means trusting God in decisions, seeking Him in uncertainty, and relying on Him in every season of life. While the world pushes independence, God calls men into relationship. And in that relationship, a man finds clarity, courage, and direction. When he stops striving to stand on his own and chooses instead to walk with God, he becomes the kind of man who can endure, lead, and fulfill his purpose with strength that never runs dry.

Noah did not endure the flood by strength, intelligence, or human determination. In a world collapsing under its own corruption, it was the favor of God that preserved him. Grace reached Noah before the ark was ever built, before obedience was ever proven. It was grace that called him, grace that sustained him, and grace that carried him through judgment. Noah walked with God because God had first extended grace toward him. His obedience was the response, not the cause. This is the order that must never be reversed. When a man forgets grace, pride begins to grow, and his walk becomes about proving himself instead of trusting God. But when he remembers that everything began with God's mercy, his life remains humble, steady, and dependent. True manhood is not built on self-reliance, but on surrendered reliance. A godly man walks with God not to earn grace, but because he has already found it and that grace becomes the strength that carries him through every storm.

When a man truly understands grace, he no longer sees obedience as a burden, but as a response of love. Grace is the power to stand. It confronts the heart, corrects the will, and calls a man higher than his flesh ever could. A careless man treats grace as permission, but a godly man recognizes it as transformation. The same grace that forgives sin also trains the heart to turn from it. It awakens conviction, strengthens discipline, and produces a deep desire to walk in a way that honors God. A man shaped by grace does not ask how close he can get to sin without falling - he asks how fully he can surrender without holding back. Grace teaches him to deny ungodliness, to resist compromise, and to live with intention before the Lord. It anchors his life in humility, because he knows he stands only by the mercy of God, yet it fuels his obedience with strength that comes from above. Grace is not passive - it is active, forming a man who lives with reverence, walks with purpose, and obeys with a willing heart.

Many misunderstand grace as though it lowers God's standard, as if His holiness bends to accommodate human weakness. But true grace is not a permission slip for compromise, but a divine strength that calls a man higher. Grace meets a man in his brokenness, but it refuses to leave him bound there. It awakens his spirit, convicts his heart, and gives him the power to walk in obedience where he once walked in failure. God's standard remains holy, unchanging, and pure, and grace is the very force that enables a man to rise toward it. A man who truly understands grace does not become careless - he becomes transformed. He no longer asks how close he can get to sin, but how fully he can honor God. Grace reshapes his desires, strengthens his resolve, and teaches him to live with purpose and discipline. It lifts him from where he was, but it also leads him to where God has called him to be. Grace is not the lowering of the bar; it is the hand of God lifting a man up to reach it.

Noah's grace was active, visible, and proven through obedience. When God spoke, Noah did not hesitate, negotiate, or delay; he moved. The ark he built was not just a structure of wood; it was a testimony of trust, a declaration that he believed God enough to act on His word. True grace compels a man to align his life with what God has spoken. A man who truly understands grace will not use it as permission to remain unchanged. Instead, he will see it as divine empowerment to obey when obedience is costly, difficult, or misunderstood. Noah labored for years without visible proof of rain, yet he stayed faithful because grace had anchored his heart in trust. That same grace calls men today to rise, build, and walk in obedience even when others do not understand. Grace is not the absence of responsibility—it is the strength to fulfill it. When a man walks in true grace, his life becomes evidence that faith is real, obedience is possible, and God is worthy to be followed without hesitation.

A man who has truly received grace understands that it is a calling to live intentionally. Grace does not remove responsibility; it reveals it. Grace awakens a man to the reality that he now belongs to God, and with that belonging comes a responsibility to walk in a way that honors Him. It is not pressure that drives him, but gratitude. He does not obey to earn grace, but because grace has already been given. God's favor equips a man to carry what he could never carry on his own. Where responsibility once felt heavy, grace now provides strength, wisdom, and endurance. A faithful man does not shrink back from what is required; he leans into it, knowing that the same grace that saved him will sustain him. He becomes dependable, steady, and obedient not by his own power, but by the power of God working within him. Grace does not make a man passive; it makes him faithful. It turns responsibility into purpose and transforms duty into a life of devotion.

A godly man understands that no amount of talent can replace the necessity of God's favor upon his life. He may be skilled, disciplined, and experienced, but he knows that ability alone cannot open doors that only grace can unlock. While others may rely on reputation, connections, or past success, a godly man remains anchored in the awareness that God's presence is his greatest advantage. Because of this, he recognizes that every victory, every opportunity, and every measure of progress is ultimately a result of God's mercy working on his behalf. This keeps his heart tender and dependent, never self-sufficient or hardened by success. He does not boast in what he has built, because he knows it is grace that sustained him while building it. And when he faces weakness or limitation, he is not shaken, because his trust has never been in himself. A godly man lives with a steady reliance on God, fully convinced that with God's favor, even his smallest steps can carry eternal impact.

Grace has a way of bringing a man low in the best possible way. It strips him of pride and silences the inner voice that tries to take credit for what only God could sustain. When a man truly understands grace, he stops comparing himself to others and starts examining his own heart. He realizes that his strength is not self-made, his righteousness is not self-earned, and his position is not self-secured. Every step he stands on is supported by the patience of God, every victory is covered by mercy, and every opportunity is sustained by faithfulness that he did not deserve. This kind of understanding produces a quiet humility that shapes how a man lives and treats others. Instead of looking down on those who fall, he remembers how many times grace has held him up when he could have fallen himself. Grace teaches him to walk carefully, gratefully, and dependently before God. It reminds him that he is not standing because he is better - he is standing because God has been good.

When a man forgets grace, pride quietly begins to take its place. He forgets the prayers he prayed when he was weak, the mercy that covered his failures, and the hand of God that carried him through what he could not survive on his own. When a man no longer recognizes his dependence on God, he begins to drift from the One who sustained him. But the righteous man guards his heart when he looks at every victory and sees God's fingerprints all over it. He knows that doors were opened he did not deserve, strength was given when he had none left, and wisdom came in moments he could not have figured out on his own. This remembrance keeps him humble, grounded, and grateful. Instead of exalting himself, he honors God as the source of every good thing in his life. And because he remembers grace, he remains steady - never lifted up by pride, but always strengthened by the awareness that without God, he would have nothing, and with God, he can walk in true victory.

Noah's life reveals that grace is a powerful force that strengthens a surrendered man to stand when others fall. In a generation consumed by corruption, grace gave him the courage to live differently without apology. It steadied his heart when no one else understood his obedience, and it anchored his identity in God rather than in the approval of men. Grace made him firm when compromise was easier, faithful when wickedness was common, and obedient when the cost was high. That same grace carried Noah through years of unseen labor, giving him patience to keep building and faith to keep trusting before a single drop of rain had fallen. Grace strengthened his hands for the work, his spirit for the waiting, and his heart for the unknown. It was not weakness that sustained him - it was divine strength flowing through a life fully yielded to God. And that same grace is still available today, enabling a man to stand, to build, and to trust even when the world around him refuses to believe.

Every righteous life begins not with effort, but with grace. A man does not wake up one day and decide to become righteous by his own strength; he is first met by the mercy of God. Grace reaches him before he has proven anything, before he has built anything, before he has earned anything. It is God who initiates, God who calls, and God who supplies what the man could never produce on his own. Until a man receives what God gives, he will struggle to become what God desires. The same grace that forgives him also strengthens him, upholds him, and teaches him to walk uprightly. He does not carry the weight of obedience alone; he is sustained by the very hand of God. Every step of righteousness is supported by grace, and every act of obedience is fueled by what God has already poured into his life. When a man understands this, he stops striving to earn God's approval and starts walking in the strength God provides, building his life not on self-effort, but on the unshakable mercy of the Lord.

Grace is the soil where godly character takes root and begins to grow. A man cannot produce true integrity, obedience, endurance, or faithfulness through pride or self-effort alone. When a man encounters the goodness of God his motives are purified, his desires are realigned, and his strength is no longer rooted in himself but in the One who called him. Grace softens the heart, making it teachable, responsive, and willing to walk in truth even when it is difficult. Where grace is received, character is formed. Integrity grows because grace teaches a man to value what God values. Obedience becomes natural because grace awakens love for the One who leads him. Endurance is strengthened because grace reminds him he is sustained, not abandoned. Faithfulness takes root because grace reveals that God is faithful first. A man shaped by grace does not live to prove himself - he lives to honor God. And in that place, his life becomes steady, fruitful, and marked by a quiet strength that cannot be shaken.

A man who truly finds grace does not elevate himself; he humbles himself before God. He understands that every step forward, every victory won, and every lesson learned came not by his own power, but by the hand of God working in his life. He recognizes that his strength was sustained by God, his growth was guided by God, his wisdom was given by God, and his survival was secured by God. Such a man lives with a constant awareness of how much he has been helped. He remembers the moments when he was weak, when he almost gave up, when he did not know the way and how God carried him through. This remembrance keeps his heart soft and his spirit thankful. Instead of boasting in what he has become, he points to the One who made him. He knows that without God's mercy, he would have fallen, without God's guidance, he would have been lost, and without God's strength, he would have failed. So he walks forward in humility, giving all glory to God for everything he has overcome.

This kind of man becomes steady because he walks with a quiet awareness that every step is taken under the eyes of God. While others are shaken by criticism or inflated by praise, he remains grounded, because his validation does not come from the crowd. In the hidden places where no one else is watching, he chooses integrity, because he understands that God sees what men overlook. His confidence is not the self-promoting confidence of a man trying to elevate himself, but the steady assurance of a man who knows he has been called and upheld by God. He does not have to force doors open or strive to secure his place, because he believes that what God has ordained cannot be taken from him. This trust produces a calm strength within him that does not panic in uncertainty or crumble under pressure. He stands firm because he leans on the One who is unshakable. And in that dependence, he becomes a man who is both humble and immovable, anchored in the quiet confidence that God is enough.

In evil times, courage alone is not enough to carry a man through. Courage may help him stand for a moment, but grace is what enables him to stand consistently. Grace strengthens him where his flesh is weak, steadies him when pressure rises, and guards his heart when temptation whispers. When the world around him drifts further from truth, it is grace that anchors him in righteousness. It is not his willpower that keeps him clean, but the quiet, sustaining power of God working within him - teaching him to say no to sin and yes to obedience even when no one else understands. A man who walks in grace is not easily shaken by the condition of the culture. While others compromise, he remains firm. While others mock obedience, he continues to follow God with humility and conviction. Grace equips him to live righteously without needing approval. In a collapsing world, he becomes a steady light not because he is stronger than other men, but because he depends on a strength that is not his own.

Be a man who finds grace in the eyes of the Lord. Do not build your life on pride, performance, or personal strength alone, because those foundations will eventually crack under pressure. Grace is what anchors a man when life shifts, when trials come, and when his own ability is not enough. When a man recognizes his need for God, he positions himself where grace can reach him, shape him, and establish him in righteousness. Every righteous life begins with grace, and every faithful man is sustained by it. Grace is not only what saves a man but is what teaches him, strengthens him, and keeps him steady through every season. It gives him the power to remain faithful when others fall, to stand firm when pressure rises, and to walk upright when compromise is easier. A man who lives under grace walks with quiet confidence, knowing that God is the source of his strength. And because he depends on God, his life becomes consistent, his character becomes rooted, and his faith becomes unshakable.

"A MAN WHO HEARS GOD"

Genesis 6:13 says, "And God said unto Noah, 'The end of all flesh is come before me...'" This verse shows us that God does not reveal His heart to just anyone - He speaks to those who are aligned with Him. A man who hears God is a man who has made room for Him. Spiritual sensitivity is cultivated through obedience, humility, and a desire to know God deeply. This kind of man becomes a vessel for direction in uncertain times. While others were unaware of what was coming, Noah received clarity because he was listening. God still speaks today, but many miss His voice because their hearts are crowded or distracted. A man who hears God must guard his inner life, keeping it clean, surrendered, and attentive. When God finds a man who will listen, He will also trust him with instruction, purpose, and responsibility. Just as Noah was called to build according to God's word, so every man who hears God is called to act on what he hears.

God revealed His plans to Noah before the flood ever appeared on the horizon. While the world moved forward consumed with its own routines and distractions, Noah walked in a different awareness. God entrusted him with warning, direction, and purpose because his heart was tuned to listen. This is the power of spiritual sensitivity: it allows a man to see beyond the natural and prepare for what others overlook. In a world that cannot see what is coming, God is still looking for men who will listen, believe, and prepare. When a man values God's voice above the noise of culture, he gains access to divine insight that positions him ahead of circumstances rather than beneath them. Spiritual sensitivity is cultivated through relationship, obedience, and separation from the distractions that dull the soul. A man who learns to hear God will not be caught off guard by life's storms because he is already being guided before they arrive. While others scramble in confusion, he moves with clarity and purpose.

A man who hears God does not drift through life reacting to every voice around him. He is not driven by pressure, emotion, or the shifting opinions of people. Instead, he becomes anchored in a deeper awareness - the voice of God guiding his steps. While others move impulsively, he moves intentionally because he has learned to discern when God is speaking. His life is no longer accidental; it becomes directed, purposeful, and aligned with something eternal. This kind of man understands that hearing God is not a one-time event, but a cultivated relationship. He learns to slow down, to separate from the noise, and to value God's voice above all others. When God leads, he follows. When God corrects, he humbles himself. When God prepares him, he yields to the process, even when he does not fully understand it. Because of this, he is not caught off guard by life - he is prepared for it. God goes before him, and by learning to hear, he walks in clarity, confidence, and divine direction.

Noah's ability to hear God was not a sudden gift reserved for a moment of crisis; it was the result of a consistent walk with Him. Day after day, Noah lived in fellowship with God, honoring Him in quiet obedience when no one else was watching. That steady relationship sharpened his spiritual sensitivity. When God spoke, Noah recognized His voice because it was not unfamiliar to him. Spiritual hearing is cultivated in the daily decisions to pray, to listen, to obey, and to set aside the noise of the world for the presence of God. A surrendered heart is what keeps a man aligned with the voice of God. Reverence positions him to listen, and obedience confirms what he has heard. When a man consistently yields his will to God, his spirit becomes tuned to divine direction. Then, when critical moments come, he is not scrambling for guidance - he is already walking in it. A man who walks with God will hear God and walk in confidence even when the world around him is uncertain.

Many men ask God for direction but hesitate when it comes to devotion. They want clear answers without cultivating a close relationship, and guidance without yielding their will. A man who only seeks God in moments of confusion will struggle to hear Him clearly, because spiritual clarity is not built in crisis, but in communion. It is in the quiet, consistent place of prayer, humility, and reverence that a man learns to recognize the voice of God. God often speaks most clearly to the man who has already settled obedience in his heart. When a man comes with a yielded spirit - already willing to obey whatever God says - his heart becomes aligned with heaven. Obedience sharpens discernment. Surrender removes interference. And devotion opens the door to divine direction. The man who walks closely with God does not just receive instructions - he lives in step with them, guided not only by what God says, but by who God is.

A man must develop an ear for God's voice because spiritual clarity is cultivated through intentional pursuit. God is always speaking, but not every man is positioned to hear. When a man consistently gives his attention to God's Word, he begins to recognize the tone and direction of God's voice. As he spends time in prayer, not just speaking but listening, his spirit becomes more sensitive, more alert, and more responsive. The voice of God grows clearer to the man who values it enough to seek it daily. In a world filled with noise, distraction, and competing voices, a man must train his heart to listen beyond what is loud and immediate. The man who learns to quiet his soul and disciplines himself to listen will begin to hear what others miss. He will receive direction when others are confused, peace when others are troubled, and conviction when others drift. A man who develops an ear for God's voice walks guided, anchored, and aligned with the will of God.

The world is loud, and its voice is relentless. It speaks through fear that tries to paralyze, pride that tries to elevate self above God, pressure that demands conformity, and temptation that pulls the heart away from righteousness. It fills a man's life with constant noise until his spirit becomes crowded and unfocused. If he is not careful, he will begin to mistake the urgency of the world for the leading of God. The louder the world becomes, the easier it is for a man to drift from stillness, and without stillness, he loses the clarity needed to recognize the voice of the Lord. God's voice is often found in quiet places, in moments of surrender, in a heart that has chosen to listen rather than react. A man who desires to hear God must be willing to turn down the volume of the world and draw near with intention. He must guard his mind, discipline his attention, and create space for God's presence. When he does, he will discover that God has been speaking all along.

Hearing God requires separation from the noise that constantly surrounds a man's life. The world is filled with opinions, pressures, distractions, and demands that fight for attention and shape decisions if left unchecked. A man who desires to hear God must be willing to step away from all of it. He must learn to be still, to quiet his thoughts, and to create space where God's voice is not competing with everything else. In that stillness, clarity begins to form. The confusion fades, the pressure loosens, and the direction of God becomes more discernible to a heart that is no longer crowded. It takes discipline to silence the voices that pull at a man's mind and emotions, especially when they feel urgent or important. But the man who masters this discipline positions himself to hear what truly matters. When he chooses God's voice above every other voice, he is gaining divine direction. He is strengthened, aligned, and prepared to walk with confidence, knowing he has heard from God.

Noah lived in a generation that had lost its moral direction, yet he refused to let that corruption become his compass. While others allowed the culture to shape their thinking, Noah chose a higher authority. He did not adjust his convictions to fit the crowd but instead anchored his life to the voice of God. He did not follow the shifting opinions of people; he followed the unchanging word of the Lord. Because Noah valued God's voice above all else, he was able to hear clearly and obey faithfully. The culture around him may have mocked, questioned, and resisted, but Noah had already settled in his heart who he would listen to. That decision gave him clarity when others were confused and direction when others were lost. A man who listens to God will not be easily swayed by the pressure of the crowd. When God's voice becomes greater than the culture's influence, a man gains the strength to stand alone if necessary and, in doing so, he becomes a vessel through which God can accomplish something eternal.

Direction is found in the unchanging voice of God. A man who values public opinion above God's Word will always feel pulled in different directions, because people are inconsistent and culture is unstable. What is praised today may be rejected tomorrow. But when a man settles it in his heart that God's Word is final, he finds clarity. A man who builds his life on what God says becomes unshakable. Storms may come - criticism, pressure, rejection, and misunderstanding - but they do not move him, because his foundation is secure. He is not adjusting his convictions to fit the moment; he is standing on what is eternal. While others are tossed back and forth by opinions, he walks with confidence, knowing that God's Word will outlast every voice that rises against it. Direction comes when a man stops asking, "What do people think?" and starts asking, "What has God said?" For the man who builds on that foundation will not only stand - he will endure.

When God spoke to Noah, He did not leave him with a vague warning or a general sense of danger - He gave him clear, specific instruction. God told him exactly what to build, how to build it, and what to do. This reveals something powerful about the nature of God's voice: it is not only corrective, it is directive. A man who truly listens to God will be guided into obedience. The voice of God is not meant to create fear, but to produce action rooted in faith. This truth still stands today. When God speaks, He leads. He does not expose sin without also calling a man to repentance. He does not reveal danger without also providing direction. The problem is not that God is silent, but that many men stop at conviction and never move into obedience. Noah did not just hear God - he responded. He built when it had never rained, he obeyed when it made no sense, and he trusted when no one else believed. That is the kind of man God is looking for: a man who does not just recognize His voice but follows it.

A man who truly hears God cannot remain unchanged by what he hears. The voice of God is given to direct, correct, and lead. Every instruction from God carries with it a call to movement. Whether it is a step of faith, an act of surrender, or a decision to turn away from sin, the man who values God's voice will respond with action, not delay. Obedience is the evidence that God's voice has been honored. It proves that His word holds authority in a man's life above comfort, fear, and personal preference. Many may hear, but few will move not knowing it is in the moving that transformation takes place. When a man obeys, he aligns himself with the will of God, and heaven begins to shape his path. But when he resists, he hardens his heart and dulls his spiritual hearing. A man who walks with God understands this: every time God speaks, a decision follows. And the man who chooses obedience does not just hear God - he walks with Him.

Noah stood in a place where faith had to rise above sight. He heard the voice of God speak of rain when the earth had never seen it, of judgment when the world felt secure, and of an ark when there was no visible reason to build one. Yet he chose to believe before there was proof. This is the mark of a spiritually sensitive man - he does not wait for evidence before he trusts God's word. He understands that circumstances eventually align with what God has already spoken. A man who walks with God builds when others question, prepares when others ignore, and obeys when others delay. Faith is proven in those moments when nothing around him confirms what God has said, yet he remains steady. The world may not understand his actions, but heaven recognizes his obedience. In time, what was once unseen becomes undeniable, but by then, the faithful man has already positioned himself under God's promise because he chose to believe before the evidence appeared.

This kind of man will often walk a lonely road. When he obeys God without hesitation, some will mock his warnings, and some may even reject him altogether. But his life is not built on the shifting opinions of people - it is anchored in the unchanging voice of God. He understands that truth is not validated by majority agreement, and righteousness is not determined by public acceptance. A man who has truly heard from God cannot afford to be ruled by human approval. If he does, he will dilute his obedience, silence his convictions, and eventually drift from his calling. Instead, he must stand firm, even when misunderstood, knowing that obedience to God is always worth the cost. His responsibility is not to be accepted - it is to be faithful. In time, the same voice that led him will sustain him, vindicate him, and use his life as a testimony. Because in the end, it is far better to stand approved by God and questioned by men than to be celebrated by men and found unfaithful before God.

God is not silent. He still speaks through His Word that reveals truth, through His Spirit that convicts and guides, and through the wisdom He gives to those who seek Him with a sincere heart. His voice may not always come with noise or spectacle, but it is steady, faithful, and clear to the man who is listening. When a man opens his life to God, he begins to recognize that divine guidance is not rare - it is constant. Scripture becomes more than words on a page; it becomes direction.

The Spirit becomes more than a concept; He becomes a present guide. And wisdom becomes more than knowledge; it becomes the ability to walk rightly before God. But a man must guard his heart if he wants to continue hearing that voice. A hardened heart resists truth, a dulled conscience ignores conviction, and a careless attitude toward holy things slowly silences spiritual sensitivity. That is why he must remain tender before God - quick to respond, quick to repent, and quick to obey.

Spiritual sensitivity is the discipline of a man who refuses to be ruled by impulse, ego, or emotion, and instead chooses to be led by truth. When pride rises up and demands to be heard, a spiritually sensitive man has the strength to be silent and listen for the voice of God. When impatience presses him to act quickly, he has the restraint to wait until God gives direction. This kind of man is powerful, but his power is governed by wisdom, humility, and reverence. In a world that rewards noise, speed, and self-promotion, spiritual sensitivity sets a man apart. It gives him the courage to stand still when others rush ahead, and the conviction to obey God when the crowd pressures him to compromise. He is not easily shaken because he is not led by the moment, but by the Spirit. His strength is seen in his ability to discern and to respond with obedience. This is the kind of strength that builds lasting character - a strength that does not need to prove itself to men, because it is already anchored in the will of God.

A man who truly hears God becomes a man of direction. While others are pulled in a hundred different directions by trends, opinions, and pressures, he is anchored by a higher voice. He does not feel the need to chase what is popular or react to every report of fear, because his decisions are guided by obedience. When God speaks, it brings clarity, and that clarity produces stability. His life is shaped by the steady leading of the Lord. Because his steps are ordered by God, he walks with a quiet confidence that cannot be shaken by changing circumstances. He may not always understand every detail of the path ahead, but he trusts the One who directs it. This kind of man is not easily distracted or discouraged, because he knows where his direction comes from. While others wander, he advances. While others hesitate, he moves forward in faith. His strength is not in knowing everything, but in knowing the One who is leading him and that is what keeps him steady, focused, and unwavering.

Be a man who hears God. In a world filled with noise, opinions, and constant distraction, spiritual clarity is developed through intentional separation and devotion. A man who truly hears God has learned to quiet his soul and to value time in God's presence. When a man begins to prioritize God's voice above all else, his life gains direction, stability, and purpose that cannot be shaken by the chaos around him. In a confused generation, God is still searching for men like Noah - men who are sensitive enough to hear, faithful enough to obey, and strong enough to stand. These men may walk paths that others question but they carry a confidence that comes from knowing they have heard from God. When God speaks, they respond without hesitation, trusting that His way is higher and His plan is sure. This kind of man becomes a pillar in uncertain times - a steady voice, a faithful leader, and a living testimony that even in the midst of confusion, God still speaks to those who are willing to listen.

| 7 |

"THE MAN WHO BELIEVES THE WARNING"

Hebrews 11:7 tells us that Noah was "warned of God of things not seen as yet," revealing a powerful truth that faith responds to God before circumstances confirm what He has spoken. Noah was warned of things not yet seen, yet he moved with reverent fear and obedient action. He did not wait for the sky to darken or for rain to begin before he took God seriously. This is the kind of faith that does not require visible proof to move forward. It believes that if God has spoken, that is reason enough to act. This kind of faith still calls to men today. A man of God does not wait until consequences are obvious before he obeys; he responds when God speaks. Obedience before evidence requires a deep trust in God's character. It means building when no one understands, preparing when no one else sees the need, and standing firm when the world dismisses the warning. Noah's life reminds us that true faith is not passive - it moves, builds, and prepares.

True faith is not built on what a man can see, but on who God has proven Himself to be. Like Noah, who moved with fear and reverence at the word of God concerning things not yet seen, a man of faith responds to God's voice before the evidence appears. He does not need the sky to darken with rain before he starts building. This kind of faith separates the man who merely listens from the man who obeys.

Real faith reveals itself most when the path is unclear and the outcome is uncertain. It is easy to believe when the blessing is in hand, but it takes strength to believe when all you have is a word from God and the responsibility to act on it. A man walking in this faith will move forward when others hesitate, stand firm when others doubt, and obey when others delay. his is not passive belief - it is active trust. It is the kind of faith that builds, prepares, and moves before the world sees any reason to do so, and in the end, it is the kind of faith that stands vindicated by God.

Noah believed God concerning things that had not yet happened. The flood was not visible, the skies were still clear, and the world around him carried on as if nothing would ever change. Yet when God spoke, Noah responded in obedience. While others relied on what they could see, Noah built his life on what God had said. That kind of faith does not require visible proof; it requires a settled heart that knows God is true. This is the faith every man must learn to walk in. There will be moments when God warns, leads, or calls you forward into something that cannot yet be confirmed by natural sight. In those moments, faith builds, prepares, and obeys before the rain ever falls. A man who walks with God does not wait for the storm to prove the word - he trusts the word enough to prepare for the storm. And when the day comes that what was once unseen becomes reality, it will not be panic that fills his heart, but peace, because he acted on God's voice when others ignored it.

A man of faith understands that truth is established by the voice of God. While the world shifts with opinions, trends, and pressures, the righteous man stands anchored in what heaven has already spoken. When God speaks, it settles the matter in his heart. Even when others question, mock, or misunderstand he moves forward, knowing that obedience to God will always lead to life, even when it costs him comfort or acceptance. This kind of man learns to value God's word above every competing voice. He refuses to let public opinion reshape what God has made clear. Like the faithful men of scripture, he stands when others bow and obeys when others hesitate. His strength is not in being agreed with, but in being aligned with God. Over time, his life becomes a testimony that God honors those who trust Him fully. While the world chases approval, the righteous man walks in conviction because he knows that one word from God carries more authority than the approval of a thousand voices.

Faith is proven not in what a man says he believes, but in how he responds when God speaks without explanation. Many claim trust in God, yet hesitate when obedience requires uncertainty. They wait for visible confirmation, for circumstances to align, or for others to agree. But faith does not stand on evidence - it stands on the authority of God's word. A man of faith understands that if God has spoken, the outcome is already settled, even if the path is not yet visible. He moves forward not because he sees clearly, but because he trusts completely. True faith obeys in the tension between promise and manifestation. While others delay, analyze, and negotiate, the faithful man acts. He knows that waiting for proof is not faith - it is dependence on sight. Faith honors God by responding immediately, trusting that obedience will reveal what hesitation never could. When a man chooses to obey before he sees, he places his confidence where it belongs - not in circumstances, but in the unchanging voice of God.

Noah's obedience proved what he truly believed. When God spoke of a coming judgment, he responded with action. While others lived as though nothing would change, Noah built according to a word that had not yet been seen. Day after day, board by board, he demonstrated that faith is not measured by agreement, but by alignment. He didn't wait for evidence to confirm God's warning; he let God's word become his evidence, and he ordered his life around it. That is the kind of faith every man must pursue. Real faith does not stay hidden in thoughts or confined to words - it steps forward in obedience. It restructures priorities, redirects decisions, and withstands the pressure of doubt and opposition. A man of faith does not merely acknowledge what God has said, he lives as though it is already true. When obedience becomes visible, belief becomes undeniable. In the end, it is not what a man claims to believe that defines him, but what he is willing to build, change, and surrender in response to God's voice.

A righteous man does not treat God's warnings as optional suggestions - he receives them as lifelines from heaven. While others may delay obedience, a righteous man responds quickly, knowing that delayed obedience can lead to unnecessary struggle. He values the voice of God more than his own comfort, and he also recognizes that every warning carries purpose. God does not warn to harm, but to shield, to guide, and to prepare a man for what lies ahead. A righteous man sees divine instruction as protection from unseen dangers and preparation for greater responsibility. He understands that obedience in the moment positions him for blessing in the future. Instead of resisting correction, he embraces it, knowing that it is shaping his character and securing his path. In this way, he walks not only in awareness, but in wisdom - guarded, guided, and grounded in the truth that God's warnings are acts of love.

Some warnings come through scripture, where truth is written plainly for the man who is willing to read and receive it. Some come through conviction, that inward stirring that unsettles the soul and refuses to let compromise feel comfortable. Others come through godly counsel, when a voice of wisdom speaks what a man may not want to hear but desperately needs. And some warnings come through the quiet dealings of the Holy Spirit, not loud or forceful, but persistent and clear to a heart that is sensitive to God. However they come, these warnings are moments where heaven reaches into a man's life to redirect, correct, and preserve him from paths that lead to loss. A wise man does not harden his heart, make excuses, or push away what challenges him. Instead, he leans in, listens, and responds with humility and obedience. He recognizes that ignoring God's voice today can lead to consequences tomorrow, but receiving it can lead to protection, growth, and alignment with God's will.

The danger for many men is not the absence of God's voice, but the dulling of their own ears. God has already spoken through His Word, through conviction, and through correction but familiarity can breed neglect. A man may hear warnings about pride, lust, anger, bitterness, laziness, compromise, and rebellion, yet convince himself there is still time to deal with it later. But each delay hardens the heart a little more, making what was once clear feel distant. The Spirit's prompting grows quieter not because God has stopped speaking, but because the man has grown comfortable resisting what he already knows is right. Delayed obedience is a slow drift into disobedience. God calls men to respond when He speaks, not when it feels convenient. A righteous man understands that immediate obedience protects his heart, sharpens his discernment, and keeps him aligned with God's will. The longer a man waits, the more he risks losing sensitivity to truth.

Noah's life reveals that warning is mercy in action. When God spoke to him about the coming flood, He was not trying to frighten him, but to prepare him. Direction came before destruction. Instruction came before judgment. In the same way, when God places conviction in a man's heart, when He speaks through His Word, or sends a warning through circumstances, it is not to condemn him but to rescue him. A wise man does not ignore those moments but recognizes them as divine opportunities to align himself with God before consequences take hold. Many men wait until the storm has already broken to seek God, but Noah responded while the skies were still clear. Warning is God's grace giving a man time to change course, to build what will sustain him, and to walk in obedience before it is too late. The man who listens early will stand strong later. But the man who delays risks losing what could have been saved. When God warns, He is not closing a door - He is opening one.

Manhood requires a kind of faith that is not swayed by the laughter of men. When Noah built the ark, there was no visible evidence that rain was coming - only the word of God. To the world, his obedience looked irrational, excessive, even embarrassing. Yet Noah was not building based on public opinion; he was building based on divine instruction. A man who fears God must settle this in his heart that what looks foolish to a blind world is often wisdom in the eyes of heaven. Faith will always put a man at odds with a culture that does not honor God. The same voice that calls a man to righteousness will expose the emptiness of the world's approval. A man cannot wait until obedience is popular before he moves - he must move when God speaks. True manhood stands firm when mocked, stays steady when misunderstood, and continues building even when no one else sees the purpose. Because in the end, the laughter of men fades, but the reward of obedience stands.

A man who fears mockery will eventually bow to it. The opinions of others become a louder voice than the command of God, and what begins as hesitation turns into quiet disobedience. But a man of faith understands that obedience is not validated by applause. God does not require a crowd's agreement before He gives instruction. There are moments when obedience will look strange, uncomfortable, and even foolish to those who do not hear what you hear. Some of the greatest assignments a man will ever receive demand isolation of conviction. He must be willing to stand alone when others doubt, to believe when others mock, and to build when others laugh. The depth of faith is forged not in the comfort of agreement, but in the tension of standing firm without it. A man who walks closely with God learns that obedience often separates before it elevates. And if he remains faithful in that lonely place, what was once mocked will one day stand as a testimony that he chose God's voice over the noise of men.

The world often mocks what it cannot discern. It laughs at holiness because it does not understand purity, questions conviction because it has grown comfortable with compromise, and belittles obedience because it resists authority. Faith appears foolish to those who measure life only by what they can see, control, and explain. But a man who walks with God learns early that if a man builds his life on the approval of the crowd, he will constantly adjust his convictions to avoid their laughter but in doing so, he will drift further from the voice of God. There will be moments when obedience requires silence while others speak, faith while others doubt, and courage while others mock. In those moments, a man must remember that God does not ask for agreement from the crowd - He asks for obedience from His servant. When a man chooses the voice of the Lord over the noise of the world, he steps into a deeper walk of faith, one that may not always be understood by others, but will always be recognized by God.

Noah's faith was never meant to stop with Noah. When Noah believed God's warning about what was coming, he did not treat it lightly or delay his response. While the world continued in ignorance, Noah moved in obedience, and that obedience created a place of safety not just for himself, but for his entire household. His faith took form in action, and that action became a refuge. It reminds us that real faith is not passive - it prepares, it moves, it builds according to what God has said, even when no one else understands. A man must recognize that what he listens to, what he obeys, and what he builds in response to God can become a covering for those connected to him. When a man walks with God, he is not just shaping his own future -he is influencing the direction, protection, and spiritual climate of his family. Faithful obedience creates an atmosphere where others can be preserved, strengthened, and guided. In this way, a man's faith becomes a shield, a shelter, and a legacy for those under his care.

A man must never treat his faith as something casual or secondary, because it carries weight far beyond his own life. Every decision he makes sets a direction not only for himself but for those connected to him. His faith becomes the atmosphere of his home. When he walks in obedience, he creates stability. When he disciplines his life, he builds strength into his family. When he prays, he invites God's presence into places that would otherwise be empty. A man may think his private choices are isolated, but in truth, they echo into his marriage, shape his children, and quietly establish the course of his future. This is why surrender is not weakness but responsibility. A man who humbles himself before God is securing his legacy. His repentance teaches his children honesty before God. His consistency teaches them endurance. His reverence teaches them what truly matters. Long after his words fade, the pattern of his life will remain. A man who takes his faith seriously alters the trajectory of generations.

Faith in what cannot yet be seen is active courage, the kind that chooses obedience when there is no visible evidence and no immediate reward. A man walking by faith often finds himself moving forward with nothing but the word of God to stand on. Like The Bible teaches, faith is the substance of things hoped for and the evidence of things not seen. Courage is what keeps a man laying bricks when he cannot yet see the finished structure. There is also courage required to remain faithful over time. Anyone can be excited at the beginning, but it takes a steady, unwavering heart to continue when the promise still feels distant. Faith refuses to measure God's faithfulness by present circumstances. It chooses trust over doubt, discipline over discouragement, and perseverance over quitting. A courageous man of faith understands that just because he cannot see movement does not mean God is not working. He stays committed, knowing that in due season, what was once invisible will become undeniable.

In a world that delays, debates, and dismisses truth, the man who believes God without needing visible proof stands apart. Noah did not wait for rain before he built - he responded to the voice of God before the first drop ever fell. While others mocked and continued in their own ways, Noah's reverence moved him to action. The kind of faith God recognizes is a faith that moves, builds, and prepares even when it stands alone. Noah became more than a man who survived a storm; he became a witness to a generation that refused to listen. His life declares that one man, fully surrendered to God, can stand firm when everyone else falls away. He shows us that obedience is about conviction. When a man chooses to believe God at His word, he positions himself for preservation, purpose, and legacy. Even if no one else understands, even if no one else follows, the man who walks in reverent faith becomes living proof that God rewards those who trust Him and act on what He has spoken.

Long before the storm clouds gather, the man of faith is already building, already preparing, already aligning his life with what heaven has spoken. He does not need the agreement of others to move forward. While the world mocks and questions, he stands firm, anchored in reverence for God. He understands that obedience before the storm is what preserves him in the storm. Faith is not passive; it is active, decisive, and courageous. It builds when others are idle. It listens when others ignore. It acts when others hesitate. A man of faith sees beyond the natural and responds to the unseen reality of God's truth. He builds what God told him to build, even when it looks foolish to those around him, because he knows that what God has spoken will surely come to pass. In the end, it is not the opinion of the crowd that matters - it is the approval of God. And the man who believes the warning, who obeys before the evidence appears, will stand when others fall, because he trusted what others refused to hear.

| 8 |

"A MAN WHO MOVES WITH REVERENCE"

Noah was not shaped by what was easy, popular, or accepted - he was shaped by holy reverence. While the world around him continued in normal routines, unmoved by the warning of judgment, Noah allowed the voice of God to interrupt his life and redirect his priorities. Hebrews 11:7 reveals that when God spoke of things not yet seen, Noah did not hesitate or dismiss it as unlikely - he moved with faith. Godly fear anchored him. It kept him steady when others were careless, focused when others were distracted, and obedient when others refused to listen. His reverence made him sensitive to God's voice and serious about God's instruction. A man who walks in this kind of fear is not controlled by the opinions of people or the pressure of culture. He understands that God's word carries eternal weight, and he responds accordingly. Noah did not negotiate with God or delay until it was convenient - he obeyed because he believed. That is the difference holy fear makes. It produces action, not excuses.

A man who moves with reverence does not treat the voice of God as a suggestion or a distant opinion, but as absolute truth that demands response. Reverence shapes the way he thinks, speaks, and lives. It anchors his heart in the reality that God is holy, righteous, powerful, and true. Where there is reverence, there is careful obedience. Where there is reverence, there is a refusal to compromise. This kind of man walks with an awareness that every step matters before God. Noah's generation ignored the warning, but Noah respected it. That reverence moved him to act when there was no visible evidence, to build when there was no rain, and to prepare when others mocked. A man who fears God like this is not controlled by the crowd or distracted by delay. He is steady, focused, and obedient because he knows that God's word will stand. Reverence gives him the strength to live differently, to stand alone if necessary, and to align his life with what heaven has already declared.

Holy fear is not a paralyzing dread that causes a man to hide from God; it is a deep reverence that causes him to draw near with humility and obedience. This kind of fear steadies a man's heart. It silences pride, corrects careless living, and awakens a seriousness about how he walks before God. When a man carries holy fear, he understands that God's words are not suggestions but divine instruction, and he treats them with weight and urgency. Noah walked in this kind of fear. While others ignored the warning, Noah honored the voice of God and moved in obedience. Holy fear gave him clarity when the world was confused, and conviction when others were compromised. It anchored him in a time of widespread corruption and kept him faithful to an unseen reality. A man who fears God this way does not need the approval of people, because he is governed by a higher authority. He knows that when God speaks, the wisest response is not delay, debate, or doubt but immediate and faithful obedience.

The world often misunderstands a man who walks carefully before the Lord, labeling him as too serious, too rigid, or out of step with the times. But what the world calls excessive, heaven calls essential. A reverent man understands that life is not casual when it comes to the things of God. He does not treat holy matters lightly, nor does he allow culture to redefine what God has already declared sacred. His posture is not driven by fear of man, but by a deep awareness of God's authority, holiness, and truth. This kind of man is anchored, not swayed - steady because he values God's voice above every other voice. A foolish man handles sacred things without care, speaking loosely, living casually, and crossing lines God never permitted. But a wise man bows his heart before the Lord long before he ever bows his knee in public. His reverence shapes his decisions, guards his conduct, and directs his path. He orders his steps according to God's Word, not convenience, emotion, or pressure.

Many men drift not because God has stopped speaking, but because they have stopped trembling. The voice of God becomes familiar, and what was once holy becomes common in their ears. In that casual posture, the heart grows dull, and sin no longer feels dangerous. But a man who walks with God understands that every word from Him carries weight. He does not treat divine instruction lightly, because he knows that what God says is not a suggestion - it is life or death. Noah stands as a witness against delay. He did not wait for the first drop of rain before he moved; he responded when the warning was still unseen and the command seemed unreasonable. That is the difference between a man who merely hears and a man who believes. Faith responds early. Faith moves when others mock. Faith builds in private what will be revealed in time. A man of faith understands that reverence is proven not in what he feels, but in how quickly and seriously he responds when God speaks.

Noah was warned about something he had never seen, yet he obeyed as though it was already happening. That is what reverence does in a man's life. It moves him beyond what his eyes can confirm and anchors him in what God has declared. Reverence gives a man the ability to act on truth before it becomes visible reality. He does not need proof to begin preparing - he needs only the word of the Lord. In a world driven by evidence, reverence teaches a man to be driven by conviction. Reverence gives him the strength to obey when no one else understands and to move forward when others stand still. Noah built while others questioned, prepared while others mocked, and obeyed while others ignored the warning. That is the power of a heart that takes God seriously. A reverent man does not delay obedience waiting for approval; he aligns himself with heaven immediately. He knows that what God has spoken is already certain, whether or not it has appeared.

A man who truly fears God is no longer governed by the shifting opinions of people. Noah lived in a generation that likely mocked his obedience, questioned his sanity, and rejected his message, yet he kept building. He understood that the voice of God carries more weight than the approval of a crowd. When a man values divine instruction above human opinion, he becomes steady, unshaken, and immovable in his assignment. This kind of fear is not weakness - it is strength anchored in reverence. It produces a boldness that does not need applause to continue and does not collapse under pressure to conform. Noah feared God too much to compromise, too much to delay, and too much to turn back. And that same posture is what God is seeking today - a man who will obey even when misunderstood, who will stand even when isolated, and who will build what God commanded even when no one else believes. When a man fears God rightly, he is finally free from being ruled by man.

The fear of man is a subtle trap that weakens conviction and bends a man toward compromise. It causes him to measure his decisions by opinions, approval, and acceptance rather than truth. He begins to ask, "What will people think?" instead of seeking, "What has God said?" And in that shift, his strength is slowly replaced with hesitation. But the fear of God anchors a man in truth, steadies his heart, and gives him the courage to stand when standing is costly. A man who fears God understands that pleasing God will often require disappointing people, but he chooses righteousness anyway. When voices rise against him, he returns to what God has spoken and stands firm on that foundation. His reverence becomes his strength, and his obedience becomes his testimony. While others bend to fit the moment, he stands because he is grounded in eternity. The fear of God makes a man unshakable, because his life is built on the authority of God's word rather than the instability of human opinion.

When a man truly understands that his assignment comes from God, he does not approach it casually or treat it as something optional. Like Noah, he moves with a deep awareness that obedience is not based on feelings but on reverence. Holy fear produces that kind of focus. It strips away excuses, silences procrastination, and reminds a man that what God has entrusted to him carries eternal weight. This kind of reverence sustains endurance when the work becomes long and unseen. Noah labored for years without applause, without visible results, and without the approval of those around him but he did not quit. Why? Because holy fear kept him serious about his assignment. A man who fears God understands that quitting is not an option when God has given a command. He stays steady, committed, and faithful, knowing that every act of obedience matters. In the end, it is not bursts of inspiration that fulfill God's will - it is consistent, reverent obedience that carries a man all the way to completion.

Every man needs holy seriousness in his life - not a heavy spirit that crushes joy, but a focused heart that understands purpose. This kind of seriousness is steady, disciplined, and anchored in the awareness that life is a stewardship before God. A man who carries holy seriousness moves with clarity, knowing that eternity is shaped by how he lives today. A man cannot afford to be casual with his calling, careless with his family, or lazy with his faith and still expect to finish strong. Reverence teaches him that what God placed in his hands matters too much for neglect. It causes him to show up when it's hard, to stay faithful when no one is watching, and to guard what has been entrusted to him. This kind of man understands that strength is not just seen in bold moments, but in consistent obedience. And because he treats his assignment with honor, he positions himself to finish his race with integrity, leaving behind a legacy that reflects the seriousness with which he walked before God.

When Noah moved with reverence toward God, he built more than an ark; he built a place of safety for everyone connected to him. His fear of the Lord positioned his family under divine protection in the middle of judgment. A man's decisions, his discipline, and his obedience create an atmosphere that either protects or exposes those under his care. Noah didn't just save himself - his reverence made room for his family to be preserved. When a man honors God, he becomes a source of covering, direction, and stability for his household. His consistency builds trust. His obedience invites God's hand. His reverence establishes order where chaos would otherwise rule. A man who fears God is not just securing his own future - he is shaping the destiny of those connected to him. Whether he realizes it or not, his life is either building an ark or leaving his household exposed. Walk with God in such a way that those around you are safer, stronger, and more secure because of your obedience.

When Noah laid each piece of the ark in place, there was no applause, no evidence of rain, and no visible urgency to the natural eye. What seemed like daily routine was actually divine strategy unfolding. A man who walks in reverence does not measure his obedience by what others see, but by what God has spoken. He knows that every act of faithfulness is building something greater than the moment. In time, what Noah built in private became the refuge that saved his family in public. This is the power of reverent obedience - it turns hidden faithfulness into visible deliverance. A man must understand that the disciplines he commits to today, the prayers he prays, and the standards he refuses to compromise are not just for now - they are shaping a future covering. When the storms come, it will not be last-minute effort that sustains him, but long-term obedience. What a man builds with God in secret becomes the very place God uses to protect, sustain, and carry him through what others cannot survive.

Reverence guards a man from the quiet rise of pride by keeping his eyes fixed on God instead of himself. When a man truly fears the Lord, he does not measure his life by his own accomplishments, but by his accountability to heaven. He understands that every ability, every victory, and every open door came from the hand of God. This awareness dismantles self-exaltation before it can take root. Holy fear reminds him that his life, his calling, and his strength are entrusted to him, not produced by him. Because of this, his heart remains low even when his life is elevated. He walks carefully, not carelessly, knowing that pride precedes a fall and that God resists the proud but gives grace to the humble. Reverence becomes a constant guard over his thoughts, his decisions, and his motives. It keeps him sensitive to correction and quick to give God the glory. A man who walks in holy fear does not drift he stays anchored in humility, steady in obedience, and aligned with the One who gave him everything.

Many men do not fall suddenly - they drift. What was once holy becomes common, what once stirred conviction becomes routine, and what once demanded reverence becomes something handled casually. Familiarity dulls the edge of conviction if it is not guarded by honor. When a man treats sacred things as common, he begins to lose sensitivity to the very voice meant to guide him. What once corrected him no longer moves him, and what once humbled him no longer reaches him. A wise man approaches God with fresh reverence, even in familiar places. The more a man is entrusted with spiritual truth, the more carefully he must walk before God. Reverence keeps a man sharp, humble, and responsive. It protects his heart from pride and his life from hidden compromise. A man who honors what is holy will remain steady where others fall, because he never forgets that what he handles is sacred, and the God he walks with is not to be taken lightly.

Noah did not stand above his generation with pride - he stood apart from it through obedience. When others dismissed the warning, he believed it. When others continued in comfort, he moved with conviction. His faith was not hidden; it took form in daily, costly obedience. Every strike of the hammer on the ark echoed a message the world could not ignore: God had spoken, and a man believed Him. Noah's life became a living sermon, not through words alone, but through unwavering action. In choosing to obey when it made no sense to the natural mind, he drew a clear line between belief and unbelief, between those who trusted God and those who trusted themselves. In the same way, when a man chooses righteousness in a culture of compromise, when he walks in truth while others follow deception, his life becomes a testimony that cannot be silenced. Obedience declares that God is right, even when the majority disagrees. It reveals that faith is not passive - it responds, it moves, it builds.

A man who moves with reverence does not delay obedience while waiting for full understanding. He recognizes that God's wisdom is higher than his own, and that trust is proven in action, not explanation. When God speaks, reverence responds. Noah built what had never been seen, prepared for what had never happened, and committed himself to a command that made no sense to the natural mind. His obedience was not rooted in evidence, but in confidence in the voice of God. This is the posture every man must learn. Reverence produces a steady, unquestioning obedience that does not fluctuate with feelings or circumstances. A man who fears God more than he fears uncertainty will move when others hesitate. He understands that delayed obedience is still disobedience, and that God honors those who act on His word, even when the outcome is unseen. When a man reaches this place, he no longer needs constant reassurance - he only needs direction. And once he hears, he moves.

This kind of man is rare, but he is necessary in every generation. While others compromise and make peace with sin, he draws a line and stands firm. He understands that sin is not something to manage but something to crucify. His life is marked by a deep awareness that God sees, God knows, and God judges righteously. Because of this,

his obedience is intentional, disciplined, and rooted in love for God. This man knows he has been entrusted with an assignment, and he does not treat it lightly. Whether leading his family, stewarding his calling, or standing in the gap during difficult times, he carries a holy weight in his spirit. He lives with eternity in view, knowing that one day he will give an account before God. That reality shapes his decisions, sharpens his priorities, and strengthens his resolve. This is the man heaven can trust - the man who does not drift with the culture, but stands anchored in truth, faithful to God until the end.

A man who moves with reverence is governed by a holy awareness that God sees, God speaks, and God requires. This kind of man walks with intention, measuring his steps against the holiness of God. His reverence produces wisdom, and his wisdom produces strength. He bows before God, and because he bows, he stands strong before everything else. Like Noah, his reverence becomes visible through obedience. When God speaks, he does not argue - he builds. When instruction comes, even without full understanding, he responds with faith-filled action. His life becomes proof that he trusts God beyond what he can see. That reverence becomes the foundation that protects his home, the discipline that guards his character, and the legacy that outlives him. This man moves carefully, knowing that every decision carries weight before a holy God. And because he lives with that awareness, his life is built on faith, sustained by obedience, and secured by reverence.

| 9 |

"A MAN WHO OBEYS COMPLETELY"

The testimony spoken over Noah in Genesis 6:22 reveals a level of obedience that few men ever reach, "Thus did Noah; according to all that God commanded him, so did he." This was not casual obedience - it was complete surrender. Noah did not filter God's voice through his own comfort, logic, or preference. He didn't negotiate with divine instruction or reshape it to fit his understanding. When God commanded, Noah acted. This kind of obedience is the evidence of a heart that trusts God fully, even when the outcome is unseen and the process is difficult. This is the kind of obedience God still seeks in men today. Partial obedience may satisfy the flesh, but it does not fulfill the will of God. A man of faith does not pick and choose which commands to follow - he submits completely because he knows that God's wisdom is higher than his own. True manhood is revealed when a man obeys God fully. Like Noah, his life becomes a testimony that obedience is the proof that his faith is real.

A man who obeys completely understands that God's commands are divine authority spoken with purpose and power. When God speaks, a faithful man responds with reverence, not resistance. Noah stood in a generation saturated with corruption, yet he refused to let the darkness around him take root within him. While others ignored God, Noah listened. While others rebelled, Noah submitted. This kind of man understands that obedience is not always easy, but it is always right. Noah built the ark when there was no rain, followed instructions that defied human logic, and remained faithful when no one else stood with him. He proved that righteousness is not determined by the majority but by alignment with God. A man who obeys completely moves in faith, trusting that God's wisdom is higher than his own. In a world that constantly pressures compromise, this man stands firm, knowing that obedience is not only his responsibility - it is his protection, his testimony, and his path to walking with God.

Partial obedience is not the pattern of a righteous man, because righteousness is not measured by what a man is willing to do for God, but by what he refuses to withhold from God. Many desire the benefits of obedience but stop short of full surrender. A divided heart produces inconsistent obedience, and inconsistent obedience cannot sustain a life that pleases Him. The righteous man understands that every command from God carries weight, and every area of life must come under His rule. The life of Noah reveals that true faith is seen in complete obedience, not selective response. He did not negotiate with God's instructions or modify them to fit his comfort - he obeyed fully, even when it cost him everything. That is the kind of faith that moves heaven and preserves a man in the midst of judgment. Real faith does not obey halfway; it yields completely. And the man who learns to obey God in full will walk in a strength, clarity, and covering that partial obedience can never produce.

Noah did according to all that God commanded him. Every instruction mattered, whether it seemed significant or small, visible or hidden. A man who walks with God understands that nothing God says is optional. What others might overlook, he esteems. What others might minimize, he carries out with reverence. A godly man pays attention to the details because he recognizes that obedience is not just about the outcome, but about the relationship. Each command is an opportunity to trust, to submit, and to demonstrate that God's wisdom is higher than his own. When a man obeys fully, he builds a life that is stable, ordered, and aligned with heaven. There is power in that kind of obedience - a strength that does not waver when tested. Just as Noah's ark was built plank by plank according to divine instruction, so a man's life is built decision by decision through faithful obedience. And when the storms come, it is not partial obedience that sustains him - it is his complete obedience to every word.

Complete obedience is rooted in humility, because it requires a man to lay down his own understanding and trust the wisdom of God. Pride insists on explanations, demands clarity, and resists anything it cannot control. But humility bows before the authority of God and says, "If You have spoken, that is enough." This kind of humility is a settled confidence that God's way is higher, wiser, and always right. Noah walked in that kind of humility. He obeyed because he trusted the voice that spoke to him. While others likely questioned, mocked, or dismissed what he was doing, Noah remained steady, anchored in obedience to God rather than influenced by the opinions of men. That is the posture every man must learn. When humility leads, obedience follows without delay. And when a man trusts God more than he trusts himself or the crowd around him, he positions his life to be preserved, directed, and used by God in ways that reach far beyond his own understanding.

Obedience is the visible evidence of an invisible faith. A man can speak confidently about what he believes, but it is his actions that reveal the truth of his heart. When God speaks, faith answers with obedience. It steps forward even when the path is unclear, and it continues even when the process is long. Words may inspire, but obedience proves. A man who truly believes God will align his life with what God has said, regardless of cost or convenience. This is what made Noah's faith undeniable. Noah did not simply agree with God's warning - he acted on it. Every strike of the hammer, every day of labor, every moment of endurance declared that he trusted what he had not yet seen. His obedience turned belief into reality. In the same way, a man's daily choices testify to the condition of his faith. When he obeys in the small things and the unseen places, he builds a life that speaks louder than words. Faith that is real will always produce obedience that is consistent, steady, and unshaken.

Noah stood alone in his generation, yet he stood right. While others continued in sin, he chose holiness. While others mocked, he kept building. His obedience was not influenced by popularity, pressure, or opinion - it was anchored in reverence for God. This is the difference between a man who follows the world and a man who fears the Lord. One adjusts to the culture, the other stands firm in conviction. True godly manhood is proven in seasons where obedience costs something. It is easy to follow God when others are doing the same, but it is a different kind of strength to remain faithful when no one else is. Noah prepared for what he had not yet seen because he trusted the word of God more than the comfort of the present. A man who fears God does not drift with the careless or compromise with the crowd—he walks with God regardless of the environment. His faithfulness becomes a testimony, his obedience becomes a witness, and his life becomes a line drawn between righteousness and rebellion.

Godly manhood is not built on strength alone, but on a man's willingness to listen closely to the voice of God and respond with precision. A man who ignores divine instruction may still appear strong outwardly, but his foundation is unstable. When a man gives careful attention to God's Word, he gains wisdom beyond his own understanding - wisdom that guides his decisions, shapes his character, and guards his household. Noah stands as a powerful witness to this truth. He did not merely hear God - he took Him seriously enough to act on every detail. His obedience was not partial or convenient; it was complete and unwavering. Because of this, his life became a covering over his family in a time of judgment. In the same way, a man today becomes a shield for those entrusted to him when he honors God's instruction with reverence and urgency. The safety, direction, and spiritual strength of his home are deeply connected to how seriously he listens to and obeys the voice of God.

Many men do not fail from lack of exposure to truth, but from a lack of surrender to it. Truth reaches their ears, stirs their conscience, and even brings moments of conviction but it stops short of governing their lives. They hear what is right, they acknowledge what is true, and they may even speak it boldly among others, yet inwardly they hold back areas they are unwilling to yield. A man who only agrees with God publicly, but resists Him privately, builds a divided life that cannot stand. Truth was meant to be obeyed at the deepest level. Complete obedience requires more than agreement - it requires surrender of the whole man. It means the mind yields its thoughts, the heart yields its desires, and the will yields its direction to God's authority. There are no hidden rooms, no reserved corners, no private exceptions. A man who walks in true obedience does not pick and choose which parts of God's Word to follow; he bows fully to the whole counsel of God.

Noah's obedience was not easy but quite costly. Day after day, he labored on something no one around him understood, pouring out strength, time, and focus into a calling that brought more questions than applause. True obedience will always require something from a man. It may strip away convenience, challenge his comfort, and even separate him from the approval of others. Yet a godly man does not measure obedience by how easy it feels, but by how faithfully it aligns with God's command. He understands that whatever obedience costs, disobedience costs far more. Disobedience may seem easier in the moment, but it leads to loss, regret, and distance from God's purpose. A man must decide which cost he is willing to bear - the temporary sacrifice of obedience or the lasting consequences of ignoring God. In the end, obedience is never wasted. It shapes the man, honors God, and secures a future that disobedience can never provide.

A man who obeys completely does not negotiate with sin because he understands its nature. Sin pulls, deceives, and hardens the heart little by little. The man of God does not stand at the edge of compromise asking how close he can get without falling; he steps back entirely, choosing separation over subtle surrender. His obedience is decisive, rooted in reverence for God and a deep awareness that even small compromises can open doors to greater ruin. He also recognizes that delayed obedience, selective obedience, and partial obedience are disguised rebellion. To obey only when it is convenient, comfortable, or understandable is to place self above God. But a man of complete obedience bows his will fully, trusting that God's commands are not burdens but protection and life. He moves when God speaks, follows where God leads, and submits even when the path is unclear. His life becomes a testimony that true faith is not measured by what he agrees with, but by what he obeys.

Complete obedience is proven over time, not in a moment of enthusiasm. Many men begin with passion but fail in perseverance. Noah's obedience was a sustained commitment. Day after day, with no visible rain and no public support, he continued building exactly as God commanded. He did not allow delay to weaken his resolve or repetition to dull his focus. This is where true obedience is tested - not in starting strong, but in staying faithful when the work becomes ordinary, slow, and unseen. A godly man understands that finishing is just as important as beginning. Half-built obedience does not fulfill God's command. Consistency is the discipline of faith in action, choosing to obey again today just as you did yesterday. It means refusing to grow careless, refusing to drift, and refusing to quit when the process feels long. The man who completes what God has assigned to him becomes a vessel God can trust. He does not just respond to God's voice - he carries it through to completion.

There are many men who begin with fire in their hearts. Conviction is strong and their desire to obey God is sincere. But when pressure comes that initial fire begins to fade. Distractions creep in quietly, pulling their focus away from what God said. What started as a clear calling becomes clouded by comfort, fear, or compromise. Beginning well is important, but the true measure is whether he remains faithful when the cost increases and the excitement fades. Noah stands as a witness to a different kind of strength - the strength to stay under command until the assignment is complete. He did not build halfway and walk away. He did not allow the passing of years or the silence of results to weaken his resolve. He stayed aligned with God's instruction day after day, moment by moment, until what God spoke was fully carried out. This is the kind of endurance that defines a godly man. He understands that obedience is not proven at the start, but at the finish.

Obedience is often God's shield long before the storm arrives. Genesis shows us that Noah moved with reverence at the warning of God, even though no rain had yet fallen and no flood had ever been seen. His obedience was not based on visible evidence, but on trust in God's word. In the same way, a man who walks with God must learn to respond to divine instruction before circumstances make sense. What feels unnecessary in the moment may be the very thing that preserves his life later. A wise man understands that delayed obedience can open doors to unseen danger. God sees the hidden traps, the storms forming in the distance. When a man chooses obedience early, he is stepping into divine preservation. While others wait for visible signs before they act, the godly man moves at the voice of God. By the time the storm becomes visible, it is often too late to prepare. But the man who obeyed beforehand stands secure, not because he avoided the storm, but because he was ready for it.

A man's obedience is never isolated; it carries weight beyond his own life. When Noah obeyed God, he was not just building an ark - he was building a place of preservation for his family. His faithfulness became their covering. His consistency became their stability. His reverence for God created a pathway for others to be protected in a time of judgment. In the same way, a man today must understand that his choices shape the spiritual climate of his home. When he walks in obedience, he invites strength where there could be weakness, order where there could be confusion, and direction where there could be drift. This is why obedience can never be treated as a small or casual thing. A man who obeys God becomes a pillar for those connected to him. His life provides covering, not just through words, but through example. His decisions influence the future of his household, setting a course that others will follow, whether for good or for harm.

Complete obedience is strength brought into alignment with divine authority. A man who submits to God is placing his life into the hands of the One who sees the end from the beginning. True strength is revealed when a man has the power to choose his own way yet willingly lays it down to follow God's command. That kind of surrender requires courage, discipline, and trust, and it produces a life that is steady, directed, and anchored in truth. When a man yields his will to God, he is not diminished - he is empowered. His decisions gain clarity, his path gains purpose, and his life gains eternal weight. A surrendered man is not easily shaken, because he is no longer governed by impulse, pride, or fear, but by the voice of God. This is where real power is found - not in resisting God, but in walking with Him. A man is never more powerful than when his will is fully surrendered to the Lord, because in that place, heaven's strength begins to flow through his life.

Noah's life reveals that God entrusts purpose to the man who proves faithful in obedience. Before the ark was ever built, before the rain ever fell, there was a man who chose to take God at His word and follow it without compromise. Noah did not wait for confirmation from the world or approval from others - he moved at the command of God. God does not hand greater assignments to those who treat His current instructions casually. He looks for the man who will carry out what has already been spoken with precision, humility, and consistency. Many men desire greater purpose, influence, and calling, but overlook the foundation that makes those things possible. Purpose is not given to replace obedience; it is built upon it. When a man proves that he can be trusted with what God has already said, he positions himself for what God will say next. True advancement in the kingdom does not begin with opportunity - it begins with obedience.

A man who obeys God completely does not need a platform to be a witness - his life becomes the message. Like Noah, he may walk a path that few understand, building according to divine instruction while others question, mock, or ignore. Yet his consistency speaks louder than words. His decisions, his discipline, and his reverence for God declare that faith is lived out in daily submission. Complete obedience is not merely an outward act; it is the evidence of a transformed heart. It reveals a man who has chosen God's will above his own, truth above comfort, and righteousness above convenience. This kind of obedience forms character that God recognizes and honors. It produces stability in a shifting world and establishes a legacy that reaches beyond one lifetime. A man who walks in this way becomes a visible reminder that real faith still exists. His life proves that godly manhood is not defined by words or appearance, but by an unwavering commitment to obey God fully, no matter the cost.

| 10 |

"A MAN WHO BUILDS BY FAITH"

God told Noah, "Make thee an ark of gopher wood" (Gen. 6:14), and in that command we see that Noah did not design his own calling - he received it. A godly man understands that his life is not self-assigned but God-directed. In a world that celebrates personal ambition, a man of faith learns to quiet his own desires long enough to hear the voice of God. Before he builds anything - career, ministry, family, or legacy - he seeks divine instruction. He recognizes that what God ordains carries purpose, provision, and power that human ideas can never produce. This kind of life requires humility and surrender. A man must be willing to lay down his own plans in order to take up God's. Noah could have questioned the assignment or reshaped it to fit his preferences, but instead, he obeyed exactly as he was told. In doing so, he became part of God's redemptive plan for generations. When a man builds according to God's voice, his work becomes obedience with eternal impact.

Noah's ark did not begin with tools in his hand, but with a voice from God that defined the assignment. This is the foundation of all righteous work: it must originate from divine instruction. A man can be busy, productive, and even admired, yet still be building something God never asked for. Noah did not build because it made sense, he built because God spoke. When a man learns to wait for the voice of

God before he moves, he protects himself from wasted effort and misdirected strength. The word of God gives both direction and purpose, ensuring that what is built carries eternal weight. Noah's ark stood because it was built according to God's word, not human reasoning. In the same way, a godly man must seek God first, listen carefully, and then build with obedience. When God speaks, the work may seem slow, costly, or misunderstood, but it will be right. And what is built on His instruction will not only stand through the storms - it will preserve life, purpose, and legacy for generations to come.

A man who builds by faith submits his vision to God's design. He understands that what God commands carries wisdom beyond human understanding. Noah followed divine instruction with precision, trusting that God's pattern was perfect. In the same way, a godly man resists the urge to reshape God's will to suit his comfort. He does not build according to what is popular or easy, but according to what is right. Faith anchors him in obedience, even when the blueprint stretches his patience and challenges his reasoning. This kind of faith requires humility and trust. A man must accept that God sees what he cannot see and knows what he cannot know. Noah's obedience was not partial or selective - it was complete. Every measurement, every detail, every step mattered because it came from God. When a man builds this way, his life becomes something that can withstand storms and preserve others. What is built according to God's design carries lasting strength, eternal purpose, and divine approval.

Many men quietly wrestle in the hidden place of the heart where ambition and surrender collide. They desire God's hand of blessing, yet they cling tightly to their own plans, shaped by preference, pride, and personal vision. But true faith does not present a finished blueprint and ask heaven to sign off on it. Faith lays every plan on the altar and invites God to examine, correct, or even dismantle it. A man of faith understands that what is built outside of God's will may succeed in the eyes of men, but it will not stand in the eyes of God. Blessing is not found in convincing God to endorse our direction - it is found in aligning our lives with His. Faith is not control; it is surrender. It is the willingness to abandon personal agendas in exchange for divine instruction. When a man submits to God's blueprint, he steps into a design that carries eternal weight and purpose. What heaven initiates, heaven sustains. This is the difference between striving and building, between forcing outcomes and following obedience.

God gave Noah precise instructions because heaven does nothing without purpose. The measurements, the structure, the rooms, and the single door carried divine intention. What may seem small to a man can be critical to God, because God sees what the man cannot. A godly man learns to respect the details of God's voice. He does not treat instruction casually or assume he can improve on what God has already designed. He understands that when God speaks, every word carries weight, and every command is connected to something greater than what is immediately visible. When destiny is attached to obedience, details are never insignificant. The strength of the ark and the preservation of Noah's family all depended on his willingness to follow God exactly. In the same way, a man who walks with God must learn that precision in obedience produces power in outcome. The blessing is often hidden inside the details, and the breakthrough is often secured by the parts others would overlook.

Noah could not afford careless construction because what he built would be tested by judgment waters. Every beam, every measurement, every layer of pitch mattered because the storm would reveal the strength of his obedience. In the same way, a man cannot afford to build his life casually. Character must be formed with intention, convictions must be rooted deeply in truth, and his walk with God must be strengthened in the hidden places. A godly man understands that the strength of his life is not proven in calm seasons but in violent ones. Just as the ark was built to withstand what had never been seen before, a man must prepare for battles he has not yet faced. His family depends on the strength of what he builds. His calling depends on the stability of his foundation. His convictions must be anchored so firmly in God that they do not bend when pressure comes. Careless living leads to fragile structures, but disciplined obedience produces enduring strength.

Faith is not proven in what a man says he believes; it is proven in what he is willing to build in obedience to God. Noah did not simply agree with God's warning - he responded to it. Day after day, he labored on something that had never been seen before, in a season when there was no visible evidence that rain was coming. Every strike of his hammer was a declaration that God's word was more real to him than the opinions of men. His faith took form in wood, structure, and perseverance, showing that real belief always moves a man to action. This is the kind of faith that separates a godly man from a passive one. Faith is not idle agreement; it is active obedience. When a man truly trusts God, he will build what God told him to build, even when it is costly, slow, or misunderstood. Like Noah, his work will speak before the storm ever arrives. And when the rain finally falls, it will reveal that what he built in obedience was not wasted effort but the very thing that preserved his life and the lives connected to him.

Real faith is never passive; it always expresses itself through action. A man may declare that he trusts God, but if that trust does not lead him to obey when it is difficult, to build when it is inconvenient, to prepare when nothing seems urgent, and to endure when results are delayed, then his faith has not yet matured into its full expression. True faith steps forward even when the path is unclear. It labors without applause, follows without full understanding, and stands firm when others turn away. Faith must move from the mouth to the hands. It must take on form through obedience, discipline, and perseverance. When a man truly believes God, his life begins to align with that belief - his decisions change, his priorities shift, and his actions reflect heaven's instruction. Just as Noah built the ark long before the rain ever fell, a man of faith works in response to God's word, not visible evidence. This kind of faith produces results that words alone never could. It builds, it prepares, it endures.

Noah built while others ignored the warning. Day after day, he labored in obedience to a voice that most people refused to hear. While his generation laughed, dismissed, and continued in their own ways, Noah remained steady. He did not measure truth by public opinion or slow his obedience to match the comfort of others. A man of God cannot afford to stop building because of mockery, silence, or resistance. The pressure to conform will always try to compete with the call to obey. But purpose is not sustained by approval - it is sustained by conviction. Noah's consistency declared that he feared God more than he feared man. In the same way, a godly man must keep working, keep preparing, and keep obeying, even when his environment offers no support. What God has spoken is enough. And in the end, it is not the voices of the crowd that matter, but the fulfillment of what God commanded him to build.

Sometimes obedience will set a man apart in ways that make him appear strange, misunderstood, or even foolish in the eyes of the world. Noah labored day after day on an ark when there was no visible sign of rain, no evidence of a coming flood, and no support from the culture around him. A man who walks with God must accept that obedience will often separate him from the approval of men, but what he loses in popularity he gains in purpose, protection, and alignment with heaven. A man who fears God more than he fears opinions becomes unshakable. Like Noah, he builds when others question, prepares when others ignore, and stands firm when others compromise. His confidence is not in being understood, but in being obedient. And in the end, what seemed strange to the world becomes the very thing God uses to preserve, deliver, and establish His will. True strength is found in a man who can stand alone with God, knowing that obedience is always worth it.

Building by faith will always demand patience because what God ordains is rarely completed in a moment. Noah did not see immediate results for his obedience; he saw years of labor, repetition, and steady progress. Day after day, he cut the wood, shaped the structure, lifted the weight, and sealed the ark according to God's instruction. There were no crowds applauding, no visible rain to validate the work - only the quiet assurance that God had spoken. This is where true faith is tested. A man who builds by faith must be willing to continue when the work feels slow, when the results seem distant, and when the process stretches longer than expected. A godly man understands that preparation seasons are not wasted seasons. Every act of obedience, every hidden sacrifice, and every moment of persistence is shaping something greater than he can see. Just as the ark was formed piece by piece, so is a man's character, calling, and legacy built over time.

Many men begin with passion, but passion alone cannot carry a man to completion. The work of God will test more than a man's excitement - it will test his endurance. When the weight increases, when progress feels slow, and when the results are not yet visible, that is where many turn back. But a man of faith does not measure his assignment by how easy it feels; he measures it by who gave the command. Faith is not proven at the starting line - it is proven in the long, unseen stretch where quitting feels easier than continuing. A man of faith keeps building when the work becomes heavy. He keeps showing up when motivation fades and when the reward is still out of sight. Like Noah, who labored day after day without visible evidence of rain, a godly man remains steady under pressure. He trusts that every act of obedience is laying another piece of the structure God commanded him to build. And in time, what was built in quiet endurance will stand as a testimony that real faith does not quit.

Noah's obedience reached far beyond his own life - it became a shelter for his family. Every board he cut and every step of obedience he took was building more than an ark; it was building protection for those entrusted to him. A godly man must understand that his faithfulness is never isolated. When he walks in obedience, he creates an atmosphere of safety, order, and divine covering over his household. His decisions shape the spiritual climate of his home, and his alignment with God becomes a shield for those connected to him. This is the weight and privilege of true manhood. A man who obeys God does not just secure his own future - he helps establish direction, stability, and legacy for generations to come. His consistency becomes a guide, his reverence for God becomes a standard, and his faith becomes a foundation others can stand on. Just as Noah's obedience preserved life, a man's faithfulness today can guard his family from destruction and lead them toward righteousness.

A man must never underestimate what God is building through his obedience. What feels like small, repetitive, unseen work in the present may be part of a divine structure that stretches far beyond his understanding. Day after day, choice after choice, he is laying beams of faith, sealing gaps with obedience, and strengthening what God has assigned him to build. The hands that labor in quiet obedience are participating in something eternal. God often hides greatness inside what looks ordinary so that a man learns to walk by faith and not by sight. What looks like wood and pitch today may become deliverance tomorrow. The discipline, the prayers, the integrity, and the unseen sacrifices are forming a covering that can preserve lives beyond his own. When the storms come - and they will - what he built in obedience will stand as a refuge. This is why he must remain faithful, even when the work feels slow and unnoticed, because God is not just building for the moment - He is building for generations.

Godly manhood is not measured by ambition or by the words a man speaks about his future, but by the work he is willing to do under the authority of God. Many men desire strength, leadership, and purpose, but few submit themselves to the process that produces it. True manhood is revealed in the daily choices to follow, to submit, and to construct a life that aligns with heaven's blueprint rather than personal preference. Desire can inspire a man, and vision can direct him, but only faith put into action can transform him. A godly man does not wait for perfect conditions or constant motivation; he picks up the responsibility God has given him and begins to build. He labors in prayer, disciplines his life, orders his steps, and stays faithful even when the progress feels slow. Real strength is formed not in what a man hopes to become, but in what he consistently builds through obedience. When a man commits to building under God's authority, his life becomes proof that his faith is active and producing lasting fruit.

While the culture around him drifted further into compromise, Noah stayed anchored to divine instruction. He did not adjust the blueprint to gain acceptance or avoid criticism. He understood that God's pattern was not up for negotiation. When the world normalizes what God has condemned and questions what God has established, a godly man stands firm. His strength is not found in blending in, but in holding fast to what God has spoken. This kind of commitment requires courage, conviction, and reverence for God above all else. Noah's obedience proved that righteousness is unwavering. He built in alignment with heaven even when it set him apart on earth. A righteous man is not swayed by pressure or fear of rejection. He is governed by the word, not the world. And because he remains faithful to God's pattern, his life becomes a testimony that truth does not change with time. It stands, just as Noah's ark stood, as evidence that obedience to God will always rise above the corruption of any age.

Every man is building something, whether he realizes it or not. With every decision, every habit, and every response to God's voice, he is shaping a life that will speak long after he is gone. Scripture reminds us through the life of Noah that what a man builds must come from God's instruction, not his own imagination. A structure built on pride, fear, or self-will may rise quickly, but it cannot stand the testing of time or judgment. True strength is found in building what God has spoken, even when it is slow, unseen, or misunderstood. When a man builds by faith, he aligns his life with heaven's blueprint, trusting that obedience today will produce fruit tomorrow. What he builds in private - his integrity, discipline, and devotion - will eventually become visible in his legacy. A man who builds according to God's command is not just creating something for himself; he is establishing something that can preserve, protect, and influence generations. When the storms come, only what was built by faith will remain.

A man who builds by faith is not driven by recognition, but by reverence. Each step, each sacrifice, each moment of perseverance declares that his trust is not in the opinions of men, but in the word of the Lord. What he leaves behind is not merely proof that he tried - it is proof that he obeyed. And what is built in obedience carries power beyond the present moment. Noah's ark was not just a structure; it was a vessel of preservation, a covering for his household, and a bridge into the future God had prepared. In the same way, a man who builds by faith is shaping more than his own life - he is influencing generations he may never see. His obedience creates stability where there could have been destruction, direction where there could have been confusion, and legacy where there could have been loss. When a man chooses to build according to God's design, his work becomes more than effort - it becomes a divine instrument that carries purpose, protection, and promise into the generations to come.

| 11 |

"A MAN WITH A LONG ASSIGNMENT"

Noah's assignment was a lifetime of obedience stretched across years of unseen progress. God gave him clear instruction, but not immediate results. Day after day, Noah had to rise and continue building, cutting, shaping, and assembling what others did not understand. His faith was not proven in a single act, but in sustained commitment. A godly man must learn that true obedience is not measured by how he starts, but by how he continues when the work is long, the progress is slow, and the reward is not yet visible. This kind of assignment requires endurance anchored in trust. Noah had to believe that God's word was true even when circumstances gave no evidence of it. He had to remain faithful through repetition, silence, and time. In the same way, a man walking with God must develop the strength to stay consistent when the assignment stretches beyond comfort. Long obedience builds deep character. It forges patience, strengthens resolve, and proves that a man's faith is not temporary, but enduring.

Genesis 6:3 reveals that God was working with mankind within a measured season. His patience had a boundary, His warning had a timeframe, and His call required a response before that window closed. While others continued in corruption, Noah understood that when God speaks, a man must respond with urgency and reverence. A wise man discerns the season he is in and aligns himself with God's command before the opportunity to obey passes. Genesis 6:22 shows the strength of Noah's character, "Thus did Noah; according to all that God commanded him, so did he." Noah did not begin the work and grow weary, nor did he abandon the assignment when it became long and difficult. He stayed faithful until every instruction was fulfilled. Endurance is the proof of true obedience. Many will start, but few will finish. But the man who walks with God will remain steady, committed, and faithful until the assignment is done, knowing that completion honors God just as much as beginning.

A man with a long assignment must come to terms with the pace of God. Heaven is not rushed, and purpose is not produced overnight. What God builds in a man - and through a man - is often formed through years of steady obedience, repeated effort, and quiet consistency. The process may feel slow, hidden, and even unnoticed, but it is never wasted. Every act of faithfulness, every unseen sacrifice, and every disciplined step is shaping something far greater than the moment itself. Just because the work is long does not mean God has stepped away. In fact, it is often in the long seasons that God is most deeply involved, refining character, strengthening endurance, and establishing unshakable faith. A man who understands this will not quit when progress feels slow. He will remain steady, knowing that God is present in every stage of the process. The assignment may be long, but so is the faithfulness of God - and that faithfulness will carry him all the way to completion.

Noah's obedience was not proven in a single moment, but in the repetition of faithful labor. Day after day, he kept cutting, shaping, lifting, preparing, and building while the world around him lived as though nothing would ever change. There was no applause, no visible sign of rain, and no confirmation from the outside that his work mattered. godly man must understand that obedience often requires continuing the work when it feels unnoticed, uncelebrated, and slow. What God has spoken is enough reason to keep building. There will be days when the assignment feels heavy and the progress seems small. There will be moments when the hands grow tired and the mind questions how much longer the work will take. But like Noah, a man must let obedience carry him when emotions grow weak. Steady obedience is what moves a man forward when excitement fades. Each act of faithfulness, no matter how small it appears, is a step toward the fulfillment of God's purpose.

A righteous man does not measure his commitment by how easy the journey feels, but by how true the calling remains. He understands that fatigue is not a signal to quit, but a test of what truly lives within him. Many begin with passion, but only a few continue with perseverance. A godly man stays when others walk away. His strength is not found in comfort, but in conviction. Endurance is not optional in manhood; it is essential. It is forged in the quiet days, the unseen battles, and the moments when quitting feels easier than continuing. A righteous man knows that what God has entrusted to him is worth the struggle. He does not abandon his post because the process is difficult - he stands firm because the assignment is divine. Through endurance, his character is refined, his faith is strengthened, and his legacy is built. He finishes what he starts, not because it is easy, but because he understands that lasting impact is only given to those who refuse to give up.

Many men know how to begin with passion but far fewer learn how to remain steady when the work becomes ordinary and the progress feels slow. Starting often draws strength from emotion, but finishing draws strength from discipline, commitment, and reverence for God. Noah did not have the luxury of building only when he felt inspired. Day after day, he returned to the same assignment, shaping, lifting, and preparing according to God's command. His faith was not proven in a moment of enthusiasm, but in a lifetime of consistency. Noah's endurance is what set him apart. He did not walk away when the task grew heavy or when the world around him failed to understand. He stayed with the assignment until God said it was finished. Finishing requires a settled heart, a disciplined mind, and a deep conviction that God's word is worth obeying to the very end. A man who learns to remain faithful over time becomes a man God can trust, because he is anchored in obedience until the work is complete.

Long assignments strip away surface-level commitment and reveal the true condition of a man's heart. When the days stretch on and the results are not immediate, a man begins to discover whether he is driven by conviction or convenience. Shallow obedience fades when the cost increases, but deep obedience remains anchored because it is rooted in reverence for God, not the ease of the task. Faithful manhood is not proven in moments of excitement, but in seasons where endurance is required and no applause is given. A man who only obeys when the path is light has not yet carried the full weight of responsibility that comes with true obedience. Real strength is formed when he continues to show up, continue to labor, and continue to submit when the work feels heavy and unseen. Long assignments teach him discipline, humility, and unwavering trust. They shape a man who does not quit when challenged, but who stands steady until the assignment is finished.

Great assignments are not proven in moments of excitement but in seasons of endurance. A man may feel strong when the vision is fresh, but it is the passing of time that reveals whether his strength is real or shallow. Legacy is formed day after day of choosing obedience when progress feels slow and when the reward seems distant. Character is not shaped by one decision, but by a pattern of decisions made under pressure, fatigue, and time. The man who stays faithful in the ordinary is the man God can trust with the extraordinary. It is the daily choosing of what is right, the repeated surrender of one's will to God, and the quiet discipline of staying the course that produces lasting fruit. Many men desire impact, but few are willing to embrace the process that creates it. Yet the man who commits to long obedience will find that over time, his life becomes a structure that cannot be shaken - a testimony that speaks not of quick success, but of proven faithfulness before God.

Noah's ark was not formed in a moment of inspiration, but through countless moments of obedience. Each beam cut, each board set in place, each day of labor was a declaration that he trusted God's word more than what he saw around him. In the same way, a man's life is not shaped by one great decision alone, but by the steady accumulation of many small ones. Every choice to obey when it is inconvenient, every moment he chooses discipline over comfort, and every time he honors God in private builds something far greater than he can see in the moment. What seems small in the present is often significant in eternity. The days may feel repetitive, the progress may seem slow, but heaven measures differently than man. God is not only concerned with the finished work; He is watching the process of building. When a man stays committed to obedience day after day, he is constructing a life that can carry purpose, protect others, and stand when the storms come.

A man must not despise slow progress, because God often works in ways that do not satisfy the urgency of the flesh but perfectly develop the strength of the spirit. What feels like delay is often divine design. In the slow seasons, patience is built, faith is stretched, and character is formed through repetition, endurance, and quiet obedience. The man who keeps showing up, keeps trusting, and keeps doing what is right when nothing seems to be changing is becoming stronger than he realizes. God is using the process to root him deeply so that when elevation comes, he will not be easily shaken. Quick success without inner development produces instability, but slow growth creates endurance, wisdom, and restraint. God is far more concerned with who a man becomes than how quickly he arrives. The hidden work, the unseen battles, and the long stretches of consistency are shaping a man into something lasting.

When the assignment stretches longer than expected, discouragement will whisper that the effort is unnoticed and will attempt to measure worth by visible results and public recognition. But faith does not draw its strength from what can be seen or applauded. A man of faith understands that silence from the world does not mean absence from God. A faithful man continues because he knows who gave the assignment. He does not require constant affirmation to remain steady, because his confidence is rooted in God's awareness, not man's attention. What others overlook, God examines closely. What others forget, God remembers fully. In seasons where progress feels slow and unseen, faith anchors a man to the truth that his labor is not wasted. It is forming strength, building character, and preparing him for what lies ahead. So he keeps working, not because it is easy, but because he trusts God sees and that is enough.

Noah did not build for the approval of men; he built in reverence to the voice of God. While the world around him continued in disbelief, distraction, and indifference, Noah remained anchored in divine instruction. His confidence was not drawn from the crowd's understanding but from the certainty that God had spoken. A man of faith must be unmoved by misunderstanding, undistracted by silence, and undeterred by the absence of applause. When God has given instruction, that word becomes enough. There is a strength that comes when a man no longer needs to be seen to stay faithful. Hidden obedience, quiet discipline, and steady commitment are the marks of a life built before God rather than before men. The crowd may never understand the calling, but their approval was never the source of direction. A godly man builds because God said build. He moves because God said move. And in the end, it is not the voice of the crowd that will matter - it is the approval of God that will stand forever.

Endurance reveals whether a man's obedience is rooted in emotion or conviction. It is easy to respond when the vision is clear, the fire is strong, and the motivation is fresh. But true obedience is not proven in the beginning; it is proven in the middle, where the work becomes routine, the excitement fades, and the outcome is still unseen. This is where many turn back, not because the command changed, but because their patience weakened. A man of faith, however, continues to obey because he trusts the One who gave the command, even when progress feels slow and the reward feels distant. Endurance builds a strength in a man that cannot be shaken by time, silence, or delay. He is no longer working for recognition or immediate reward; he is working because he fears God and honors His word. What begins as simple obedience grows into a life of proven faithfulness, and in time, what was once unseen will stand as a witness that enduring obedience always produces a harvest.

A godly man must learn that responsibility is not a burden meant to break him, but a weight designed to shape him. A disciplined man keeps his heart guarded while his hands remain faithful. He does not allow the demands of life to corrupt his spirit. Instead, he stays rooted in humility, gratitude, and reverence before God, understanding that who he becomes under the weight is more important than what he accomplishes through it. There will be a cost to carrying responsibility well. Comfort will often have to be sacrificed. Ease will have to be set aside. There will be days when the work feels heavy and goes unnoticed, when rest seems distant and the reward unclear. Yet a godly man keeps building. He keeps his heart clean so that bitterness cannot take root, and he keeps his focus steady so that distractions cannot pull him away. In doing so, he becomes a man God can trust - one who not only carries responsibility, but carries it with strength, integrity, and unwavering faith.

Long obedience requires vision that reaches beyond what a man can currently see, feel, or measure. When God gave Noah the assignment to build the ark, there was no visible evidence of rain, no sign that the flood was near, and no confirmation from the world around him. Yet Noah continued because he anchored his life to what God had spoken, not to what he could observe. This is the kind of vision a godly man must develop - a forward-looking faith that holds tightly to God's promise even when the present moment feels ordinary, slow, or uncertain. Without that vision, the weight of daily obedience can begin to feel meaningless, and the temptation to stop becomes stronger. A man who loses sight of God's promise will eventually struggle to remain faithful in the process, because endurance is sustained by purpose. Vision reminds him why he started. Vision strengthens him when progress seems invisible. Vision keeps his heart aligned when distractions try to pull him away.

Every man must come to the place where he settles the question of duration in his heart. Faithfulness is proven in the quiet, unseen decision to remain steady when the assignment stretches longer than expected. It is easy to commit when the path is clear and the strength is fresh, but true obedience is revealed when fatigue sets in and when understanding is limited. A man who is called by God must learn that the length of the assignment is not his to control - only his obedience is. Faithfulness means showing up even when nothing around him seems to affirm that his labor matters. A man with a long assignment must build endurance in his spirit. He must obey when he is tired, stand when he is misunderstood, and continue when time feels heavy. There will be moments when quitting feels reasonable and when slowing down feels justified. In the end, it is not the man who starts strong who is honored, but the man who remains faithful until God says the work is finished.

Noah's endurance was not just effort - it was evidence. Every day he continued building, he proved that his faith was real. Noah did not have visible proof that the flood was coming yet he kept building because he believed the word God had spoken. His persistence became a testimony that he trusted God more than he trusted what he could see. A godly man must understand that true faith carries him beyond the moment of instruction into a lifetime of obedience. It is one thing to hear God's command; it is another to remain under that command until the assignment is complete. Noah did not treat obedience as a temporary response - he lived under it daily. His endurance declared that God's word was worth his life, his strength, and his years. In the same way, a man's persistence today will reveal what he truly believes. When he refuses to quit, even when the work is hard and the results are delayed, his endurance becomes living proof that his faith is genuine.

A man with a long assignment must settle in his heart that the call of God is not measured by speed, but by faithfulness. Like Noah, who built the ark over many years, he must keep building when progress feels slow and when results are not yet visible. There will be days when the labor feels unnoticed and the cost feels high, but a faithful man does not measure his assignment by comfort. He measures it by obedience. He keeps his hands steady, his heart aligned, and his focus fixed on God, knowing that every act of obedience is building something eternal. The weight of a long assignment will test a man's patience, discipline, and endurance, but it will also refine his character and deepen his faith. And when the assignment is complete, the reward of faithfulness will far outweigh every moment of weariness. What was built in quiet obedience will stand as a testimony that he did not turn back, did not grow careless, and did not abandon what heaven placed in his hands.

| 12 |

"A MAN WHO WORKS WHILE OTHERS MOCK"

Noah lived in a generation that had turned its heart away from God, yet he refused to let the condition of the world dictate the condition of his soul. While corruption spread and violence became normal, Noah walked in reverence, obedience, and quiet strength before the Lord. He did not blend in with the rebellion around him, nor did he grow silent under its pressure. Instead, he stood as a preacher of righteousness, declaring through both his words and his life that God was still holy and still to be feared. Before the rain ever fell, Noah's life was already speaking. He did more than build a structure - he became a living witness that God still speaks and still calls men to repentance. Though many ignored him, heaven did not. His faithfulness proved that one man, fully surrendered to God, can stand as a light in the darkest times. A godly man must understand that his life is always preaching something, and when he walks faithfully with God, he declares truth even to those who refuse to hear it.

A man of God must come to terms with the truth that righteousness is not measured by applause, but by alignment with God. There will be moments when obedience places him outside the approval of others, but righteousness has never been about fitting in - it has always been about standing firm. Noah lived in a generation that rejected God, yet he refused to adjust his life to match their rebellion. His obedience drew a clear line between him and the spirit of his age, proving that a man cannot walk with God and blend in with sin at the same time. When a man is truly committed to God, he will speak differently, live differently, and choose differently. This separation is evidence that he has heard from God and values divine approval over human acceptance. Like Noah, his assignment will require him to stand out, even when it costs him comfort, reputation, or understanding. But in the end, it is far better to stand alone with God than to stand with the crowd and be found outside His will.

Noah stood in a generation that had no appetite for truth, yet he carried a message that could not be silenced. He preached righteousness when corruption was normal, and that kind of stand demanded real courage. There were no crowds cheering him on, no culture affirming his convictions, and no visible evidence that his labor would be rewarded. Still, Noah spoke what God said and built what God commanded. His strength came from knowing that obedience to God outweighs agreement with men. A man of God must learn this same resolve - to speak truth even when it is unwelcome, to stand firm when righteousness makes him stand alone, and to keep moving forward without needing validation from a world that does not understand his calling. This kind of faith shifts a man's focus from earthly approval to divine approval. Noah did not measure success by how many listened, but by how faithfully he obeyed. He understood that God sees what others ignore and honors what others mock.

Every godly man will face seasons where his obedience sets him apart in ways others cannot understand. People who have not heard what he has heard will question his discipline, misinterpret his priorities, and sometimes even mock his convictions. Like Noah building before the rain ever came, a man of God must learn to move at the pace of divine instruction, not public opinion. When God has spoken, that word becomes his anchor, his direction, and his authority, even when it makes him stand alone. A man who has truly heard from God cannot afford to let confused voices silence clear instruction. If he waits for everyone to understand, he will delay what God has already commanded. If he seeks approval, he will weaken his obedience. Faith requires him to keep working, keep building, and keep moving forward, even when the crowd is watching with doubt instead of support. In time, what was mocked will become evident, and what was questioned will be proven.

A man who lives for the approval of people will slow down, compromise, or turn back under pressure. But a man who has settled his heart before God will remain steady. He understands that obedience is not validated by public opinion but by divine instruction. Mockery becomes a refining fire, separating shallow desire from genuine conviction. In those moments, a man must decide whose voice will carry more weight - God's or the crowd's. Ridicule may bruise pride, but it cannot stop a man who is anchored in purpose. Every insult becomes an opportunity to strengthen his resolve, and every misunderstanding becomes a chance to deepen his dependence on God. Faithfulness in the face of ridicule is not weakness; it is quiet strength under pressure. It proves that his identity is not built on acceptance but on obedience. And in the end, the same man who was mocked for his faithfulness will stand approved before God, knowing he chose eternal reward over temporary applause.

Noah's obedience exposed the difference between natural sight and spiritual understanding. To those around him, his labor looked unnecessary, excessive, even foolish. He was building for rain that had not fallen, for judgment that had not yet appeared, and for a future no one else could see. A man of faith must come to terms that if he walks with God, there will be seasons when his decisions cannot be explained to those who do not hear God's voice. Faith often requires a man to move ahead of visible evidence. It calls him to commit before the outcome is clear. The world measures wisdom by what can be seen and proven, but God measures wisdom by obedience to His word. What looks foolish in the eyes of men may be alignment with heaven's plan. A godly man must not allow the opinions of others to silence what God has spoken within him. If God has given instruction, that is enough. In time, what was mocked will be understood, and what seemed unnecessary will be revealed as essential.

A man must understand that mockery often rises in the absence of revelation. Those who laughed at Noah could not see what he saw, hear what he heard, or understand what God had spoken. Their perspective was limited to the present, while Noah was building for a future shaped by divine warning. In the same way, when God places an assignment in a man's life, it will not always make sense to those around him. Their laughter is the sound of human reasoning trying to interpret what can only be understood through spiritual discernment. A man who walks with God must learn to value revelation over approval. He must keep building, even when the noise of ridicule surrounds him. Mockery does not cancel the command of God, nor does it delay what God has already set in motion. The man who endures this pressure proves that his confidence is not in the crowd, but in the One who called him. In time, the same voices that mocked will be silenced by the evidence of obedience.

The enemy uses ridicule as a slow pressure to make a man question whether his obedience is worth it. What begins as external criticism can become internal doubt if a man is not watchful. The whisper says, "This is pointless... no one sees... this will not matter." But those words do not come from God. They are designed to disconnect a man from the assurance that God's instructions are purposeful, even when they are not publicly affirmed. A faithful man must learn to resist that erosion by anchoring his heart in God while keeping his hands committed to the work. Even when the noise surrounds him, he stays steady while building, praying, and moving forward. Confidence is not maintained by circumstance but by communion with God. And when a man refuses to let ridicule rewrite what God has spoken, he becomes unshakable - finishing what others mocked and proving that what was built in faith will stand when the voices have gone silent.

Noah's hammer echoed with conviction while the voices around him echoed with doubt. Every strike into the wood was a declaration that he trusted what God said more than what people thought. His obedience became a language louder than ridicule, a steady rhythm of faith that refused to be silenced. A godly man must come to this same place, where his actions are no longer controlled by the noise of others but anchored in the voice of God. There will always be voices that question, criticize, and try to weaken a man's resolve, but obedience answers them without saying a word. Every step taken in alignment with God's will becomes evidence of where a man's trust truly rests. Noah did not stop to defend himself; he stayed focused on the assignment. In the same way, a godly man must learn that consistency in obedience carries more weight than any explanation he could give. When his life reflects faith in action, it becomes a testimony that cannot be argued with.

Noah did not build the ark in a burst of inspiration but through years of steady, unseen labor. Day after day, he worked under the weight of a word that had not yet manifested, surrounded by a generation that neither understood nor believed. The skies gave no sign, the ground offered no confirmation, and yet he kept building. The nature of real faith does not depend on visible progress or public approval. It is anchored in the voice of God, choosing obedience even when the evidence has not yet appeared. There will be times when obedience isolates him, when the results are delayed, and when criticism grows louder instead of quieter. But faithfulness is proven in those very moments. It is the decision to keep showing up, keep building, and keep trusting when nothing around him affirms his direction. The man who refuses to quit in the face of misunderstanding becomes a testimony that obedience is steadfast, unwavering, and rooted in a confidence that God's timing is always right.

A heavy assignment requires a deeper foundation. It demands a man who is anchored in what God has spoken, not in how he is perceived. When the word of God settles in a man's heart, it gives him something unshakable to stand on. It steadies him when recognition is absent and strengthens him when affirmation is withheld. There will be times when a man is misunderstood, overlooked, or even criticized for doing what is right. In those moments, his calling is tested. Will he slow down when the clapping stops, or will he continue when the only witness is God? True strength is revealed when a man keeps building without recognition, keeps serving without applause, and keeps moving forward when no one is cheering him on. When God has spoken, that word must carry more weight than every opinion around him. A man who learns to obey in silence will be trusted with greater things, because he has proven that his faithfulness is not for display - it is for God alone.

When a man has truly heard from God, his direction is not determined by the opinions of others but by the conviction placed within him. Like Noah building the ark in a generation that could not comprehend his obedience, a man of God must learn to stand firm when his calling sets him apart. Mockery may test his patience and expose his vulnerabilities, but it also reveals the depth of his commitment. A man who guards his mind disciplines his thoughts, refusing to rehearse the words that seek to weaken his faith. Instead, he strengthens his spirit through prayer, truth, and unwavering focus on what God has spoken. The noise of others will always try to compete with the voice of God, but the man who remains anchored will not be moved. He does not seek validation from the crowd because his confidence is rooted in divine instruction. And in time, what was once mocked will stand as evidence that a man who refuses to surrender will always outlast the voices that tried to stop him.

Noah teaches us that a man does not need a righteous culture to live a righteous life. He lived in a generation filled with corruption, violence, and spiritual blindness, yet he chose a different path. While others drifted with the current of sin, he anchored himself in obedience to God. This reveals that a man's character is not determined by the environment around him, but by the convictions within him. The darkness of the generation may surround him, but it does not have to define him. A godly man must understand that ridicule, isolation, and misunderstanding often accompany obedience. Noah kept building while others mocked, questioned, and ignored him. Yet his consistency became his strength. He did not allow the noise of the crowd to silence the voice of God. In the same way, a man today must guard his heart and stay committed to what God has spoken, even when it sets him apart. When a man refuses to compromise, he becomes a testimony that righteousness is still possible.

A godly man must guard his heart when ridicule comes. The voices of others may question or misjudge his obedience, but he cannot afford to let their words reshape his spirit. Instead, he must keep his hands busy with the work God has given him and keep his inner life clean before the Lord. When his focus remains on obedience, his spirit stays anchored, and his peace remains intact. He must also remember that his calling is not to prove himself right in every conversation, but to remain faithful in every assignment. Mockers may try to pull him into arguments, provoke his pride, or stir anger within him, but a disciplined man refuses to be distracted. He understands that anger and pride can damage what obedience is building. So he walks humbly, speaks carefully, and continues steadily in the path God has set before him. In doing so, he becomes a testimony not of winning debates, but of enduring faithfulness - a man whose life speaks louder than the noise around him.

A man who anchors his life in God's truth understands that obedience matters more than recognition. While others chase acceptance, he pursues alignment with heaven. He knows that it is better to stand approved before God in quiet faithfulness than to be celebrated by people while drifting from divine purpose. A man must settle within himself whose voice will guide his steps. If he lives for the approval of people, he will constantly adjust his convictions to fit their expectations, becoming a servant to opinions rather than a servant of God. But when he chooses to honor God above all, he is set free from that pressure. He can walk in boldness, humility, and clarity, unmoved by praise or criticism. His identity is no longer shaped by the crowd but by his calling. And in the end, when every voice is silenced and every opinion fades, it is God's approval that will matter most and the man who lived for it will stand secure.

In a world that measured worth by popularity, Noah measured his life by faithfulness to God's voice. He stood alone if necessary, building what others mocked and preparing for what others denied. His legacy was not built on the shifting opinions of men, but on the unchanging word of God. That is why his name still speaks. Popularity has a short memory, but obedience leaves a testimony that echoes beyond a lifetime. A man must understand that every decision is shaping what will remain when his life is finished. Temporary acceptance can feel rewarding in the moment, but it cannot carry eternal weight. When a man trades obedience for approval, he gains applause but loses authority, gains recognition but forfeits legacy. But when he chooses to stand with God, even if he stands alone, he builds something that cannot be erased. The man who seeks eternal approval will outlast the voices that once tried to silence him, because what is built in obedience is preserved by God Himself.

There will come a day when what was done in quiet obedience will stand as undeniable wisdom. Noah's ark was not applauded while it was being built - it was questioned, mocked, and misunderstood. But when the rain began to fall and the waters rose, the very thing that drew ridicule became the only place of safety. In the same way, a man of God must understand that the value of obedience is often hidden until the appointed time when God allows the results to speak. A man must therefore commit himself to building by faith, not by public opinion. He must keep working, keep obeying, and keep trusting even when there is no visible evidence that it matters. The proof of obedience is not always in the present moment - it is revealed in the future when God brings His word to pass. So he must not quit under pressure or abandon his assignment under mockery, because in due time, obedience will stand justified, and faithfulness will speak louder than every voice that once doubted it.

A man who continues to work while others mock reveals that he has settled in his heart that the opinion of God outweighs the approval of men. While others seek validation from the crowd, he seeks alignment with heaven. He understands that obedience is not measured by applause but by faithfulness. So he keeps building when it is lonely, keeps standing when it is uncomfortable, and keeps preaching when no one seems to listen. When the work is finished, the voices that once laughed will no longer matter, because the only voice that will carry eternal weight is the voice of God. His approval is not temporary, not shallow, and not fading. It is lasting, powerful, and full of reward. A man who lives for that approval walks a narrow road, but it is a road that leads to purpose, preservation, and peace. And when he stands before God, he will not regret the rejection he endured, because he will understand that every moment of obedience was building something far greater than the crowd could ever see.

| **13** |

"A MAN WHO PROTECTS HIS HOUSE"

Genesis 7:1 says, "And the Lord said unto Noah, 'Come thou and all thy house into the ark; for thee have I seen righteous before me in this generation.'" When a man lives in obedience, reverence, and consistency before God, he is not only building his own relationship with the Lord; he is establishing a spiritual covering that guards his household. Noah did not just believe God for himself - he obeyed God in a way that created safety for his family. His righteousness became a refuge. This is the weight and privilege of godly manhood. A man's decisions, disciplines, and devotion have the power to shape the spiritual climate of his home. When he prays, he is strengthening the walls around his family. When he obeys, he is opening a door for protection, favor, and direction to flow into the lives of those connected to him. Just as Noah's obedience brought his household into safety, a man today must recognize that his faith can become a shield and his obedience a covering for those under his care.

When God spoke in Genesis 7:1, He acknowledged Noah as both a righteous man and a covering for others. Noah's obedience created a place of refuge not only for his own soul, but for everyone connected to him. This shows that God sees a man as a gateway. His faith, his decisions, and his obedience carry weight beyond himself. This kind of leadership is both a privilege and a burden. It means that a man cannot afford casual obedience or partial surrender. What he allows, tolerates, or neglects can affect the spiritual direction of his household. But the opposite is also true - what he builds in righteousness can become protection, stability, and blessing for generations. Noah did not just enter the ark; he led his family into it. In the same way, a godly man must take responsibility for the spiritual atmosphere of his home. He must lead in faith, stand in obedience, and move when God speaks, knowing that his response can open the door for others to experience safety in God.

A godly man does not live unto himself; he understands that his life is tied to others. His decisions echo beyond his own soul and into the hearts and futures of those entrusted to him. His household should feel that there is a man standing in the gap on their behalf. Through his words, his integrity, and his daily walk, he becomes a living example of what it means to follow God with sincerity. This kind of man refuses to be careless about spiritual matters at home. He does not assume that things will turn out right - he labors in faith to see that they do. His obedience becomes a guiding light, his consistency builds trust, and his reverence for God shapes the atmosphere of his house. His wife is strengthened by his leadership, his children are anchored by his example, and those under his influence are challenged to rise higher. A godly man understands that influence is not accidental - it is cultivated. And when he walks closely with God, everyone connected to him has the opportunity to walk in that same light.

Leadership begins at home. A man may carry influence in public spaces, earn respect among peers, and even be seen as a voice of strength in the world, but if his house is neglected, his foundation is cracked. God designed leadership to be a responsibility rooted in love, consistency, and presence. The measure of a man is not first how he stands before crowds, but how he shows up daily for those under his care. Integrity is proven in how he speaks, how he listens, how he leads when there is no applause. A man who leads his home with patience, truth, and humility builds something eternal. His example becomes a living blueprint for those watching him most closely. When a man aligns his home under God's order, his public influence carries weight because it is backed by authenticity. But when the private life is in disarray, public honor is hollow. Leadership that pleases God begins not on platforms, but in living rooms where love is practiced, character is tested, and legacy is formed.

Noah did not build the ark in response to rain - he built it in response to a word from God. While the sky was still clear and the ground was still dry, he moved with urgency because he understood that obedience is the truest form of protection. Faith does not wait for visible evidence; it responds to divine instruction. A man who desires to guard his household must be prophetic in his posture, discerning the voice of God before danger ever takes shape. What looks like overreaction to others is often divine wisdom in motion. Real covering is established long before crisis arrives. Noah's family was preserved because he took God seriously. The call of true manhood is to lead with conviction before circumstances demand it. A man who waits for the storm has already waited too long. But a man who obeys early builds a place of safety in advance. His obedience becomes a refuge and his faith becomes the unseen structure that holds his family secure when the world begins to shake.

A man cannot force salvation into the heart of his family, because every soul must stand before God and respond for itself. True covering is the quiet, consistent witness of a life aligned with God. When a man walks in righteousness, prays with sincerity, and honors God in private and public, he creates a spiritual environment that speaks louder than words. His life becomes a living testimony that faith is real, obedience matters, and God is worthy of reverence. In that atmosphere, hearts are softened, not pressured. Faith is invited, not imposed. Children see what devotion looks like, a wife experiences what spiritual leadership feels like, and a home becomes a place where

God's presence is welcomed rather than ignored. A righteous man establishes a culture where truth is respected, and God's voice is not drowned out by the noise of the world. While he cannot choose for his family, he can lead in such a way that choosing God becomes clear, compelling, and deeply personal for those under his influence.

Noah's ark was never just a structure of wood and pitch; it was a living sermon built in obedience to God. Every beam he lifted, every board he fastened, and every layer of pitch he spread was a visible declaration that God's word could be trusted even when it made no sense to the world around him. His work spoke louder than his words. Day after day he showed his household that faith is not merely believed, it is built. As his family watched him labor, they weren't just seeing a man build an ark -they were witnessing a man build conviction, discipline, and trust in God. That kind of leadership creates an atmosphere where faith can grow and be passed down. A righteous man may not be able to force belief into the hearts of his family, but he can construct a life so aligned with God that it becomes impossible to ignore. In the end, the ark stood not only as a vessel of salvation, but as a testimony that one man's faithful obedience can prepare a way for others to be preserved.

When a man refuses to let the spirit of the age define his home, he establishes a boundary that darkness cannot easily cross. The world may shift, compromise, and call evil good, but a man anchored in God stands as a gatekeeper over his family. While others drift with the current, he builds according to divine instruction. His obedience becomes a covering. His conviction becomes a compass. Noah's family was surrounded by wickedness, yet they were not abandoned to confusion. When a man leads with righteousness, he creates a place of refuge in the middle of chaos. His home becomes an ark in a storm, not because trouble is absent, but because God's direction is present. The man who stands firm gives his family identity, stability, and hope. He reminds them that while darkness may surround them, it does not have to shape them. And when the storms come, they will not be lost, because they were led by a man who refused to let the spirit of the age define their home.

Every man is building something, whether he realizes it or not. His words, his decisions, his habits, and his priorities are laying bricks every single day. The question is not if he is building - but what he is building. A man who walks with God builds an atmosphere of safety, where his family knows they are covered, not just physically, but spiritually. His presence brings clarity, not confusion, because his life is anchored in truth. When a man chooses faith over fear, even in uncertain times, he becomes a steady foundation his family can stand on. But when a man neglects his spiritual responsibility, the structure begins to weaken. Confusion replaces direction, fear replaces faith, and the voices of the world begin to shape the culture of his home. A house may be full of activity, yet empty of God's presence. A man must be intentional to build a home where God is honored not occasionally, but consistently. This means guarding what enters his home, modeling righteousness, and leading with humility and conviction.

When a man chooses to walk in alignment with God's voice, he positions himself as a gateway through which divine protection, wisdom, and direction can flow. His obedience invites God's hand into places his strength alone could never reach. It builds a spiritual hedge around his family, guiding them away from unseen dangers and into paths of purpose. What he submits to God, God entrusts with influence. The decisions he makes in private echo loudly in the lives of those he leads. When a man chooses integrity over compromise, faith over fear, and obedience over convenience, he creates a ripple effect that shapes his household's future. His consistency becomes their stability, and his surrender becomes their safety. A man must understand that his walk with God is not just personal - it is foundational. Every act of obedience lays another brick in the covering over his family, ensuring that those connected to him benefit from the doors he opens through faithfulness.

A man cannot afford careless living because his life is never his alone. Every decision he makes echoes beyond himself and into his home, into his relationships, into the lives of those who quietly watch and follow his lead. When he compromises, even in small ways, it creates cracks in the foundation others are standing on. But when he chooses faithfulness - when he walks in integrity, humility, and obedience to God - he builds strength into others. His consistency becomes a steady voice. His discipline becomes a pattern worth following. When a man bows his will to God, he steps into a position where heaven backs his life. His prayers carry weight. His obedience creates protection. Just as a strong wall guards a city, a surrendered man becomes a spiritual barrier against the attacks that would try to reach his family. His life becomes a place of refuge, where those under his care can find safety, strength, and the quiet assurance that someone is standing watch in faith.

Noah stood as a righteous man in an unrighteous generation. In a world consumed by corruption and compromise, his life became a testimony that God still finds those who walk uprightly before Him. God sees what others ignore. He measures a man not by the noise around him, but by the obedience within him. Noah's consistency, his reverence, and his faithfulness became the very thing that distinguished him in the eyes of God. While the world drifted further into darkness, Noah remained anchored in truth and that difference mattered more than popularity, acceptance, or approval. His walk with God became a covering for his family. This is the weight and the beauty of true righteousness: it invites divine intervention. When a man chooses to live right before God, he becomes a doorway through which protection, mercy, and grace can flow into those connected to him. Noah didn't just survive the storm; he led others through it because he had already chosen to walk with God before the rain ever began.

A man who is serious about protecting his house cannot afford to let culture dictate what crosses his threshold, because not everything that is common is harmless. Trends may be popular, but popularity has never been the standard of righteousness. There are voices, influences, and attitudes that quietly erode the strength of a home, and a wise man learns to recognize them before they take root. He knows that what he allows in today will shape what his family lives with tomorrow. Discernment becomes his guardrail and his weapon. He listens beyond words, watches beyond appearances, and tests what enters his environment with spiritual awareness. There will be moments when he must say no, when he must close doors others leave open, and when he must take a stand that is misunderstood by those around him. But a man who discerns well builds a house that is not easily shaken. His courage to stand apart becomes the very thing that keeps his household secure.

There are moments in a man's life when love requires a line to be drawn. Not every voice deserves influence, not every spirit deserves access, and not every pattern belongs under his roof. When a man says, "Not in this house," it is a declaration of responsibility. He understands that what he allows will shape what grows. Like Joshua who boldly declared, "As for me and my house, we will serve the Lord," a godly man establishes spiritual boundaries that honor God and protect those entrusted to him. His conviction becomes a covering, his discernment becomes a shield, and his obedience becomes a foundation his household can stand on. Guarding a home is not passive - it is intentional, watchful, and rooted in truth. A godly man pays attention to what enters through conversations, influences, attitudes, and environments. He rejects what corrupts and embraces what strengthens. This kind of leadership is not loud, but it is firm; not harsh, but it is unwavering.

The ark was built through years of faithful preparation. Every board Noah placed, every instruction he followed, was an act of love expressed through obedience. In the same way, a man's daily choices matter more than he realizes. His work ethic, his prayer life, his discipline, and his willingness to obey God are not isolated acts - they are laying the foundation for something that can shelter and sustain his family in seasons they cannot yet see. Preparation is often quiet, unseen, and uncelebrated, but it carries eternal weight. A godly man understands that what he builds today can become someone else's refuge tomorrow. His consistency becomes their covering. His obedience becomes their protection. His surrender becomes their strength. Just as Noah's ark stood firm when the storm came, a man who prepares with God at the center is creating a legacy that can withstand pressure, uncertainty, and time. That is not selfish labor - it is love in its strongest, most sacrificial form.

A house without spiritual leadership becomes vulnerable. When there is no one guarding the atmosphere, no one seeking God for direction, and no one standing watch in prayer, influences begin to slip in unnoticed. But when a man humbles himself before God, everything begins to shift. As he bows before the Lord and aligns his life with His Word, he becomes a vessel through which God establishes order, peace, and protection within the home. His prayers cover his household, his obedience sets a standard, and his consistency builds a foundation others can stand on. Even when words are few, his walk speaks loudly. The atmosphere shifts when a man aligns his life with God, because heaven moves in response to agreement, not just desire. When his heart, words, and actions come into unity with God's will, what surrounds him begins to reflect what is above him. In that kind of home, those under his care are sheltered by the unseen covering that flows from a life surrendered to God.

God did not call Noah into the ark alone; He called his entire household with him. Noah's obedience built more than an ark; it built a covering. His faith created space for his family to be preserved in a time of judgment. This is the power of a life surrendered to God - it reaches further than the man himself and touches everyone connected to him. A man must understand that his decisions are not his alone. His obedience or compromise, his discipline or neglect, his faith or fear - all of it echoes into the lives of those entrusted to him. One righteous man can shift the direction of a household, alter generational outcomes, and create a refuge in the middle of chaos. God is still looking for men like Noah - men whose lives speak loudly in heaven, men whose obedience invites divine covering over their families. When a man chooses to walk with God, he is not just securing his own future; he is helping shape the destiny of those who walk beside him.

A man who protects his house understands that his role goes far beyond providing walls and a roof - he is called to establish a covering. This covering is built through his relationship with God, not just his strength or effort. He leads with faith when circumstances are uncertain, trusting God's direction over his own understanding. He guards with wisdom, discerning what should be allowed in and what must be kept out. His prayers are not casual or occasional, but carried with burden, knowing that what he intercedes for in the spirit can shape what unfolds in the natural. His obedience is not partial or convenient; it is rooted in conviction, because he knows that compromise weakens the very covering his household depends on. His life becomes a declaration, "As for me and my house, we will honor the Lord." He chooses to build a home where God is welcomed, respected, and obeyed. In doing so, he doesn't just protect his house - he positions it under the covering of God's favor, peace, and purpose.

| 14 |

"A MAN WHO LEADS HIS FAMILY"

In Genesis 7:7, we see a powerful picture of what true spiritual leadership looks like. Noah did not step into the ark alone - he brought his family with him. This was not accidental; it was the fruit of a life lived consistently before God. A man's walk with God is never meant to be isolated. When it is genuine, it creates a visible path that others can follow. Noah didn't just hear from God - he responded in a way that positioned his entire family for preservation. His life preached louder than any sermon he could have spoken. In a world that was corrupt and resistant, his consistency gave his family something stable to anchor to. A godly man must understand that his decisions, his discipline, and his devotion help determine the spiritual direction of his home. When he walks closely with God, he creates a pathway of safety, faith, and purpose for those behind him. His obedience today can become the very thing that carries his family through tomorrow's storms.

A godly man must come to grips with the weight and the honor of responsibility. His choices now carry influence beyond himself. The way he walks with God, the way he speaks, the way he responds under pressure, and the priorities he sets all become a pattern that others will follow. A man can no longer afford to live casually when lives are connected to his leadership. His obedience can create covering, stability, and direction, while his neglect can open doors to confusion and weakness. A godly man leads with awareness that his decisions shape the spiritual atmosphere of his household. When he seeks God, he is building a foundation for those entrusted to him. When he chooses righteousness, he is setting a course that others can safely follow. His life becomes a testimony that faith is not just spoken but lived. In this, a man matures beyond self-centered living and steps into purposeful leadership, knowing that his direction today can influence generations tomorrow.

Noah's faith was something he lived out in plain sight. When he heard from God, he did not delay, debate, or dilute the instruction. He believed it fully, and his belief moved him into action. Every strike of the hammer, every board set in place, and every day spent building the ark was a declaration that he trusted God's word above the opinions of men. His family didn't have to wonder what he believed - they could see it in how he lived, how he worked, and how he refused to quit even when the world around him did not understand. This is the kind of faith that shapes a household. A godly man does not lead with empty words, but with visible conviction. His devotion becomes a pattern others can follow. When his family sees him pray, obey, stand firm, and endure, it builds something in them that words alone cannot produce. And when the time came to enter the ark, his family followed not just because they were told to, but because they had witnessed a man who truly believed what God had said.

True leadership is revealed in what is lived daily - when decisions are difficult, and when consistency is required. His children are not only listening to what he says about God; they are watching how he responds under pressure, how he treats others, and how he prioritizes his time. When they see him pray, it teaches them that God is real, present, and necessary. His life becomes a living testimony that faith is a way of walking. His wife must see conviction in him - a steadiness that is not shaken by circumstances or culture. A godly man sets the spiritual tone of his home by making God the foundation, not an accessory. This means that his decisions, his discipline, and his direction are all rooted in his relationship with God. When a household sees that God is honored daily it builds an atmosphere of trust, strength, and covering. In that environment, faith is not forced; it is formed. And the man who lives this way leaves more than words behind - he leaves a legacy of authentic, unwavering devotion.

Family leadership begins where personal obedience begins. A man sets the direction of his home not merely by what he says, but by what he lives. His daily choices preach louder than his words ever could. When he walks in integrity, his family sees what righteousness looks like in real time. When he prays, they learn dependence on God. When he repents, they learn humility. But when he lives carelessly while demanding discipline, he creates confusion instead of clarity. A man cannot lead his family into a place he refuses to walk himself. A man cannot call his family to holiness while entertaining compromise in secret places. True leadership carries the weight of consistency. It is a steady, visible commitment to honor God in private and in public. When a man chooses to live what he expects, he builds trust, stability, and spiritual authority in his home. His family is far more likely to follow a life they can clearly see than words they only occasionally hear.

Noah's leadership was proven in a lifetime of steady obedience. He did not build the ark in a day, and he did not follow God only when it was convenient. He showed up daily with commitment, even when there was no visible sign that the rain was coming. That kind of consistency builds trust, not only with God, but with those who are watching closely. A man who walks faithfully over time becomes a pillar in his home; someone whose actions speak louder than his words. His family learns that obedience is a decision made again and again. In a world that shifts constantly, a man's consistency becomes an anchor for his household. When fear rises, when uncertainty shakes the foundations of life, his steady walk with God gives his family something firm to stand on. They see a man who does not quit, does not waver, and does not abandon what God has called him to do. That kind of leadership creates security. It teaches that stability is not found in circumstances, but in a life rooted in obedience to God.

A godly man understands that true leadership is built on trust in God and a heart shaped by Him. He does not raise his voice to be heard; he raises his standard to be followed. His faith anchors his decisions, his wisdom guides his actions, and his humility keeps him teachable before God. Strength in a godly man is steady, reliable, and sacrificial. Those under his care are not burdened by his presence; they are strengthened by it, because they see in him a reflection of God's character. He creates an atmosphere where growth is possible, where correction is given with love, and where truth is lived, not just spoken. Instead of dominating his home, he disciples it - investing time, prayer, and intentional example into those entrusted to him. His life becomes a living blueprint of what it means to walk with God. And in that kind of leadership, his family does not follow out of fear - they follow because they see a man who is following God.

There are moments in a man's life when silence is no longer an option, when he must rise with conviction and declare, "We are going God's way." This is the sound of responsibility. It is the understanding that the direction he sets will shape the lives entrusted to him. A godly man sees what compromise can cost, what disobedience can destroy, and he chooses a higher path out of reverence. His stance becomes a line drawn in the sand, not to elevate himself, but to protect his household from what could pull them away from God's will. True leadership demands courage - the kind that stands firm when others bend, the kind that chooses obedience when it is unpopular. A man who leads his family toward God must be willing to be misunderstood, to go against the current, and to carry the weight of that decision with humility and strength. He does not lead by forcing, but by faithfully walking the path himself. His consistency builds trust, and his conviction builds security.

Noah's family stepped into safety not because they each received the command individually, but because one man heard God and chose to obey. Long before the rain ever fell, Noah had already built a place of refuge through his surrender. Every board placed, every day endured, every act of faith became a covering for those connected to him. This reveals a powerful truth: when a man aligns himself with God, his life begins to create protection beyond himself. A man's surrender is never isolated. It carries weight, influence, and consequence. When he walks in obedience, he builds something his family can step into—peace in chaos, direction in confusion, and safety in judgment. His prayers become a shield, his discipline becomes stability, and his faith becomes a refuge. God honors a man who says yes, not just for his own sake, but for the sake of those entrusted to him. The ark did not begin when the flood came - it began the moment Noah chose to obey.

God never intended for leadership to be silent when souls are being shaped. A father's voice carries weight, forming direction, identity, and understanding in the hearts of those under his care. He must teach truth clearly, not leaving his family to learn God's ways by accident or assumption. Wisdom should flow from his lips in daily conversation, in correction, in encouragement, and in moments of decision. His words should illuminate the path, pointing consistently toward righteousness. When he explains the ways of God, he builds spiritual foundations that storms cannot easily shake. A godly man understands that correction must come with love and that teaching requires patience. He steps into his role with intentionality, knowing that his voice can either shape or leave a void. Leadership is to ensure that those entrusted to him are not left wandering. When a man faithfully instructs his family in the ways of God, he becomes a living compass, aligning his household with truth, purpose, and divine order.

Instruction alone is not enough to shape a godly home - example is what gives it weight. A man can speak truth, quote scripture, and lay down principles, but if his life does not reflect what he teaches, his words lose their authority. True leadership is not proven by what is said in moments of teaching, but by what is lived in the quiet, unseen moments of daily life. When a man walks in integrity, his actions echo louder than his voice. His consistency becomes a testimony, and his faith becomes visible in the way he treats others, handles pressure, and honors God when no one is watching. A man's family learns not only from his instruction, but from his demonstration. They watch how he responds to difficulty, how he prioritizes God, and how he lives when tested. If he teaches patience but lives in anger, or speaks of faith but walks in fear, the contradiction weakens his influence. But when his life aligns with his words, it creates clarity, trust, and direction within the home.

Leadership is not only about guiding in the present - it is about discerning what is coming before it arrives. Noah stood in a generation that was blind to its own destruction, yet he saw what others refused to acknowledge. While the world dismissed the warning, he responded with obedience. Spiritual alertness is what separates a passive man from a prepared one. A man who leads well does not wait for visible evidence of trouble; he listens for the voice of God and acts on it. When others laugh, doubt, or delay, he remains steady, because his awareness is rooted in faith, not in popular opinion. A man must be awake - spiritually sensitive to danger, compromise, and the subtle shifts that threaten his household. This awareness is not fear-driven but faith-driven. It produces action. It builds, prepares, and positions his family for what lies ahead. Strength in leadership is not proven in the moment of crisis, but in the quiet seasons of preparation before the storm ever forms.

Faith is not proven in panic, but in preparation. Long before the first drop of rain fell, Noah was already building in obedience, moving at the word of God when there was no visible evidence of a flood. In the same way, a man of God must take his assignment seriously before pressure forces him to. He must build his life on truth when things are calm, strengthen his relationship with God when things are stable, and establish order in his home before chaos ever tries to enter. Preparation is not optional - it is the evidence of wisdom and obedience. He must pray before the crisis, not just react in desperation when trouble arrives. He must teach his family the ways of God before confusion and compromise knock at the door. A godly man leads with foresight, not hindsight. He understands that what is built in private will stand in public, and when the rain finally comes his house will not be shaken, because he did not wait for the storm to get serious about what God already called him to do.

A man can supply food, pay bills, and provide comfort, yet still leave his household exposed if he neglects the spiritual and emotional weight of leadership. True covering means standing as a guardian over what God has entrusted to him - watching over the atmosphere of the home, setting the tone for righteousness, and leading with a heart anchored in truth. It is not enough to build a house; he must build a place where God is honored, where peace is protected, and where faith is lived out daily. His presence should bring order, his words should bring life, and his example should point his family toward God. Spiritual direction, emotional stability, moral clarity, and faithful love are the pillars of that covering. A man who leads well prays over his household, speaks wisdom into confusion, corrects with grace, and remains steady when life becomes uncertain. His strength is not just in what he provides with his hands, but in what he cultivates in the hearts around him.

Noah's leadership reveals that true faith is not silent - it is seen, lived, and proven over time. His obedience to God was not a momentary decision but a sustained walk that his family witnessed day after day. He built the ark before there was rain, trusted God before there was evidence, and moved forward before there was understanding. His family may not have grasped every instruction, but they saw a man who was unwavering in his devotion. That kind of faith creates a foundation of trust, where those under his leadership can follow not because they understand everything, but because they believe in the God he serves. A man's faith should shape the atmosphere, guide decisions, and establish direction within his home. Like Noah, a godly man leads by example, showing that obedience to God is worth following even when the path is unclear. His life becomes a testimony that draws his household closer to God, not by force, but by the undeniable evidence of a faith that stands firm through every season.

A man who leads his family will often carry weight that no one else can see. In the quiet moments, he wrestles in prayer over decisions, protection, provision, and direction. Like a watchman in the night, he stays alert even when others rest, bringing every concern before God. His strength is not found in having all the answers, but in trusting the One who does. When weariness tries to settle in, he leans deeper into faith, knowing that unseen battles are often the most important ones he will fight. Leadership is not always loud or recognized, but it must always be faithful. A godly man keeps showing up, keeps praying, and keeps guiding even when misunderstood or unappreciated. His quiet endurance becomes a covering over his household, and his faithfulness builds a foundation his family can stand on. In time, the man who refuses to quit, who remains steady under pressure, becomes a living testimony that true leadership is about obedience to God and unwavering devotion to those entrusted to his care.

The greatest gift a man can give his family is not the illusion of perfection, but the reality of surrender. A surrendered man does not pretend to have all the answers but lives in daily dependence on God. He acknowledges when he falls short, and models repentance instead of pride. In doing so, he teaches his family that strength is not found in flawless performance, but in a heart that continually returns to the

Lord. His surrender becomes a living testimony that God's grace is sufficient, even in weakness. When a man walks in surrender, his life becomes a compass pointing his household toward God. He obeys when obedience is costly and stands firm when pressure rises. His leadership is not built on control, but on submission to a higher authority. Through his example, his family learns that true authority flows from alignment with God's will. A surrendered man may not be perfect, but he is powerful because his life is anchored in obedience, shaped by humility, and guided by the hand of God.

Noah did not wander into the ark by accident - he walked in with purpose, conviction, and direction. His faith was not passive; it moved, it obeyed, and it led. When the waters of judgment came, Noah was not scrambling for safety for he had already prepared a path for his household. His obedience became their covering. His trust in God became their rescue. A man's faith is not meant to end with him, but to extend outward, creating a refuge for those God has placed under his care. A godly man today must live with visible, consistent faith that others can follow. His decisions should point toward God, his words should carry truth, and his life should reflect a steady trust in the Lord. Leadership in the home is not about control, but about setting a course that honors God and walking it first. When a man lives this way, his family does not have to guess where he stands. They see it. They trust it. And through his example, they come to know that in his house, God will be honored, obeyed, and lifted above all.

| 15 |

"A MAN WHO PREPARES BEFORE THE RAIN"

Noah teaches us that righteousness is not proven in the storm - it is revealed there. The real work happens long before the rain ever falls. While the world lived unaware and unconcerned, Noah was already moving in obedience, laying plank upon plank in quiet faith. There was no visible evidence, no storm clouds forming, no applause from others - only the voice of God and a man willing to trust it. This kind of faith separates the prepared from the overwhelmed. When the storm finally came, Noah was not scrambling - he was ready. His obedience had already secured what the crisis would demand. In the same way, a godly man prepares his life, his family, and his spirit before the pressure arrives. He prays before the battle, he builds before the need, and he listens before the urgency. Faith is not reactive; it is proactive. And the man who walks with God today will stand firm tomorrow, not because the storm is weak, but because his obedience was already strong.

Genesis 7:4–5 reveals a powerful truth about the nature of faith: God speaks before He moves, and the faithful man responds before he fully sees. Noah was given a warning of something the world had never witnessed - a coming flood - and yet he did not delay, debate, or dilute the instruction. Scripture declares that he "did according unto all that the Lord commanded him." That kind of obedience is not casual; it is rooted in reverence. A faithful man does not wait for confirmation from culture or comfort from circumstances - he moves at the sound of God's voice. Obedience is his response, not his struggle. While others question, he builds. While others ignore, he prepares. His faith is proven not by what he says, but by what he does when God speaks. This is the mark of a man who walks with God: he trusts divine instruction even when it defies human understanding. Noah did not argue about the timing, the method, or the magnitude - he simply obeyed.

Preparation rooted in faith is anchored in trust. When God spoke to Noah, he did not respond with panic, but with steady obedience. There were no visible signs of rain, no evidence of a coming flood, yet Noah built the ark with unwavering commitment. His preparation was not a reaction to fear, but a response to revelation. Faith gave him the vision to act before the storm arrived. In the same way, a man who walks with God does not wait for pressure to force his hand - he moves when God speaks, trusting that obedience today will sustain him tomorrow. A man of faith understands that preparation is obedience in advance. It is choosing discipline before the battle, prayer before the crisis, and alignment before the shaking begins. While others delay until circumstances demand action, the faithful man prepares because he believes what God has said. And when the rain finally falls, the man who prepared in faith will stand secure, not because he feared the storm, but because he trusted the voice of God.

Many men do not move until pressure forces them to, but by then the damage has already begun. They wait until the storm clouds gather before they pray, until tension fills the home before they lead, and until things begin to break before they seek God with urgency. But spiritual responsibility was never meant to be reactive - it is meant to be proactive. A wise man does not wait for the rain to fall; he prepares while the sky is still clear. The man who builds before the flood is the man who stands when it comes. He invests in his marriage before it strains, pours truth into his children before confusion takes root, and orders his life under God before chaos tries to take hold. This kind of preparation says, "I believe what God has spoken about tomorrow, so I will act today." Strength is not proven in the storm alone; it is revealed by the decisions made long before it arrives. A faithful man does not scramble when the pressure hits - he stands, because he has already built something that can endure.

A man who prepares before the rain prays before the crisis. He does not treat prayer as a last resort, but as a daily foundation. In the quiet seasons - when the skies are clear and the winds are still - he is already seeking God, already building strength in the secret place. He understands that storms do not create faith; they reveal it. So he develops a relationship with God before the pressure comes, learning His voice, anchoring his heart, and establishing spiritual discipline long before trouble ever reaches his door. When the storm finally arrives, he is not scrambling for direction - he is standing on what he has already built. The altar he raised in peace becomes his refuge in battle. Because he prayed before the crisis, he now has confidence in the crisis. His family is not left exposed to his uncertainty but covered by his preparation. This is the wisdom of a godly man: he prepares in advance, seeks God early, and builds a life that can withstand the rain when it inevitably falls.

Noah's obedience looked strange long before it looked wise. While others lived their lives without concern, he labored daily on something that made no sense to the natural eye. There was no rain, no storm clouds, and no evidence yet Noah built anyway. His confidence was not in what he saw, but in Who had spoken. Faith anchored him when understanding could not. In the same way, a faithful man must learn to move at the sound of God's voice, even when obedience sets him apart. What looks unnecessary to the world may be essential in the spirit, and what seems foolish today may be revealed as wisdom tomorrow. A man who walks with God cannot be governed by the opinions of men. Noah did not pause construction to explain himself, nor did he seek validation from those who doubted him. He understood that divine instruction carries greater weight than public approval. When God speaks, obedience is the only proper response.

There are assignments from God that will not make sense to the crowd while you are building them. When a man begins to construct a life of prayer, discipline his character, invest in his marriage, and train his children in truth, it may look unnecessary to those who live by sight instead of faith. Just as Noah built before there was any evidence of rain, a wise man builds his life on what God has said, not on what others can see. The rain will eventually reveal what obedience was preparing all along. Build your prayer life until it becomes your strength in secret. Build your character until integrity stands when pressure comes. Build your marriage with intentional love and truth so it can endure storms. Build your children on the Word so they are anchored when culture shifts. And above all, build your house on the foundation of God's Word, because when the rain comes only what was built according to His instruction will stand.

Wise men do not wait for crisis to awaken their obedience - they build before the storm ever forms on the horizon. They establish their homes in truth, anchoring their families in the Word of God while there is still calm. They cultivate discipline in daily living, they lead with love that is consistent, and they bring order where chaos would otherwise take root. A faithful man understands that spiritual covering is woven into the fabric of everyday life through prayer, instruction, and steady devotion. What is built in quiet seasons will be what stands in violent ones. A man who delays obedience until the storm is already raging may find that hesitation carries a cost. When the winds rise and the pressure increases, the man who prepares ahead of time will not be shaken because his house has already been strengthened. Obedience today is protection for tomorrow, and the choices a man makes in peace will determine how he stands in the storm.

Preparation is an act of leadership because it requires a man to see beyond the present moment and respond to what God has revealed about the future. Noah did not build the ark when the rain started - he built it when there was no sign of a storm. That kind of obedience is not driven by fear, but by reverence. A true leader does not wait for crisis to force action; he moves at the voice of God. Noah understood that his calling was bigger than himself. His obedience became a covering for his household, shielding his family from the coming judgment because one man chose to take God seriously. Leadership carries weight, because the decisions of a man often reach further than he can see. When a man prays, obeys, and prepares, he builds an ark for others to enter. His faith becomes a refuge, his discipline becomes protection, and his consistency becomes a testimony. A prepared man is not just ready - he becomes a vessel through which God preserves and guides everyone connected to his life.

A righteous man lives with an awareness that his present actions are shaping his future reality. He does not treat today casually, because he understands that tomorrow is being constructed moment by moment through his obedience, discipline, and faith. The habits he forms become the framework of his character. The words he speaks set the atmosphere of his home. The prayers he prays invite the hand of God into his circumstances. Every decision becomes a building block in the ark of his household. He is not merely reacting to life - he is aligning himself with God's wisdom before the storm ever appears. Such a man builds intentionally, knowing that what he constructs in private will one day sustain him in public. He does not wait for crisis to start praying, leading, or correcting his course. Instead, he labors faithfully trusting that God honors preparation rooted in righteousness. When the winds rise and the waters increase, his household stands because of what was built beforehand.

Noah's preparation was not a moment of inspiration - it was a lifetime of consistency. Day after day, he built the ark under clear skies, with no clouds forming and no sign that rain was on the horizon. His obedience was not fueled by what he saw, but by what God said. That is the essence of true faithfulness: continuing the work when it feels unnoticed, unvalidated, and even unnecessary in the eyes of others. A faithful man does not require visible confirmation to stay committed; he anchors his actions in the certainty of God's word, not the uncertainty of circumstances. In the same way, a man of God today must learn to build when it's quiet, to pray when nothing seems to be changing, and to stand firm when there is no immediate evidence of breakthrough. Consistency in obedience forms the structure that will carry him through future storms. What seems repetitive and unseen is actually laying a foundation of strength, character, and trust.

Some men stop building because they measure progress by what they can see. When the results are not immediate, discouragement whispers that the effort is wasted. But God does not work on the timetable of human impatience. He often builds in silence, shaping strength where there is no applause, forming endurance where there is no evidence. What feels like delay is often divine development. A faithful man understands that obedience is not validated by visibility, but by alignment with God's instruction. Even when nothing appears to be changing, something is being established beneath the surface. Hidden seasons are not empty seasons - they are preparation grounds for future deliverance. The ark was built long before the rain fell, and what looked unnecessary became essential at the appointed time. In the same way, a wise man keeps building because he trusts the One who gave the instruction. In due time, what was built in faith will stand in the storm.

A man must learn to take divine warnings seriously, because God does not speak to impress - He speaks to prepare. His Word is not merely information; it is instruction for life, leadership, and legacy. It teaches a man how to live with integrity, how to lead with wisdom, how to love with strength and patience, how to guard his home with discernment, and how to walk uprightly before God. When a man listens closely and obeys early, he builds a foundation that can withstand pressure. But when he treats divine instruction casually, he risks facing storms unprepared. What God reveals in quiet seasons is meant to protect and guide in uncertain ones. Ignoring instruction in peaceful seasons can create pain in difficult ones. The time to align your life is not when everything is shaking, but when everything is still. A wise man does not wait for crisis to force obedience - he chooses obedience while there is still time to prepare. A faithful man knows that obedience today can spare him sorrow tomorrow.

Noah prepared before the flood because he trusted that what God said about tomorrow was more certain than what he could see today. The sky was clear and the ground was dry, but Noah built anyway. That is the essence of faith: not reacting to what is visible but responding to what is revealed. A man of God does not wait for evidence to align before he obeys; he aligns himself with God's word and lets his obedience become the evidence. Faith builds when others doubt, moves when others hesitate, and stands when others dismiss the call. A wise man understands that the voice of God carries more weight than the noise of the world. A man of conviction does not follow the shifting winds of culture, but firmly orders his life, his home, and his decisions according to unchanging truth. When a man chooses God's command over cultural consensus, he becomes like Noah - building something that may not make sense today but will stand when the storm finally comes.

Preparation also requires sacrifice. Noah did not build the ark in comfort or convenience; he invested years of unseen labor, physical exhaustion, and unwavering focus on a word from God. His obedience required the surrender of reputation, as others likely questioned and mocked what they did not understand. Yet Noah understood that divine instruction outweighs human opinion. Real preparation is not proven in ease, but in sacrifice - when a man gives his time, strength, and resources to align with what God has spoken, even when it stretches him beyond what feels reasonable. Every man who desires to build something that lasts must come to the same crossroads. Comfort must be laid down so calling can be picked up. Pride must be surrendered so obedience can take root. Convenience must give way to discipline, and the approval of others must lose its grip when it competes with the voice of God. Sacrifice is not loss when it is given to the purposes of God - it is investment.

The rain came exactly as God said it would - not early, not late, but in perfect alignment with His word. And when it came, Noah was not found scrambling in fear or rushing to obey what he had long delayed. While others lived unaware and unprepared, Noah had already settled the matter in his heart: if God spoke, he would act. So when the floodwaters rose, what overwhelmed the world did not overwhelm him. The same rain that brought judgment upon the earth became the very thing that lifted the ark. There is a powerful lesson in that: what you do before the storm determines how you stand in it. Obedience in the unseen seasons becomes stability in the shaking seasons. A wise man does not wait for pressure to build character - he builds it daily through faithfulness to God's voice. When the rains of life begin to fall those who have already been walking with God will not panic. They will stand firm, because preparation grounded in faith transforms chaos into confirmation.

The call to every man is to build when the skies are still clear. Strengthen your spirit in the quiet place, before the battle ever reaches your door. A wise man does not scramble in the rain - he prepares in the sunlight. He teaches his children truth before confusion has a voice, plants conviction in their hearts before the world tries to rewrite it and roots his life so deeply in God that when the winds come, they find nothing loose to carry away. Preparation is not fear - it is faith in action, obedience before evidence, and trust that what God has revealed about tomorrow requires movement today. Love your wife with intention before distance has a chance to grow. Lead your home with clarity before chaos tries to settle in. Put your house in order not out of pressure, but out of purpose because storms do not create strength, they reveal it. When the rain begins to fall, it will expose what was built in secret. The man who prepared will stand steady, not because the storm is weak, but because his foundation is strong.

A righteous man does not wait for the storm to start building - he builds when the sky is still clear, because his confidence is not in the weather but in the word of God. What God reveals about tomorrow becomes his assignment today. Faith moves him to act before there is visible evidence, and obedience anchors him when others hesitate. While others delay, question, or drift, he prepares with quiet conviction, laying one plank at a time in alignment with what God has spoken. His preparation is not driven by fear, but by trust that God sees what he cannot and knows what is coming long before it arrives. The strength of his house was formed in the unseen moments of obedience, long before the storm ever tested it. This is the mark of a godly man: he hears God, he believes God, and he moves when God speaks. And in the end, what he built in faith becomes the very thing that carries him through what others were unprepared to face.

| 16 |

"A MAN WHO ENTERS GOD SAYS ENTER"

There comes a defining moment in a man's life when preparation gives way to participation - when God no longer says, "Get ready," but declares, "Now step in." Noah lived faithfully in the hidden years, building what no one understood, obeying without applause, and trusting without visible evidence. Then in Genesis 7:1 the voice of God said, "Come thou and all thy house into the ark." The same God who commanded the building now commanded the entering. A godly man must discern not only what God told him to build, but when God is telling him to move. There is danger in hesitating when heaven has spoken. What once required patience now requires bold obedience. Every season of obedience is preparing you for a moment of entrance. The ark was not Noah's destination - it was his doorway into preservation, purpose, and promise. When God says "enter," it means the storm is coming, but so is His covering. It means the work you did in obscurity is about to become the place of your security.

A godly man must learn that obedience is not measured only by action, but by alignment with God's timing. It is possible to do the right thing at the wrong time and still step outside of God's will. Genesis reveals that Noah did not move when fear rose or when pressure increased - he moved when God spoke. Entering the ark too early would have been driven by anxiety, not faith. Waiting too long would have been disobedience, not patience. A mature man understands that God's voice carries both instruction and timing. The same God who gave Noah the blueprint also controlled the clock. He did not leave Noah to guess the moment - He spoke it. In the same way, a godly man must resist the urge to move ahead of God out of fear or lag behind out of hesitation. There is protection in divine timing. When God says "move," hesitation becomes danger, and when God says "wait," rushing becomes rebellion. True obedience is synchronized with heaven. It is walking in step with God's voice, not your emotions.

Many men don't miss God because they rejected His voice - they miss Him because they mismanaged His timing. They heard clearly, understood deeply, and even agreed internally, yet they failed to move when God said move. What begins as hesitation can slowly harden into resistance. Timing is not a small detail in obedience - it is a critical part of it. When God speaks, He is not only revealing what to do, but when to do it, and stepping outside of that timing can lead to missed doors, lost momentum, and unnecessary battles. Faith is not validated by how well you can repeat what God said - it is revealed by how quickly you respond when He says it. True obedience has movement attached to it. It gets up, it steps out, it acts even when conditions aren't perfect. Faith moves while the word is fresh, while the door is open, while grace is present for that moment. Don't just agree with God - walk with Him. Don't just believe the instruction - become the man who moves when it is spoken.

When God spoke to Noah and said it was time to enter the ark, everything changed. What had once been a long, demanding assignment suddenly became a place of divine preservation. The very thing Noah had labored over in obedience became the refuge that carried him through judgment. A godly man must understand that obedience is not always about immediate results - it is about trusting that what God is building through you today will sustain you tomorrow. This reveals a deeper truth about how God works in the life of a man. Often, He will lead you to build, prepare, and invest in things long before their purpose is revealed. It may feel repetitive, unnoticed, or even unnecessary in the moment. But when the storm comes, what you built in quiet obedience becomes your covering. The discipline you developed, the faith you exercised, the boundaries you established, and the voice of God you learned to follow will become your protection.

A man who walks with God learns that obedience is not just about what to do, but when to do it. There are seasons where God calls him to build in obscurity, to labor faithfully without applause, laying foundations that no one else may understand. Then there are moments when God says, "Enter," and what was once preparation becomes preservation. The same hands that labored must now rest under what was built. Discernment in timing is what separates striving from surrender. A godly man does not rush ahead in ambition or lag behind in hesitation - he moves when God speaks, trusting that every season has a divine purpose attached to it. It takes humility to step forward when it is uncomfortable, and it takes humility to step back when pride wants to be seen. A man aligned with God's timing understands that delayed obedience can cost him, but surrendered obedience will always cover him. When he learns to move at the sound of God's voice, he walks in divine protection.

Delayed obedience is not harmless - it is a silent gamble with consequences a man cannot always see. When God speaks, it is not merely instruction - it is insight into what lies ahead. What feels like "there's still time" is often an illusion, because divine timing operates beyond human perception. A man who delays obedience is not just postponing action; he is stepping outside of the covering that obedience provides. The rain may not be falling yet, but the clouds have already gathered at God's command. A wise man learns that God's voice is not a suggestion to consider, but a command to follow. Every instruction carries protection within it, even when the danger is not yet visible. What God tells you to do today may be the very thing that shields you tomorrow. Obedience positions you inside the ark before the first drop falls. But hesitation leaves the door open while judgment draws near. The difference between safety and struggle is often found in a man's response time to God's voice.

Noah's entrance into the ark was not driven by anxiety over what might happen - it was anchored in confidence in what God had said. While others may have waited until the first drop of rain, Noah moved before the storm ever arrived. His obedience was not a reaction to visible danger but a response to divine instruction. Fear scrambles when pressure rises, but faith steps forward while everything still appears calm, trusting that what God has spoken is more real than what can be seen. There is a clear difference between movement that is fueled by fear and movement that is led by faith. Fear is impulsive, driven by urgency and uncertainty, always trying to escape what it cannot control. But faith is steady, rooted in trust, and willing to act even when the reason is not fully understood. Noah did not build and enter the ark because he was afraid of the rain - he did it because he believed God. In the same way, a man walking with God doesn't wait until life forces his hand; he moves when God speaks.

A godly man must learn to move when the voice of God is clear. Faith is not built on the approval of others but on the certainty of divine instruction. Noah did not wait for clouds to gather or for the first drop of rain to fall before he stepped into obedience - he moved because God spoke. In the same way, a man of faith is willing to act when it is quiet, to prepare when it seems unnecessary, and to trust when it looks unreasonable. This kind of faith requires courage, because it will often separate a man from the comfort of agreement and place him in the tension of standing alone. When the storm finally comes, the obedience he walked out in private becomes the very thing that sustains him in public. A godly man knows that delayed understanding from others does not mean he has missed God. It simply means he has chosen to trust God early. And in that early obedience, he finds not only direction, but preservation, purpose, and the quiet confidence that comes from walking ahead with God.

This kind of obedience is not passive - it is courageous. When God calls a man to move, He is often asking him to step away from what feels safe, predictable, and understood. Like Noah entering the ark before a drop of rain had fallen, true obedience means acting on God's word even when the evidence has not yet appeared. It takes courage to endure the opinions of others, to stand firm when obedience looks foolish in the eyes of the world. Yet every step taken in faith is a declaration that God's voice carries more weight than man's approval. Courageous obedience is not the absence of fear - it is the decision that God's instruction is greater than your hesitation. Leadership, then, is revealed in the moment of movement. Many can receive a vision, but few will act when the time comes to obey it. A true leader gathers his house, speaks with conviction, and moves forward because God has spoken =not because it is easy, but because it is right.

The ark was built by one man's faith, but it became a refuge for many lives. This reminds us that a man's walk with God is never just about him. His decisions echo into the lives of those connected to him - his family, his household, and even future generations. What Noah did in private obedience became public preservation. His yes to God created a covering that extended far beyond his own life. A man must understand that his timing matters. Delay is not harmless when others are tied to your obedience. Every step of hesitation can expose others to unnecessary danger, while every step of faith can bring them into divine protection. Noah moved when God spoke, and because he did, his family stepped into safety. In the same way, a man's response to God today can build an ark for tomorrow. His obedience can become a shelter, his faith a shield, and his consistency a place of refuge. Never forget - what you do in obedience to God may be the very thing that preserves the lives of those connected to you.

There are men who delay obedience because they are waiting on clarity that God never promised to give in advance. They want the full blueprint before they take the first step, but God works differently - He leads, then reveals. Faith is not proven in having all the answers, but in moving forward when you don't. A man must understand that obedience is built on trust in a perfect God. When God speaks, He is not asking for analysis - He is requiring action. The danger of waiting is that hesitation can harden into disobedience, and what could have been a step of faith becomes a missed moment of destiny. God will always give enough light for the step you're on, but rarely for the entire path ahead. He provides just enough instruction to move, and just enough grace to sustain you once you do. The journey of obedience is where understanding grows, strength is developed, and purpose is revealed. A man who moves when God speaks will discover that provision follows obedience, not the other way around.

God's timing is never random - it is intentional, precise, and protective. A delayed response can expose a man to what obedience would have shielded him from. What feels like interruption is often divine interception. God sees what you cannot see, and He positions you ahead of what is coming. When He speaks, it is not just about where you are going, but what you are being kept from. His timing is a covering, not a constraint. The ark did not look like freedom - it looked like limitation. It closed Noah in while the world remained open. But what seemed restrictive was actually the only place of survival. Many men resist God's instructions because they do not match their idea of expansion, but God is not always expanding your space - sometimes He is securing your life. What feels like being held back is often being held safe. The walls you question may be the very boundaries preserving you. Trust that when God says enter, He is not confining you - He is guarding your future.

A man must guard his heart against the subtle trap of comfort, because what once required faith can eventually become familiar. Noah had labored faithfully outside the ark, building in obedience when there was no rain and no visible reason to continue. But when God spoke again, the assignment changed. The same man who was called to build was now called to enter. The danger is not always disobedience in action - it is hesitation in transition. When God says move, a man must move, even if it means leaving behind what he has invested in. Noah had to walk away from the tools, the structure, and the familiar rhythm of building to step into something that looked like stillness but was actually safety. Some men miss divine protection because they linger in yesterday's assignment. True obedience requires flexibility of heart and sensitivity to God's voice. A man must be willing to transition without resistance, trusting that the God who called him to build is the same God calling him to enter.

Divine opportunities are often tied to divine timing. What God opens in one season may not remain open in the next. The generation of Noah heard the warning, saw the ark being built, and had time to respond - but eventually, the door closed. The same God who showed mercy also established a moment when mercy gave way to judgment. A wise man understands that delayed obedience is not harmless; it is dangerous when it causes him to miss the window God has provided. A mature man of faith does not test the limits of God's patience - he honors it by responding quickly. When God opens a door, it is an invitation wrapped in responsibility. To ignore it is to gamble with something sacred. But to walk through it is to step into protection, purpose, and alignment with His will. The man who recognizes the moment and acts will find himself on the right side of what God is doing, while others are left outside wishing they had moved sooner.

To enter when God says enter is an act of deep trust that rises above human reasoning. It means a man has settled in his heart that God's voice is more reliable than visible circumstances. While others measure reality by what they can see, a man of faith measures it by what God has said. Noah stood in a world that looked normal, with no sign of rain and no evidence of judgment but he moved anyway. Why? Because he had heard from heaven. That is the dividing line between natural sight and spiritual discernment. One reacts to appearances; the other responds to revelation. A man led by God cannot afford to anchor his obedience in public opinion or visible proof. If he waits for confirmation from the crowd, he will miss the moment God ordained for movement. Obedience often looks unreasonable to those who lack spiritual insight, but it is always right in the eyes of God. True discernment gives a man the courage to move when others hesitate and to trust when others doubt.

There are moments in a man's life when he finds himself standing at the edge of a decision that will define more than just his present - it will shape his future, his family, and his legacy. In those moments, God is calling for obedience. When God has spoken, waiting is not always maturity; sometimes it is resistance dressed in caution. A wise man discerns the difference. He understands that there are moments when the Spirit of God is saying, "Move now." Not recklessly, but faithfully. Not blindly, but obediently. The longer a man lingers at the edge, the easier it becomes to retreat back into comfort and familiarity. But growth does not live in comfort - it lives in response. When God opens a door or issues a call, there is a grace attached to that moment that will not always remain indefinitely. Step into what God is calling you to, even if it stretches you, even if it costs you. Because sometimes the greatest wisdom a man can walk in is not found in waiting longer but in moving when God says move.

The man who enters when God says enter is not driven by impulse - he is governed by surrender. His obedience is not a reaction to pressure, but a response to relationship. He has come to understand that when God speaks, it carries intention, precision, and purpose. There is no randomness in divine instruction. What may look premature to others is actually perfectly timed in the realm of the Spirit. This man does not wait for visible confirmation because he has already received spiritual clarity. He trusts that if God has called him forward, then every step ahead has already been accounted for. He does not require the storm to validate the command. He does not need crisis to convince him to move. While others hesitate until circumstances force their hand, this man steps forward because the Lord has spoken. That is the difference between fear-driven movement and faith-driven obedience. His confidence is not in what he sees forming around him, but in what God has declared over him.

Noah's life reveals a truth that safety is not found in comfort, popularity, or visible certainty - it is found in obedience. While others lived according to what they could see and feel, Noah anchored his life in what God said. When the skies were clear, he built. When the world mocked, he stayed focused. When the time came, he entered. His security was not in favorable conditions but in divine instruction. A man who walks with God must learn to value God's voice above every other influence. There is a covering that only obedience provides. When God gives a command, it is never random - it carries protection, timing, and purpose within it. Noah did not just build an ark; he built a place of preservation through consistent obedience. Every act of faith positioned him for what was coming, even before he fully understood it. This is the posture of a man who truly walks with God: he moves when God speaks, he waits when God pauses, and he trusts when God leads.

| 17 |

"A MAN WHO TRUSTS GOD TO SHUT THE DOOR"

Noah did not wait for the rain to start before he moved; he built when there was no evidence, gathered his household when others mocked, and stepped into the ark when God called him. That is the work of a faithful man: to act on God's word even when it defies logic, culture, and comfort. Obedience is the visible expression of faith, and it requires movement, discipline, and commitment. But there comes a moment where a man must release what he cannot control. Noah could build the ark, but he could not seal it. He could enter in, but he could not secure his own protection. The scripture says, "the Lord shut him in," revealing that there are dimensions of safety, provision, and destiny that only God can accomplish. This is where surrender becomes powerful. A man must know when he has done his part and trust God to do His. When obedience is complete and surrender is embraced, a man finds himself not just doing the will of God, but being kept by the hand of God.

A righteous man is not called to control everything - he is called to obey God fully and trust God completely. Too many men exhaust themselves trying to manage outcomes that were never assigned to them. They carry the weight of results, timing, and consequences when God only asked for obedience. Noah understood his responsibility. A man walking in righteousness learns the difference between his assignment and God's authority. Noah could build the ark, but he could not command the flood. He could enter the ark, but he could not secure the future. That part belonged to God. And that is where true faith is revealed - not just in what a man does, but in what he releases. There is strength in surrender. There is peace in trusting God with what you cannot touch. When a man fulfills his part and then steps back, he makes room for God to do what only God can do. The burden lifts when he realizes that obedience is his responsibility, but outcomes belong to the Lord.

There are moments in a man's life when he reaches the edge of his own ability. In those moments, he must learn a deeper trust. Some doors are not closed by effort, wisdom, or timing, but by the hand of God alone. A man's responsibility is not to force the ending, but to remain faithful in the place God assigned him. Standing in obedience becomes an act of surrender, declaring that God is both the Author and the Finisher of every season. When God shuts a door, it is sealed with divine authority. No storm has the strength to pry it open, no enemy has the power to break through it, and no fear has the right to question it. What God closes is covered, protected, and settled. A man who understands this rests in the confidence that the same God who led him to that door has now secured it for his good. There is peace in knowing that what God has shut cannot be undone, and there is strength in trusting that every closed door is making way for a greater purpose ahead.

The moment God shut Noah into the ark was a demonstration of divine protection. When God establishes boundaries around a man, it is not because He is trying to hold him back, but because He sees what is ahead. The storm that was coming would have destroyed everything exposed to it, but what was surrendered to God's instruction was shielded by His hand. A man must learn that not every closed space is a setback; sometimes it is the very place where God secures his future. There are seasons when God will limit movement, narrow options, and shut certain doors, and it can feel like confinement if a man does not understand the purpose. But heaven calls it preservation. God knows how to protect what He intends to use. The ark was not Noah's prison - it was his provision. It carried him through what he could not survive on his own. What feels like restriction today may be the very thing that keeps him intact for tomorrow.

A man must be careful not to despise the doors God closes. What feels like rejection in the moment may actually be divine redirection. There are paths that look promising but carry hidden destruction, relationships that seem right but would erode purpose, and opportunities that appear fruitful but would pull a man out of alignment with God's will. When the Lord closes a door, it is mercy stepping in before damage can take root. A mature man learns to trust that God sees what he cannot. The same hand that closed the door of the ark secured Noah's future on the other side of the storm. What looked like confinement was actually preservation. In the same way, when God closes something in a man's life, it is not always loss - it is often protection from what could not sustain him. A wise man learns to thank God not only for open doors, but for the ones that shut, because some closures are the very thing that keep him alive, aligned, and walking in the promise God prepared.

Protection is not something a man manufactures; it is something he steps into when he aligns himself with God's instruction. Noah was not preserved because he was the strongest, the smartest, or the most admired - he was preserved because he was obedient. True protection is established from the inside out, through a life that listens to God and moves when He speaks. There is a covering that rests on a man who chooses to stand exactly where God told him to stand. It may not always look impressive to others, and it may not always make sense in the moment, but it carries a divine security that cannot be shaken. When a man steps outside of that place, he exposes himself to battles he was never meant to fight. But when he remains in alignment, even the fiercest storms lose their power over him. Safety is not found in being ahead of God or behind Him, but in walking with Him. The place of obedience may seem ordinary, but it is the only place where heaven's protection fully rests.

A man cannot expect divine protection while choosing a place God never told him to stand. The covering of God is not designed to shield rebellion, but to preserve obedience. Noah did not experience the safety of the ark while building it from a distance - he had to enter it. There was a moment when preparation had to become participation, when hearing God had to turn into moving with God. The same God who gave the instruction was the One who shut the door, but Noah had to be on the inside for that door to matter. Obedience positioned him where protection could reach him. There are blessings a man will never touch until he steps into what God has already spoken. God's protection is not found in partial obedience or delayed surrender - it is found in alignment. When a man moves where God told him to move, he steps into a place no storm can penetrate and no enemy can override. The difference is not in God's willingness to protect, but in a man's willingness to obey.

The Lord shut Noah in but only after Noah entered. That order reveals a powerful truth about how God works in a man's life. Noah had to move when God said move, step inside when it didn't make sense, and commit before there was visible evidence of rain. The security of God came after the surrender of Noah. Many men want God to lock the door while they are still standing outside, weighing options, protecting comfort, or negotiating terms. But God responds to movement, not indecision. When a man steps fully into what God has spoken, heaven responds by securing what obedience has begun. A man must understand that he cannot ask God to protect what he refuses to place in God's hands. There is no divine covering over partial obedience. Faith steps in first, even when it costs, even when it feels final, even when it separates him from what is familiar. Only then does God shut the door. And when God shuts it, no storm can break in, no enemy can pry it open, and no doubt can undo it.

There is a deep, unshakable peace that comes when a man realizes that God can shut what he never could. He may not be able to quiet every voice that rises against him, answer every question that comes his way, or gain the understanding of those who watch from the outside. But when God has spoken, approval becomes unnecessary. A man anchored in obedience does not live by applause or retreat because of criticism - he stands on the word he has received. Noah did not need to win debates or persuade a generation that refused to listen. He built, he obeyed, and he entered when God said enter. That is where true rest comes in: knowing that once a man has done what God required, the outcome belongs to the Lord. When God closes something, no voice can reopen it, no opinion can overturn it, and no opposition can break through it. A man who trusts that kind of sovereignty can walk forward without fear, because what God seals is secure.

When the Lord shut Noah in, He was drawing a line between preservation and destruction. What was inside the ark was covered, protected, and sustained by God, while everything outside was left to the judgment of the flood. In the same way, there are seasons when God deliberately removes a man from certain voices, relationships, and environments. It may feel isolating, even painful, but it is actually an act of divine protection. God knows what influences can weaken faith, distort vision, and pull a man away from his calling. So He shuts the door - not to harm him, but to preserve him. A man who walks with God must come to terms with the truth that obedience will often require separation. Not everyone will understand the boundaries God places on his life, and not everyone is meant to walk into the next season with him. Some voices must be silenced so that God's voice can be heard clearly. Some environments must be left behind so that a man can grow into who God is calling him to be.

This kind of surrender is forged in humility, not convenience. A proud man feels the need to control outcomes, to manage every door, every opportunity, every closure. He believes strength is found in holding the keys, in forcing results, in making things happen on his timeline. But humility shifts a man's posture. It teaches him that obedience is his responsibility, not the outcome. When a man truly bows his heart before God, he releases the pressure to control what only God can govern. He stops striving to open doors that heaven has not touched and stops resisting doors that God is closing for his protection. A surrendered man finds peace in this: "Lord, I have done what You asked. Now I trust what You will do." That is not passivity - it is confidence in God's sovereignty. It takes strength to step back and let God be God. It takes maturity to accept that divine timing is wiser than human urgency. In that place, a man is no longer driven by fear, pride, or the need to prove himself. He is anchored in trust.

Noah's safety was not built on his own strength, but on God's faithfulness. He did not stand at the door of the ark, straining to keep the flood out; the Lord Himself secured it. That truth speaks deeply to every man who feels the constant pressure to hold everything together. There are storms in life that no amount of effort, discipline, or determination can withstand on their own. God never intended for a man to carry that kind of weight. Instead, He calls a man to obedience, to trust, and to a place of surrender where divine strength takes over where human strength ends. When a man places his life in God's hands, he is not left to defend himself against every storm or solve every battle by his own wisdom. The same God who shut Noah in is the God who stands guard over every life surrendered to Him. His power preserves, His hand protects, and His faithfulness does not fail. A man who trusts God does not have to live in fear of what is too big for him, because he knows it is never too big for God.

A man who trusts God to shut the door does not panic when the rain begins. He remembers that it was God who warned him, God who instructed him, and God who called him into position. That kind of man is not moved by the sound of thunder or the rising of floods. The storm may shake everything around him, but it cannot shake what God has established within him. When a man is anchored in obedience, he is also anchored in peace. He understands that what God has secured cannot be undone by external forces. The flood may come with force, but it has no authority over what God has sealed. Fear loses its grip when a man fully believes that God finishes what He starts. He rests in the assurance that divine protection is not fragile - it is absolute. What God has shut, no storm can open; what God has preserved, no destruction can reach. That is the quiet strength of a surrendered man - he stands firm, not because the storm is weak, but because his God is faithful.

There are seasons when God's protection does not feel peaceful. Like Noah inside the ark, a man may hear the storm raging, feel the shifting beneath him, and sense the intensity of what surrounds him. Yet what matters most is not what he feels, but what God has secured. The door was shut by God's hand, not Noah's strength. And when God seals a man in a place, no external force can break what He has established. The noise of the storm is not evidence of danger - it is often confirmation that judgment is outside while safety is within. A mature man of faith learns not to interpret pressure as abandonment. The ark did not remove the storm; it preserved Noah through it. In the same way, God's covering does not always silence the wind or calm the waves immediately - it holds you steady in the middle of them. When a man trusts that God's promise still stands, even when his emotions are unsettled, he walks in a deeper level of faith. Protection is not always quiet, but it is always sure.

Faith is proven in the moments when feelings speak louder than truth. A man may feel confined, overlooked, or even rejected when doors close around him, but faith calls him to a higher perspective. It reminds him that not every limitation is loss, and not every closed door is defeat. What feels like restriction may actually be divine covering, shielding him from dangers he cannot see and paths he was never meant to walk. The enemy will always try to convince a man that a closed door is evidence of failure or abandonment. But a man of faith learns to ask a different question: "Is this the hand of God guarding my future?" Sometimes the greatest safety is found in divine boundaries. The door God shuts cannot be forced open by man, fear, or opposition. And behind that door, there is peace, preservation, and purpose. A wise man does not fight to escape what God has sealed - he rests in it, trusting that the same God who closed the door will open the right one at the appointed time.

The moment the Lord shut Noah in, it revealed a powerful truth about the nature of God. He does not issue commands without also securing the outcome of obedience. When God speaks, His word carries both direction and provision. Noah built the ark by faith, step by step, not fully experiencing the storm yet trusting the voice that warned him. And when the time came, it was not Noah who sealed his own safety; it was God Himself. The same God who instructs a man to move forward is the One who ensures that his obedience is not in vain. A man walking with God must understand that he is never left exposed when he follows divine instruction. The storms may come, the waters may rise, and the pressure may intensify, but God assumes responsibility for the man who trusts Him. There is a covering that comes with obedience, a preservation that cannot be manufactured by human effort. When God shuts a door, He is not limiting a man - He is securing him.

A righteous man must learn the discipline of rest after obedience. There is a holy moment when his responsibility ends and God's sovereignty takes over. He has prayed when it was hard, prepared when it was inconvenient, built when no one understood, and obeyed when it cost him something. Now comes the test that is often harder than action - the test of trust. True rest is not inactivity; it is settled confidence that God is working even when the man is still. Many men struggle here because they feel responsible for outcomes that were never theirs to carry. They try to reopen doors God has shut or force closure on things God is still working through. But a surrendered man knows that once he has obeyed, he must release the results into God's hands. Rest becomes an act of faith, not passivity. It is the quiet assurance that what God has sealed cannot be broken, and what God is shaping cannot be rushed. In that place of rest, a man is not doing nothing - he is trusting everything.

A man who trusts God to shut the door understands that safety is found in alignment with the voice of God. Noah was surrounded by silence from the sky and skepticism from men, yet he moved at the command of the Lord. When the Lord shut him in, it was a declaration that God Himself had taken responsibility for his protection. Every man must come to the place where he stops trying to control every outcome and instead chooses to stand where God has spoken. There is a sacred space where obedience meets surrender, and in that place, God becomes the doorkeeper. No force on earth can open what God has shut, and no storm can penetrate what He has sealed. A surrendered man does not panic when the winds rise or when others question his path - he rests in the confidence that he is exactly where God placed him. That is divine protection: not the absence of storms, but the presence of God securing the door.

| **18** |

"A MAN WHO SURVIVES THE STORM"

The flood came exactly as God said it would, not a moment early and not a moment late. It was not a random event or a natural accident - it was the fulfillment of a divine word. While others dismissed the warning and continued in their own ways, Noah stood on what he had heard from God. He built when it didn't make sense, moved when others mocked, and entered the ark when the skies were still clear. That is the difference between a man led by the voice of God and a man led by the opinions of the world. One prepares in obedience; the other delays in disbelief. Noah's safety was not found in avoiding the storm, but in trusting the instruction that came before it. And because he obeyed, what destroyed the world could not destroy him. This is the power of divine alignment: when a man listens, obeys, and moves at God's command, he finds himself preserved in the very place others overlooked. The storm proved that God was right, but the ark proved that God was faithful.

Genesis 7:17–18 reveals a profound truth about how God works in the life of a faithful man. The waters that covered the earth were not gentle or harmless but were instruments of judgment. Yet for Noah, those same waters became the very force that lifted him above destruction. This shows us that God has the power to take what is devastating to the world and make it developmental for His people. The storm does not have the same outcome for the obedient man as it does for the disobedient. What drowns one man can elevate another when he is positioned in God's will. This is the mystery of divine preservation. When a man walks in obedience, even adversity begins to serve a different purpose. The very thing sent as judgment becomes a vehicle of elevation. It lifts him, strengthens him, and separates him from what is being destroyed. That means you do not have to fear the rising waters if you are where God told you to be.

This is one of the great mysteries of walking with God: the same storm that buries one man can become the very thing that lifts another. It is not the storm itself that determines the outcome, but the condition of the man before the storm ever began. A man who walks in disobedience stands exposed when pressure comes, but a man who has been quietly building his life on God's word finds that what looked like destruction becomes divine elevation. The waters that covered the earth lifted the ark. In the same way, the trials that overwhelm the unprepared can become the testimony of the faithful. Pressure has a way of revealing what has been hidden in a man's life. It exposes cracks, but it also proves strength. When a man has been walking with God, trusting His voice, and obeying His instruction, pressure does not destroy him - it unveils the depth of his faith. What others call breaking is, for him, becoming. What others experience as loss, he experiences as lifting.

Obedience does not exempt a man from storms; it positions him to survive them. Noah walked with God, followed every instruction, and still found himself surrounded by rising waters and relentless rain. This is where many men misunderstand the nature of obedience. They expect that doing right will remove all hardship, but God never promised a storm-free life - He promised preservation in the midst of it. The same waters that judged the world became the very force that lifted Noah above destruction. A man of obedience must be prepared to hear the thunder, feel the shaking, and watch the waters rise without losing his trust in God. The storm is not a sign that God has failed him; it is often the evidence that God is fulfilling His word in a deeper way. God knows how to keep His man afloat even when everything around him looks like it is falling apart. The storm may surround him, but it cannot consume him, because the hand of God is beneath him, holding him up.

Obedience does not remove a man from the reality of storms - it positions him correctly within them. Noah still heard the rain, still felt the shaking of the waters, and still witnessed the judgment unfolding around him. But because he obeyed, he was not exposed to what destroyed others. A man who walks in obedience may face the same storms as everyone else, but he does not face them from the same position. There is a covering, a protection, a divine boundary that the storm cannot cross. God has never guaranteed a storm-free life, but He has promised sustaining grace in the middle of it. The waters may rise, the winds may rage, and circumstances may feel overwhelming, but obedience anchors a man in God's preservation. What destroys others refines him. What overwhelms others passes beneath him. When a man chooses to obey God, he steps into a place where the storm loses its power to consume him. The flood may come, but it cannot claim what God has already secured.

A man must come to terms with this truth: walking with God does not remove pressure - it redefines his position in the middle of it. The storms of life still form, the winds still blow, and the waters still rise, but the man who walks with God is not standing exposed. He is covered. He is anchored. He is sustained by something greater than his circumstances. What destroys others will not destroy him, not because he is stronger, but because he is held. Faith is not the absence of storms; it is the presence of God within them. It is the quiet confidence that even when everything around him feels unstable, there is a divine covering that will not break. A faithful man learns that survival is not about escaping hardship, but about enduring it with God's strength. The storm may test him, but it will also reveal what is holding him together. And when the winds finally settle, it will be evident that it was not luck, talent, or human effort that preserved him - it was the hand of God honoring the man who chose to walk with Him.

The same waters that brought destruction to the wicked became the very force that lifted Noah higher. Outside the ark, the flood was judgment, chaos, and loss. But inside the ark, that same flood became divine elevation. What crushed one group carried another. It wasn't the difference in the storm; it was the difference in alignment. When a man is rightly positioned in obedience to God, even what was sent to destroy can be used to sustain and lift him. This is the mystery of divine covering. God does not always remove the waters, but He provides a place where those waters lose their power to consume. In Christ, what should have overwhelmed you becomes the very thing that matures you, strengthens you, and moves you into your next season. The pressure becomes preparation. The storm becomes movement. The flood becomes transportation. So the question is not whether the waters will rise - they will - but whether a man has positioned himself in the place God has provided.

A man's safety is not determined by the absence of storms, but by his position in the will of God before they arrive. The waters did not create Noah's security; his obedience did. Long before the rain fell, he had already chosen where he would stand. That is the difference between preservation and destruction. When a man delays obedience, he is gambling with timing, assuming he will have another chance when pressure comes. But storms do not wait for indecision to settle - they expose it. What covers a man in crisis is not last-minute effort, but prior alignment with God. It is dangerous to treat obedience as something that can be postponed until trouble begins. By the time the winds are blowing and the waters are rising, the opportunity to prepare has often already passed. Because when the storm comes it is too late to start building what should have already been finished. The man who stands secure in the flood is the one who chose his position before the first drop ever fell.

Noah's survival was not a last-minute miracle - it was the result of early obedience. While others lived casually, anchored in what they could see, Noah lived by what he had heard from God. That is the difference between a man who is preserved and a man who is overtaken. Faith does not wait for the storm to validate the instruction; it moves at the sound of God's voice. What looks unnecessary in a season of calm often becomes essential in a season of crisis. When the flood came, Noah entered what he had already prepared. His obedience became his refuge. The ark was not built in panic; it was built in partnership with God. And that is the lesson: the time to prepare is before the pressure, the time to obey is before the evidence, and the time to build is before the need. A wise man does not wait until the rain starts falling to take God seriously. He responds when the sky is still clear, knowing that what he builds in obedience today will be the very thing that carries him through tomorrow.

Many men desire the protection of God yet resist the process that leads to it. The life of Noah shows us that divine covering is built long before the rain ever falls. While others lived casually and ignored the warnings, Noah moved with reverence and obedience. He followed instructions that didn't make sense to the natural eye but made perfect sense in the spirit. Because of that, when the storm came, he wasn't scrambling for safety - he was already secured in it. The truth is, the storm does not determine who is protected - obedience does. Many wait until trouble appears to seek God, but by then, the preparation window has often passed. Noah didn't build in the rain; he built in obedience before a single drop fell. That is the difference. If you want God's covering, you must first submit to His command. The man who survives the storm is not the strongest man, the smartest man, or the most resourced man—it is the man who listened, obeyed, and trusted God before the storm ever began.

The ark did not rise in spite of the waters - it rose because of them. What looked like overwhelming pressure was actually the very force God used to elevate Noah above destruction. While others saw judgment and chaos, Noah experienced lifting and preservation. The same waters that covered the earth carried him higher. In the kingdom of God, what surrounds you does not have to defeat you; when you are positioned in obedience, it can become the very thing that advances you. Many men are waiting for the pressure to pass before they expect elevation, but God's pattern is different. He does not always calm the storm before He moves you - He causes you to rise in the middle of it. The difficulty you feel may not be a sign that you are being buried, but that you are being lifted. If you remain where God has placed you, anchored in faith and obedience, the very weight of the situation will begin to work in your favor. What was meant to overwhelm you will instead carry you into a higher place.

A storm has a way of stripping away illusion and exposing reality. When the winds rise and the waters increase, a man no longer has the luxury of pretending. What he has built his life upon becomes unmistakably clear. If his foundation is pride, it will crack under pressure because pride cannot sustain weight. If it is pleasure, it will fade when comfort disappears. If it is rebellion, it will collapse because it was never anchored in truth. And if it is convenience, it will fail the moment obedience requires sacrifice. The storm does not create weakness - it reveals it. It uncovers what was already there, hidden beneath calm conditions. But when a man builds his life on the Word of God, the storm tells a different story. The same pressure that destroys others begins to lift him. Obedience becomes his ark, and what should have overwhelmed him instead carries him. He may feel the wind, he may see the waves, but he is not consumed by them. Why? Because his life is anchored in something eternal.

A righteous man can stand in the middle of what others cannot survive, not because he has superior strength, but because he is positioned under divine covering. When destruction comes, it exposes what a man trusted. The disobedient man leans on his own understanding, his own instincts, and his own timing, and when the waters rise, those things fail him. But the righteous man has already moved at the voice of God. He is not scrambling when the storm begins because he obeyed before it arrived. His safety was never in his strength; it was in his submission. This is the difference between striving and surrender. A man outside of God's will must fight to stay afloat, but a man inside of God's instruction is carried by what he entered through obedience. The storm may be the same, the pressure may be equal, but the outcome is completely different. One is exposed, the other is preserved. Not because one is more capable, but because one trusted God enough to step into what He provided.

Noah did not survive the flood by resisting the waters with his own hands; he survived because he remained inside what God told him to build. The ark was not just wood and pitch - it was the evidence of obedience, the covering of divine instruction, and the boundary where preservation lived. A man who steps outside of what God has built for him may feel strong for a moment, but he has stepped outside of protection. There is a deep wisdom in staying where obedience has placed you. When the pressure rises and the waters begin to surround you, your instinct may be to fight your way out, but God often calls you to remain. The safety was never in Noah's ability; it was in his position. As long as he stayed inside the ark, the storm could not consume him. In the same way, a man must learn that his security is not in his effort, but in his alignment. What God has instructed you to build - your disciplines, your convictions, your obedience - is the very thing designed to carry you through what you cannot control.

This is a word for every man under pressure: stay in the ark. Stay where God told you to be, even when the winds are howling and the waves are rising. Pressure has a voice - it tells you to panic, to abandon your post, to escape what feels uncomfortable. But faith has a stronger voice, and it says remain. Stay in prayer when your mind is restless. Stay in obedience when your flesh resists. Stay in God's Word when your emotions try to rewrite truth. The ark may not silence the storm, but it will secure your life in the middle of it. Do not jump out just because the storm is loud. Noise is not authority, and intensity is not instruction. Many men lose their covering not because God failed them, but because they stepped out of what God established for them. There is protection in staying, strength in remaining, and preservation in trusting God through what you cannot control. The storm will pass, but only what stayed anchored in God will still be standing when it does.

A man who walks uprightly before the Lord is never left to navigate the flood alone. The same God who calls a man into purpose also sustains him in pressure. When everything around him feels unstable, there is a divine stability underneath him - an unseen hand holding him steady. The storms may intensify, the winds may push, and the waves may climb higher, but none of it catches God off guard. He knows how to preserve a father carrying responsibility, a husband covering his home, a leader bearing weight, a servant walking humbly, and a son who has chosen obedience over comfort. The waters may rise, but they cannot sink what God has sealed. What God has shut in, no storm can break open. What God has established, no flood can overturn. The enemy may watch the waters increase but God is using the very same waters to lift His man higher. This is the confidence of a surrendered life: not that storms won't come, but that they cannot destroy what God Himself is keeping.

The storm may shake the ark, but it cannot cancel the promise. What God has spoken over a man's life is not at the mercy of the winds, the waves, or the chaos around him. The rain may fall relentlessly, the deep may break open with force, and everything familiar may seem to shift, but the word of God stands unmoved. The ark did not stop the storm from raging - it carried Noah through it. In the same way, a man anchored in God's promise may feel the shaking, but he will not be destroyed by it. The pressure around him does not have the authority to override the faithfulness of God within him. God remains faithful to the one who trusts Him. When circumstances become uncertain, His character remains certain. When the world changes, His word does not. Trust is not proven when the skies are clear; it is revealed when everything around a man is unstable, yet he refuses to let go of what God said. The storm may test his footing, but it cannot take his future.

A man who survives the storm is not defined by a life free of trouble, but by a life anchored in obedience. Before the flood ever came, he had already settled his heart to follow God's voice, even when it did not make sense to others. That obedience becomes the foundation that holds him when the waters rise. And in the middle of the flood, when fear tries to speak louder than faith, he chooses to trust what God promised over what he feels. Trust is not proven in calm weather; it is revealed when everything around him is shaking. A faithful man does not survive because he is stronger than the flood, but because he remains where God told him to be. He does not step outside of divine covering trying to prove his strength; he stays positioned in obedience until the storm runs its course. The waters may rise high enough to threaten everything visible, but they cannot drown a man who is hidden in God's will. When the flood passes, it will be clear that the storm does not get the final word; God does.

| 19 |

"A MAN WHO WAITS IN THE ARK"

Noah's obedience did not end when the door of the ark was shut; it continued in the silence of waiting. The same vessel that carried him above judgment also confined him to a season where nothing seemed to be happening. The rain had stopped, the violence of the storm had passed, yet Noah could not move. This is where many men struggle - not in the crisis, but in the quiet afterward. A godly man must learn that just because the pressure has lifted does not mean the assignment has changed. Waiting is not inactivity; it is disciplined trust in God's timing. Inside the ark, Noah learned that deliverance is not only about survival, but about submission to God's process. He sent out the birds, he watched for signs, but he did not force the door open. He understood that stepping out too soon could be just as dangerous as never entering at all. In the same way, a man of God must resist the urge to move ahead of divine release. Patience keeps a man aligned with heaven, not just relieved from trouble.

There are moments in a man's journey when the winds have settled, the waters are receding, and everything within him urges movement but spiritual maturity resists the impulse to act prematurely. A godly man has learned that God's timing is just as important as God's protection. Moving too soon can place him outside of the covering that preserved him. So he waits knowing that the same God who carried him through the storm will also lead him safely into what comes next. Transition is a sacred space, and it must be handled with reverence. It is in this in-between place that character is revealed and refined. A careless man rushes to open doors that appear available, but a wise man waits for God to make the way unmistakably clear. When a man honors God in the waiting, he avoids unnecessary battles and missteps. And when he finally moves, he moves with confidence, peace, and divine alignment, knowing he did not step out early but stepped out because God has spoken.

Noah understood something many men struggle to learn - timing matters just as much as obedience. The waters had receded enough for the ground to become visible, but Noah did not move at the sight of possibility; he waited for the sound of permission. Visibility can stir excitement, but it does not guarantee readiness. A man who moves simply because he sees an opening may step into something God has not prepared to sustain him. Noah teaches us that restraint is not weakness - it is wisdom. He did not let curiosity or impatience drive him out of the ark; he let God's timing lead him into his next season. In the same way, a godly man must learn to separate opportunity from assignment. Not everything that appears open is meant to be entered, and not every door that looks accessible is authorized by God. Premature movement can turn promise into pressure and opportunity into unnecessary struggle. But when a man waits for God's release, he steps into ground that is not only visible, but stable.

A man who waits in the ark is a man who has learned that timing is just as sacred as obedience. He understands that the ark was not just a place of rescue, but a place of instruction, shaping, and preservation. To leave too soon would not be an act of faith, but an act of impatience. So he waits - not passively, but with a steady trust that the same God who shut him in will also bring him out at the appointed time. This kind of man refuses to let emotion override revelation. He does not abandon what protected him simply because the storm feels like it has passed. He knows that premature movement can expose him to dangers he was never meant to face. Instead, he stays submitted to God's timing, trusting that direction will come with clarity. His patience is not weakness; it is strength under control. It is the discipline to remain where God has placed him until heaven speaks again. And when that moment comes, he will move not because pressure pushed him, but because God released him.

Waiting is a form of spiritual discipline. A man who waits well is not a man who is doing nothing; he is a man who is mastering himself. When everything in you wants to move, react, or force a change, discipline teaches you to be still and remain where God has placed you. It takes strength to resist the urge to act prematurely. It takes maturity to quiet your emotions when they are restless and fatigued. In those moments, discipline becomes the guard over your soul, keeping you aligned with God instead of being driven by impulse. Trusting God's timing is one of the hardest tests of discipline because it confronts your internal clock. Discipline anchors you in that truth. It reminds you that delay is not denial and that God is working in the waiting just as much as in the moving. A disciplined man understands that stepping out too soon can cost more than staying a little longer. So he holds his peace, steadies his spirit, and trusts that when God's time comes, it will be clear, purposeful, and right.

Waiting also requires trust. Noah had already trusted God through the flood, but now he had to trust Him in the silence that followed. It is one thing to believe God when the rain is falling and the ark is lifting; it is another thing to believe Him when nothing seems to be happening. Crisis has a way of forcing a man to depend on God, but delay tests whether that dependence is real. In the waiting, there are no visible signs, no urgent instructions - just the quiet call to remain where God has placed you. Sometimes a man can endure the storm but grow restless in the stillness that follows it. Yet the same God who shut Noah in and carried him through the waters was also carefully preparing the ground beneath him. What looked like delay was actually divine timing. If Noah had rushed out too soon, he would have stepped into something unready. The God who brings a man through the waters is also the God who knows when the ground is firm enough for him to stand.

A godly man understands that timing is as important as obedience. Even when the door appears open, he waits for divine release, because he knows that not every opportunity is permission. There is a covering in the place where God has assigned him, and stepping out too soon can remove him from that protection. What feels like delay is often preparation, and what feels like confinement is often preservation. A wise man knows that premature movement can lead to unnecessary battles. Leaving a season too early may place him in conditions his character has not yet been strengthened to handle. What appears to be freedom can quickly turn into exposure without the shelter of God's timing. So he chooses restraint over impulse, trust over frustration, and patience over pressure. He remains where God has him until the Lord speaks clearly, because he understands that true safety is not found in movement, but in alignment with God's will.

Patience is a shield that guards a man from the dangers of moving too soon. It keeps a man from making decisions rooted in frustration, fear, or weariness. The flesh is always in a hurry - it wants relief now, answers now, movement now. But patience brings restraint. It quiets the impulse to react and replaces it with the strength to stand still. A man who walks in patience understands that not every open door is from God, and not every delay is a denial. Patience also creates space for wisdom to rise above urgency. When a man slows down, he gives God room to speak clearly into his situation. What feels pressing in the moment often loses its power when viewed through the lens of time and prayer. Premature conclusions fade when truth has time to settle in the heart. Patience teaches a man to move with discernment instead of impulse, with clarity instead of confusion. In the end, patience protects his steps, preserves his purpose, and positions him to move only when God says, "Now."

Noah did not step out of the ark just because the rain had stopped or because he was tired of waiting - he sent out the raven and then the dove to discern the true condition of what lay ahead. He was not led by impatience, but by wisdom. He understood that desire is not direction. In the same way, a man who walks with God does not move simply because he feels ready or restless. He looks for evidence - confirmation in his spirit, fruit that aligns with God's word, and a peace that cannot be manufactured by emotion. Discernment guards him from stepping into something that looks open but is not yet blessed. A mature man learns to test the season before he transitions into it. He pays attention to what God is revealing, not just what he is feeling. Like the dove that returned when there was no resting place, he recognizes when it is not yet time to land. But when the dove came back with an olive leaf, it was a sign - life had returned, and the season had shifted.

The dove returned to the ark not because it lacked desire to move forward, but because it lacked a place to land. That is the tension of transition. A man can feel ready in his spirit, stirred in his heart, and eager in his steps, yet still find that the ground before him is not prepared. God, in His wisdom, will not allow a man to build on what is not yet stable. What feels like delay is often protection. What feels like resistance is often mercy. The dove's return was not failure - it was discernment. It recognized that movement without stability would lead to vulnerability. In the same way, there are seasons when God restrains a man, not to deny him progress, but to preserve his purpose. The Lord is not only concerned with where you are going, but what you are stepping onto. A premature move can undo what patience would have secured. So when there is no place for your foot to rest, do not force the next step. Return, wait, and trust the timing of God.

A man must learn to discern the difference between delay and denial, because confusion in this area can weaken his faith and distort his perspective. Delay is not abandonment, and it is not evidence that God has changed His mind. It is often the hidden work of God aligning circumstances, strengthening character, and securing a foundation that will be able to sustain what is coming. What feels like stillness is often sacred movement beneath the surface. Just as the earth must be properly settled before anything can be built upon it, so God takes time to prepare a man before placing weight, responsibility, and promise in his hands. What God is drying, settling, arranging, and establishing may not yet be visible, but it is deeply necessary. If a man moves too soon, he risks stepping onto ground that cannot support him. Delay, then, is not a punishment - it is protection. It is God ensuring that when the door opens, the man is ready and the ground is firm.

Noah waited seven more days before sending the dove again, and in that quiet waiting, he revealed a powerful truth about spiritual maturity. He did not panic when the first sign was incomplete. He did not rush ahead, nor did he abandon the process out of frustration. Instead, he allowed time for God to continue working beneath the surface. A patient man understands that waiting is not weakness; it is wisdom is the strength to trust that what God has started will reach its appointed fulfillment in due time. A patient man also knows how to revisit a matter without forcing it. Noah sent the dove again, not out of anxiety, but out of discernment. He watched, he learned, and he moved in step with timing rather than impulse. When a man walks in patience, he is not passive; he is precise. He knows that timing is just as important as action. And when he moves again, it is not from desperation, but from a place of faith, clarity, and alignment with God's unfolding plan.

When the dove returned to Noah with an olive leaf, it was not a full restoration, but it was a sign. The waters had not completely receded, the earth was not yet ready, and the door of the ark was still closed. Yet in that small, fragile leaf was a powerful message: God was working, even when Noah could not yet step into the promise. A godly man learns to recognize that hope often comes in seed form. It may not look like fulfillment, but it carries the evidence of progress. Sometimes a man struggles because he is waiting for the full picture, while God is giving him just enough light for the next step. Faith is not built on seeing everything - it is built on trusting what God has already revealed. The olive leaf teaches that partial evidence is still divine assurance. It calls a man to keep believing, keep waiting, and keep honoring God in the in-between. The one who learns to value small signs will not lose heart in long seasons. He understands that if God has started to move, He will finish what He began.

Even after the olive leaf appeared, Noah did not rush to exit the ark. That restraint reveals a depth of maturity that many overlook. It is one thing to recognize progress, but it is another to remain submitted to God's timing. The olive leaf was evidence that the waters were receding, but it was not yet the voice of God saying, "Go." A wise man understands that encouragement is not the same as instruction. Progress can lift the heart, but it must never replace the need for divine direction. When a man moves ahead of God, even good signs can lead to premature decisions. Maturity is found in the discipline to wait even when hope has appeared. A lesser man would have taken the olive leaf as permission to move, but Noah understood that obedience is not driven by signs - it is anchored in God's command. There are seasons when God allows a man to see that things are changing yet still calls him to remain where he is. That waiting teaches trust, sharpens discernment, and aligns the heart with God's voice.

Waiting in the ark can feel tight, quiet, and even frustrating. When a man knows he is built for movement, progress, and open ground, confinement can feel like delay or even denial. But what feels restrictive is often deeply intentional. The walls that seem to hold you back are actually holding back what could destroy you. A wise man learns to discern the difference between being stuck and being sheltered. There is maturity in not rushing out just because you feel ready. Readiness is not proven by impatience, but by restraint. The ark is not your destination, but it is a necessary place of preparation and preservation. To despise it is to misunderstand it. Open ground will come, but it must be ground that can sustain what you carry. Until then, the covering of God is safer than the freedom you crave. A wise man honors the season he is in, trusting that when the door opens, it will not just be an exit - it will be a release into something stable, fruitful, and ordained by God.

There is a depth of character that is only forged in the quiet places of waiting. When a man resists the urge to rush ahead of God, he steps into a refining process that shapes his inner life. Waiting strips away pride and teaches humility, because it reminds him that he is not in control of timing - God is. It cultivates patience, not as passive endurance, but as steady trust. In the stillness, a man learns to listen more carefully, to discern the voice of God above his own impulses. Restraint is developed as he chooses obedience over urgency, and dependence grows as he leans fully on God rather than his own understanding. A man who has not learned to wait will often mishandle what he once prayed for, because he lacks the maturity to steward it well. Waiting is God's way of aligning a man's character with his calling, ensuring that when the door opens, he can walk through it with wisdom and stability. The man who waits well arrives grounded and equipped to carry the very thing he asked God to give him.

A godly man must learn to discern the difference between internal pressure and divine permission. Restlessness often rises from discomfort, impatience, or the desire to escape a season that feels confining. It whispers urgency without clarity and pushes a man to act before his foundation is secure. But readiness is different - it is steady, anchored, and confirmed. A man who walks with God understands that not every urge to move is a signal to go. Sometimes, what feels like a door opening is simply a test of whether he will trust God's timing over his own impulses. When a man confuses restlessness for readiness, he risks stepping into battles he was not prepared to fight and burdens he was not assigned to carry. It is better to remain still in a season of preparation than to move prematurely into a season of struggle. The man who masters this distinction positions himself for stability, strength, and lasting impact because he is not just moving forward, he is moving with God.

Noah's waiting reminds us that God is not only the Author of beginnings, but also the Master of endings. The same God who called him into the ark was the One who determined when it was time to come out. There is a holy wisdom in recognizing that every exit must be God-ordained, just as every entrance is. A man who understands this does not force doors open in impatience, nor does he abandon his position out of restlessness. He trusts that when God shuts a door, it is for protection, and when He opens one, it is with purpose. Waiting in the ark was not confinement - it was alignment with divine timing. The man who waits knows that patience in transition is time where God preserves, prepares, and perfects what is to come. In a culture that rushes forward, the wise man understands that stepping out too soon can expose what God is still covering. So he waits in faith knowing that when God finally says "come out," the ground will be ready, the season will be right, and the next step will be secure.

| 20 |

"A MAN WHO LOOKS FOR SIGNS OF NEW GROUND"

Noah teaches us that wisdom is not driven by emotion but by discernment. The rain had stopped, the noise of judgment had quieted, and the chaos of the storm had passed but Noah did not rush out. He understood that just because the pressure had lifted did not mean the promise was ready. A man of wisdom knows that stepping too soon can undo what God preserved in the storm. There is a patience that waits for God to signal that it is safe to move forward. In the same way, many men feel the urge to move the moment hardship eases, but true discernment asks a deeper question, "Is the ground ready to sustain me?" Noah waited for evidence, not just emotion. He waited for the dove to return with a sign of new life. A mature man is one who is not led by urgency, but by clarity. Relief is God giving you a moment to breathe; release is God giving you permission to step. And the man who learns the difference will not just survive storms - he will walk wisely into the new ground God has prepared for him.

The flood had passed, but the process of restoration was still unfolding. The waters had receded, yet the ground beneath was not ready to carry the weight of a new beginning. Though his heart may have longed for movement, for fresh air, for the sound of life beyond the ark, Noah understood that timing is as important as promise. A wise man does not step forward simply because the storm is over; he steps forward when the ground is firm. Noah refused to let eagerness cause him to move ahead of God. There are seasons when everything in you wants to rush ahead, to rebuild quickly, to reclaim what was lost but just because the trial has ended does not mean the foundation has settled. Noah understood that premature movement can undo what patience has preserved. A man of faith is not driven by urgency but guided by sensitivity to God's timing. When you learn to wait, to watch, and to discern, you don't just step into something new - you step into something prepared.

When Noah sent out the dove, he was not acting on impatience - he was pursuing clarity. The waters had receded enough to stir hope, but he needed evidence that something stable had emerged beneath the surface. That is the posture of a wise man: he does not rush into a new season just because he feels ready - he seeks confirmation that God has prepared the ground. A man who moves too soon may step into something that cannot yet sustain him. Timing is where many destinies are either strengthened or strained. Just because the storm is quieting does not mean the ground is ready. The dove eventually returned with an olive leaf - a sign that life had begun again. In the same way, God will give signs when it is truly time to move forward. Until then, the strength of a man is found in his ability to wait, to watch, and to trust that when the moment comes, he will be able to walk into it with confidence, knowing the ground beneath him has been prepared by God.

There are sacred spaces in a man's journey where God has clearly brought him through something yet has not fully revealed what comes next. The storm has passed, the waters have receded, but the landscape ahead is still forming. This is where faith is tested at a deeper level. It is no longer the faith that cries out in crisis, but the faith that waits in silence. A wise man understands that just because he cannot yet see the new ground does not mean God has not already prepared it. Rushing ahead can lead a man to step onto unstable ground, while fear can cause him to retreat into what God has already called him out of. But the man who trusts God learns to stand still when necessary. He learns to listen, to discern, and to move only when God gives direction. The same God who carried him through the storm is the God who will reveal the next step at the right time. Until then, a man must anchor himself in trust, knowing that unseen ground is still secured ground when God is the one who leads.

Discernment is the quiet strength of a man who refuses to move ahead of God. It is the ability to recognize what God is revealing before everything becomes visible and settled. Noah could not step outside and survey the whole earth, yet he did not remain passive -he sent out the dove. In the same way, a discerning man looks for the evidence of movement, the subtle confirmations, the small signs that God is shifting something beneath the surface. Discernment keeps a man from acting on impulse or emotion, anchoring his decisions in what God is unfolding rather than what he immediately sees. A wise man understands that premature movement can be just as dangerous as disobedience. He learns to read the season by the signals God allows, gathering insight before stepping forward. Just as the dove returned with a sign of life, so God gives indicators to those who are attentive - peace in the spirit, alignment in circumstances, and confirmation through His Word.

Hope is a powerful force in a man's life. It lifts his eyes beyond what is and anchors him in what God has promised. But hope, when not governed by wisdom, can easily drift into impatience. A man may sense that God is leading him into something new, something greater, something different, yet sensing is not the same as being sent. There is a timing to God's purposes, and stepping outside of that timing can turn promise into pressure. Wisdom teaches a man to discern not just *what* God is doing, but when He is doing it. Hope says, "It's coming." Wisdom says, "Wait until it's time." Faith is not proven by how fast a man moves, but by how well he follows. Many mistakes are born not from lack of belief, but from moving too quickly on what has only begun to unfold. Faith does not rush ahead of God - it walks with Him, step by step, even when the pace feels slow. A mature man learns to hold hope in one hand and patience in the other, trusting that God's timing is never late and never rushed.

The dove's return was not a setback - it was revelation. When she found no place to rest, it exposed a reality Noah could not yet see from the ark: the waters had not receded enough to sustain life. In the same way, there are moments when we step forward in faith, only to find doors closed and pathways blocked. What feels like rejection may actually be divine protection, keeping us from placing our weight on something that cannot yet support us. A wise man learns to read these moments not with frustration, but with discernment. The closed door is not always a "no" - sometimes it is a "not yet." God, in His wisdom, sees what we cannot: unstable ground, hidden dangers, and unfinished seasons. When the dove returned, Noah did not force the issue - he waited. That waiting preserved life. In your own journey, what returns to you empty-handed may be teaching you when to move and when to remain until the ground is ready beneath your feet.

A righteous man does not ignore the signal of emptiness; he discerns it. When something returns without fruit, without peace, or without stability, he does not rush to force it into becoming something it is not. He understands that God's timing is not revealed through pressure, but through readiness. What comes back empty is often God's wisdom saying, "This ground is not prepared yet." A discerning man has the patience to receive that message without frustration, knowing that premature movement can damage what God intends to establish. He also understands that a promise handled too early can become a burden instead of a blessing. What was meant to bring life can turn into pressure when carried outside of God's timing. So he waits attentively. He watches, he prays, and he trusts that when the season shifts, there will be evidence of readiness. A righteous man would rather walk in delayed obedience than rushed assumption, because he knows that what God prepares, He also sustains.

Noah did not rush the process - he waited seven more days before sending the dove again (Gen. 8:10–11). In a moment where he could have acted on impatience, he chose to move in rhythm with God's timing. Faith is not only seen in stepping out, but also in holding back when necessary. A man of God learns that just because something can be done now does not mean it should be done now. Waiting becomes an act of trust, a declaration that God's timing is wiser than human urgency. Waiting is not wasted when it is guided by faith. While nothing may appear to be changing on the outside, God is aligning things beneath the surface. The dove would return differently because the timing was different. What was not ready before would soon be prepared. In the same way, when a man waits on God instead of forcing outcomes, he positions himself to move with clarity rather than confusion. Faith-filled waiting produces better decisions, stronger footing, and lasting results.

A man who looks for signs of new ground understands that delay is not the same as denial. He does not allow silence to shake his confidence or stillness to weaken his faith. Like Noah waiting patiently as the waters receded, he trusts that God is working even when there is no visible evidence. He refuses to move prematurely, because he knows that stepping out too soon can be just as dangerous as never moving at all. This kind of man lives with spiritual discernment. He recognizes that God often does His deepest work in hidden places, where roots are formed before fruit appears. Though the land is not yet visible, he believes it is coming. His hope is not based on what he sees, but on who God is. So he waits with expectation, watches with wisdom, and moves only when God reveals that the ground is ready. And when that moment comes, he steps forward with confidence, knowing that what once looked like delay was actually divine preparation.

When the dove returned to Noah with an olive leaf in her beak, it was more than a natural detail - it was a divine signal. After the judgment, after the waiting, after the silence, life was quietly pushing its way back into the earth. That leaf was small, fragile, and easy to overlook, yet it carried the weight of hope, restoration, and a new beginning. God did not announce the new season with thunder or spectacle, but with something subtle enough that only a watchful, discerning heart would recognize it. In the same way, a man walking with God must learn to pay attention to the small movements of grace. What looks insignificant to others may be the very evidence that God is turning things around. The olive leaf reminds us that new life does not always begin loudly; it often begins quietly, beneath the surface, before it is fully visible. If you can recognize and honor the small signs, you will not miss the season God is ushering you into.

A man must learn to honor small signs of hope because God rarely begins with spectacle - He begins with whispers. A single olive leaf in the mouth of a dove was enough to tell Noah that the flood was receding and that new ground was forming beneath the surface. That leaf was not the fullness of the promise - it was only a sign - but it carried within it the assurance that God was still working. A wise man does not despise small beginnings; he leans in, discerns, and gives thanks for even the faintest evidence that God is making a way forward. If you are waiting for everything to change at once, you may miss what God is already doing in pieces. Hope often arrives quietly, wrapped in moments that seem insignificant to the untrained eye. The man of faith learns to recognize them and to build on them. What begins as a leaf will one day become solid ground beneath your feet - but only if you have the discernment to see it, the patience to trust it, and the humility to honor it when it first appears.

That olive leaf in Noah's hand was more than a sign - it was a whisper from God that life was pushing its way back through the aftermath of judgment. The leaf spoke of roots still alive, of systems still functioning, of a creation that had not forgotten how to live. In the same way, there are seasons when a man looks at what has been lost - relationships, opportunities, strength, clarity - and assumes it is over. What feels like an ending can actually be a hidden beginning where life is quietly preparing to rise again. The olive leaf reminds us that restoration rarely announces itself loudly at first. It comes as a small sign, a subtle shift, a gentle return of hope. It takes discernment to recognize that what once looked destroyed is now being rebuilt by the hand of God. A righteous man learns to pay attention to these signs, to honor the small evidence of renewal instead of despising it. Because if God can bring an olive leaf out of a flooded world, He can bring purpose out of your pain and stability out of your chaos.

New beginnings are sacred, but they are not meant to be rushed. A door opening does not mean a man should run through it blindly - it means he must approach it prayerfully. Many seasons are damaged not because the opportunity was wrong, but because the timing, posture, or preparation was off. A wise man pauses long enough to seek understanding because the way you enter a season often determines what you will be able to sustain within it. Impulse is driven by emotion, urgency, and the desire for quick movement, but discernment is anchored in patience, clarity, and trust in God's voice. A man who lacks discernment may grab hold of a new beginning and mishandle it, turning what was meant to be a blessing into a burden. But a man who walks with understanding moves with intention. He knows that when the Lord opens something new, the goal is not just to step in, but to step in rightly, with wisdom, humility, and a heart that is fully submitted to His direction.

Discernment is what steadies a man in moments when everything around him is shifting. It teaches him that not every open door is meant to be walked through immediately, and not every closed door is a denial from God. There are times to wait, times to test what is in front of him, and times to move with boldness. With discernment he learns to pause without losing faith, to examine without losing momentum, and to move without losing alignment with God. Discernment also opens a man's eyes to the timing of God. What looks like delay may actually be preparation, and what feels like silence may be divine positioning. A discerning man stops measuring progress only by speed and starts measuring it by obedience. He is not rushed by the moment or shaken by uncertainty, because he trusts that God's hand is guiding every step. And when the time to move finally comes, he does not hesitate because discernment has already prepared his heart to recognize the right moment.

Every man will face seasons where the familiar has been washed away and he must learn to look again with spiritual eyes. A wise man does not rush forward simply because the storm has passed. He pauses and seeks God. He understands that not every open door is a prepared place, and not every ending signals immediate beginning. Discernment is what protects hope from becoming reckless. A man grounded in God learns to read the signs - not just what is visible, but what is stable. He does not build on wet ground, and he does not plant in soil that has not yet settled. Instead, he waits for the olive leaf - the confirmation that life is returning and that God has prepared something sustainable. In that waiting, his strength is refined, his patience is stretched, and his dependence deepens. When the time is right, he moves not with hesitation, but with confidence, because he knows he is stepping onto ground that God Himself has made ready.

A mature man does not despise the waiting place, because he understands what God is doing in it. What looks like confinement is often protection. The ark was not a prison for Noah - it was preservation in the middle of judgment. While the world outside was unstable and collapsing, God had him secured, covered, and sustained. There are seasons where movement slows, doors remain closed, and progress feels delayed, but those are not wasted moments. They are divinely appointed spaces where God shields a man from what he is not yet ready to face and from what is not yet ready for him. What protected him in one season is what prepared him for the next. The same ark that held Noah back also carried him forward. In that waiting place, his faith was strengthened, his obedience was tested, and his perspective was refined. When the door finally opened, he did not step out as the same man who entered - he came out with clarity, endurance, and readiness for new ground.

Noah teaches us that hope is refined through patience, sharpened by watchfulness, and grounded in wisdom. While the waters still covered the earth, he waited on God and watched for evidence that the season had truly changed. The dove's return was confirmation that God was moving beneath the surface before it was fully visible. A mature man does not abandon faith in the waiting, nor does he force doors open prematurely. He learns to discern what God is doing, even when the evidence is small. The man who looks for signs of new ground walks in both trust and awareness. He trusts God enough to stay when others would run, and he believes God enough to look again when others would give up. So he watches for the leaf - the subtle confirmation,the undeniable signal that God is making a way forward. And when that moment comes, he moves not out of impulse, but out of obedience. His hope is steady, his spirit is anchored, and his steps are guided by the God who never forgets His promises.

"A MAN WHO LEAVES WHEN GOD SAYS LEAVE"

There comes a moment in every man's walk with God when obedience must shift with the voice of God. Noah did not step out of the ark based on visible signs or natural reasoning. The rain had ceased but Noah remained until God spoke. That is the discipline of true obedience: not moving because circumstances look favorable but moving because God has given instruction. A faithful man learns that timing is just as sacred as direction, and that premature movement can be just as dangerous as disobedience. Leaving the place of safety requires a different kind of faith than entering it. The ark represented preservation, but it was never meant to be permanent. When God speaks a new word, staying where you were once protected can become a place of limitation. A man must be sensitive enough to discern when a season has ended, even if it once saved his life. There is courage in stepping out into a new beginning when all you have is the voice of God. But that voice is enough.

A man of God must come to terms with a truth that challenges both his patience and his comfort: timing belongs to the Lord. A man who does not discern God's timing will either step out too early in fear or remain too long in comfort. Both are forms of disobedience. There comes a moment when staying becomes more dangerous than leaving. The ark that saved Noah could not become his dwelling place forever. Comfort can quietly become confinement when a man clings to yesterday's instruction instead of seeking today's voice. Growth demands movement, and movement demands trust. When God shifts a season, He does not always remove the fear, but He does require the faith to step forward anyway. A man of God must be willing to release what once sustained him in order to walk into what God is now establishing. Timing is about alignment. And when a man aligns himself with God's timing, he will find that what once felt like risk is actually the doorway to his next level of purpose.

The ark was necessary, but it was never meant to be permanent. It was a divine provision in a season of judgment - a place where God preserved Noah when everything around him was collapsing. Yet the ark was not Noah's destiny; it was only his passage. In the same way, there are seasons in a man's life where God will place him in spaces of protection, isolation, or limitation not to confine him, but to carry him. What once felt like a refuge can become restrictive if we forget that God's purpose was never for us to settle there. The ark kept Noah alive, but it could not fulfill his calling. There comes a time when a man must recognize that what preserved him yesterday is not where he is meant to remain today. It takes discernment to know when a season has ended and courage to step into what God has next. When God calls you out, it is because there is more ahead than what is behind. The place that carried you will never compare to the place God is calling you to build.

There are seasons in a man's life where strength is not proven by movement but by stillness. It is in the ark seasons that a man learns to trust without control, to endure without answers, and to wait without knowing how long the process will last. These are the hidden places where God shapes character, strips away self-reliance, and teaches a man how to hear His voice above the noise. Entering required faith, because it meant surrendering to God's instruction even when it didn't make sense to others. It meant closing the door on what was familiar and trusting that what God was doing inside would prepare him for what lay ahead. But just as God speaks to bring a man in, He also speaks to call him out. And leaving can require just as much faith as entering. It takes courage to step out of what once protected you, to walk into a new season without the safety of what sustained you before. When God says, "Come out," He is calling a man into expansion, into responsibility, and into promise.

Some men learn how to endure a season, but they never learn how to exit it. They obey God when He says "stay," because staying feels safe, familiar, and controlled. But when God speaks again and says "move," something inside resists. The same faith that held them steady now hesitates to step forward. They begin to cling to what once protected them, not realizing that what was once a shelter can become a limitation. Safety is comforting, but it was never meant to replace calling. The wilderness kept Israel alive, but it was never their inheritance. In the same way, the place where you survived is not always the place where you are meant to build. When God calls you forward, it will require releasing what feels secure to embrace what is sacred. True obedience is proven not just in your ability to remain, but in your willingness to rise, trust again, and step into the unknown with confidence that the God who preserved you there will lead you faithfully into what's next.

Leaving the ark required more than obedience - it required faith in the unknown. When Noah stepped out, he wasn't returning to the world he once understood; he was entering something entirely new. The familiar patterns were gone, the landmarks of the past erased, and the safety he had known inside the ark was behind him. Faith is not just trusting God in confinement - it is trusting Him when He calls you into wide, open spaces where nothing feels certain. Noah had to believe that the same God who preserved him in the storm would establish him in the new beginning. The ark was a place of survival, but it was never meant to be a permanent dwelling. In the same way, you cannot build your future on yesterday's provision. Stepping into a new season means embracing change, uncertainty, and responsibility with confidence in God's voice. What lies ahead may feel unfamiliar, but it is still ordered by God. The ground may be new, but the One who leads you is the same and that is where your faith must stand.

New seasons often arrive without familiarity. The landscape changes, the ground feels dry beneath your feet, and what once made sense no longer provides direction. A man who walks with God understands that clarity is not a prerequisite for obedience. He moves not because he sees the whole path, but because he trusts the One who orders his steps. Even in barren places, there is unseen work taking place - roots stretching deeper, strength being formed, dependence on God being refined. Faith-filled obedience is not built on full explanations, but on surrendered trust. When a man chooses to obey God without having every answer, he steps into a higher level of relationship - one where trust outweighs logic and obedience outweighs hesitation. The future may feel uncertain, but God is never uncertain. What feels like a dry season is often the very ground where breakthrough is being prepared. Stay planted. Stay obedient. What you cannot see today, God is already establishing for tomorrow.

God did not bring Noah through the flood just to preserve his life - He brought him through to fulfill a purpose. The ark was not a destination; it was a transition. The same God who shut Noah in the ark also called him out of it. There was an assignment waiting on dry ground. There was a future that required faith, obedience, and vision. When God delivers a man, it is never just about what he escaped - it is about what he is now entrusted to build. You may have come through your own flood but that was not the end of your story. God preserved you for a reason. There are things He still wants to establish through your life. Like Noah, you are called to step into a new season with courage, even when the ground feels unfamiliar. The storm was necessary, but so is the rebuilding. God saved you not just to live, but to move forward, to multiply what He has placed in you, and to walk in the purpose that was waiting on the other side all along.

A man must be careful not to build his identity around what he survived. The storm was real - violent, overwhelming, and beyond his control. The ark was necessary; it was God's provision, God's covering, God's way of preserving life in a season that could have destroyed everything. And the waiting was long, stretching his patience, testing his faith, and forcing him to trust when he could not see. But survival was never meant to be the final definition of his life. What God used to protect him was not meant to permanently confine him. If a man is not careful, he will begin to cling to the very thing God designed as temporary, mistaking preservation for purpose. God's intention is not just to bring a man through the storm, but to bring him into something greater on the other side. The ark was for survival, but the earth was for dominion, fruitfulness, and forward movement. A man who defines himself by what he endured will hesitate when God calls him to step out into a new season.

When God says leave, the grace to remain is lifted. What once looked like wisdom can quietly shift into disobedience when His voice has already made the path clear. A man who lingers too long in a place God has called him out of will begin to feel the weight of that hesitation. What once protected him can begin to confine him. Doors that were once right will no longer fit his assignment. Delay is not always neutral; sometimes it is resistance dressed in caution. Discernment is the dividing line. Waiting on God is rooted in trust, but hiding from the future is rooted in fear. One leans forward in expectation; the other leans backward in hesitation. A man must search his heart honestly - am I waiting because God has not spoken, or am I delaying because I am afraid of what obedience will require? When God has spoken, the only safe place is forward. The future may be unknown, but it is not unguarded. The same God who called you out is already waiting where He told you to go.

Leaving a survival season takes courage because it requires a man to loosen his grip on what once preserved him. The ark represents structure, routine, and the comfort of knowing what to expect each day. Inside, there were boundaries, provision, and a defined space where survival was certain. But there comes a moment when what once sustained you can no longer contain your purpose. To step out is to trust that the same God who closed the door behind you is now opening a new path before you. Outside the ark, there are no walls - only wide, open space filled with responsibility and unknown territory. It is here that faith must mature beyond survival into stewardship. The familiar is replaced with the call to build, to plant, and to walk without the same visible safeguards. This transition can feel unsettling, but it is necessary for growth. A man who refuses to leave the ark will never experience the fullness of what God prepared beyond it.

Many men ask God for a new season but resist the obedience that unlocks it. They desire fresh blessings while holding on to familiar habits, hoping God will pour new wine into an old wineskin. A new season is not just a change in circumstance; it is a call to a higher level of trust, discipline, and alignment with God's voice. The same patterns that sustained you in a previous season may become the very things that hinder you in the next. What worked before will not always carry you forward. Every new season demands a fresh "yes" to God even when it stretches you, even when it costs you, even when it calls you out of comfort and into the unknown. Obedience is the bridge between where you are and where God is taking you. The man who walks into his future is not the one who simply wishes for change, but the one who yields to it. When God speaks, He is not just giving direction - He is inviting partnership. And the blessing is not found in the season itself, but in the man you become as you say yes again.

Noah did not walk out of the ark alone - he stepped into a new world with his family because he chose to obey God's timing. His obedience created a pathway not just for his own preservation, but for the future of everyone connected to him. A man's decisions are never isolated; they ripple outward into the lives of those he leads, loves, and influences. When Noah waited for God's instruction before stepping out, he demonstrated that true leadership is rooted in submission to God, not in personal urgency. His patience became protection, and his obedience became provision. In the same way, when a man aligns himself with God's timing, he becomes a door through which others can walk into promise. His obedience steadies his household, strengthens their faith, and positions them to inherit what God has prepared. There are moments when stepping too soon can bring unnecessary struggle, and moments when waiting feels costly but obedience will always yield the right outcome.

A man's courage becomes a doorway for everyone connected to his life. When he chooses to stand firm in faith, even when fear whispers otherwise, he alters the spiritual environment of his household. Courage in a man creates safety, clarity, and direction. It tells those watching him that God can be trusted beyond what is seen. Where there was hesitation, courage introduces movement. Where there was uncertainty, it establishes conviction. His faith becomes a bridge that carries his family from seasons of mere survival into places of promise and purpose. His obedience is the unseen force that sets the tone for a new beginning. When a man aligns himself with God's voice, he invites heaven's order into his home. What once felt stuck begins to move, not because of circumstance, but because of alignment. A man who obeys God becomes a catalyst for transformation, proving that one surrendered life can open doors that generations will walk through.

God did not speak to Noah merely to bring him out of confinement; He spoke to bring him into calling. When God finally spoke, it wasn't just a release from a closed door, but an invitation into a new responsibility. Noah stepped out into a cleansed world, not as a survivor alone, but as a man entrusted with purpose. In the same way, God doesn't just bring a man out of isolation, struggle, or waiting - He brings him out with intention, with direction, and with something in His hand to accomplish. The world after the flood needed more than people - it needed a faithful man who would walk with God when everything else had been wiped clean. Noah carried that mantle. His obedience in the hidden place qualified him for influence in the open place. And that truth still stands: when God speaks for you to come out, it is because there is something ahead that requires your faithfulness. When God calls you forward, He is not just changing your location - He is revealing your assignment.

There are seasons in a man's life where God allows him to dwell in a place to be shaped, to be taught, to be strengthened. That place may have been necessary, even ordained, but it was never meant to be permanent. When God says, "You have been here long enough," it is a revelation of completion. The assignment has run its course. The lessons have been learned. The grace that once sustained you there begins to lift, not because God has withdrawn His hand, but because He is extending it forward. What once felt like peace can begin to feel like pressure, not because something is wrong, but because something new is calling. A wise man discerns the shift. He does not cling to yesterday's provision when God is inviting him into tomorrow's promise. It takes courage to leave what is familiar, even when it was once fruitful, and step into what is unknown. But the same God who gave grace to remain will give grace to move. When the season changes, obedience must follow.

A man who leaves when God says leave reveals where his trust truly rests. It is easy to cling to the ark - the place of safety, provision, and preservation - because it carried him through the storm. But faith is not proven in staying where God once moved; it is proven in moving when God speaks again. The same God who said "enter" is the One who later said "come out." A faithful man understands that yesterday's provision is not meant to become today's prison. There is a deeper surrender required to step into a new season. A man who walks with God learns that seasons change, assignments shift, and methods evolve but the Lord remains constant. He does not idolize past victories or cling to former structures; instead, he follows the leading of God with open hands. Leaving is not loss when God is leading - it is alignment. And the man who can walk away when God says leave proves that his confidence is not in where he has been, but in Who is guiding him forward.

The man who obeys God in a new season stands as living proof that what tried to destroy him did not define him. The flood may have surrounded him, tested him, and stripped away everything familiar, but it did not finish him. Instead, it formed him. When he steps out of that season, he does not come out the same. He carries wisdom that can only be learned in isolation, reverence that was forged in dependence, and a renewed purpose shaped by the voice of God. What once looked like an ending becomes the very place where God prepared him for a beginning. And when God says, "Come out," the man of faith does not hesitate or cling to what was. He rises with courage, steps forward with trust, and embraces what God is unfolding next. He honors the season that sustained him, but he does not remain in it. He begins again, not as a man who barely survived, but as a man who has been refined, ready to walk forward in the fullness of God's purpose.

| 22 |

"A MAN WHO BUILDS AN ALTAR"

In Gen. 8:20, the first recorded act of Noah after stepping into a cleansed world was not ambition - it was adoration. "And Noah built an altar unto the Lord." That single decision reveals a man whose priorities were rightly ordered. The storm had passed, the ground was fresh, and opportunity lay before him, yet he refused to step into promise without first acknowledging the Lord above. A righteous man understands that survival is not his achievement - it is God's mercy. Before he builds a future, he bows in gratitude. Before he reaches for what is ahead, he remembers who carried him through what was behind. Worship becomes the bridge between deliverance and destiny. Noah teaches us that the first structure in every new beginning should be an altar. Worship keeps success from corrupting the heart and reminds you that every open door was opened by God alone. If you build the altar first, everything else you build will stand on holy ground.

When Noah stepped out of the ark into a world that had been washed, judged, and remade, he stood on ground that testified to both the severity of God's judgment and the mercy of His preservation. Everything familiar had been stripped away, and what remained was a fresh beginning. In that moment, Noah could have rushed into rebuilding his life - securing shelter, gathering resources, and establishing stability. But instead, he chose to pause and turn his attention upward. His first instinct was not to reclaim control, but to acknowledge the One who had carried him through. That decision reveals a righteous man does not let deliverance distract him from devotion. He understands that survival was not his doing, but God's grace. Noah's altar reminds us that worship must come before work, and gratitude must come before growth. Worship anchors the soul. It declares, "God, You brought me through, and everything I build from here belongs to You."

A godly man knows that the greatest foundation he can lay is not made of stone or strategy, but of reverence. Before he builds an empire, he builds an altar because what is established in worship will be sustained by God. A man who builds an altar is a man who remembers the nights when strength failed but grace did not, the moments when confusion surrounded him yet divine wisdom guided his steps. An altar declares, "I did not get here alone." It is the evidence of a heart that refuses to take credit for what only God could have done. Many men forget God once the waters recede. They cry out during the storm but grow silent in the sunshine; they pray in crisis but become casual in comfort. But Noah shows us a better way. After the flood, before building anything else, he built an altar. He understood that deliverance is not the end of dependence - it is the beginning of deeper devotion. A righteous man does not let relief erase reverence; he lets it fuel worship.

Deliverance should not make a man forgetful - it should make him worshipful. Noah did not step off the ark celebrating himself - he stepped off and built an altar. That act of worship revealed something deeper than survival; it revealed surrender. Noah understood that it was not his strength that carried him, but God's mercy. It was not his wisdom that preserved him, but God's grace. Worship anchored his heart in truth: that everything he had just lived through was not a testimony of his greatness, but of God's faithfulness. A man who worships guards his heart against the subtle poison of pride. Without worship, survival can turn into superiority, and blessing can become self-exaltation. But when a man bows before God, he remembers where his help truly came from. He is reminded that grace carried him farther than ability ever could, and that obedience itself was empowered by God's hand. Worship keeps a man low enough to stay usable and grateful enough to stay grounded.

When the storm has passed and the pressure lifts, the heart is revealed in a different way. It is easy to cry out to God in desperation, but it takes maturity to bow before Him in victory. Storms have a way of stripping a man down, reminding him of his dependence, but blessings can subtly build him back up in pride if he is not careful. What a man does after deliverance matters just as much as how he endured the trial. If he forgets the One who brought him through, success becomes more dangerous than the storm he survived. Noah teaches us that the first response to new beginnings should be worship, not self-celebration. Before building a future, he built an altar. He recognized that survival was not his achievement, but God's mercy. A righteous man keeps his heart anchored by giving honor where it belongs, especially when life begins to flourish again. Gratitude protects him from arrogance, and surrender keeps him aligned with God's purpose. When success is laid at the altar, it becomes consecrated.

An altar is a sacred place of surrender, where a man chooses to lay down his will, his plans, and even his victories before the Lord. For Noah, the altar was his first response after stepping into a cleansed world. It was his declaration that everything he had survived was not by his strength, but by God's mercy. In that moment, gratitude flowed, reverence was restored, and dependence was renewed. The altar became his way of saying, "Lord, this new beginning is not mine to control - it is Yours to lead." Every man needs altar moments - intentional pauses where he resists the urge to rush ahead and instead honors the God who brought him through. Before building dreams there must be a moment of surrender. At the altar a man remembers that his life, his family, and his future are not self-made, but God-given. When a man learns to build altars before he builds anything else, he ensures that whatever he builds will stand on a foundation of humility, gratitude, and divine alignment.

A godly man understands that before anything is established in his hands, something must first be established in his heart. The altar represents surrender, gratitude, and reverence. It is where ambition is laid down and priorities are rightly ordered. He refuses to chase opportunity at the expense of obedience, because he knows that success without God is ultimately failure. Like the faithful men of Scripture who paused to worship before they moved forward, he builds a place for God before he builds a platform for himself. In doing so, he acknowledges that every ability, every open door, and every ounce of strength comes from the Lord. Storms may come but what is built on a life of worship has roots that reach deeper than circumstances. He is not shaken by success nor crushed by setbacks, because his identity was never in the empire - it was in the God he honored first. A man who builds altars before empires builds something that can endure, because it is anchored in the One who never fails.

When there is no altar, there is no surrender; when there is no surrender, there is no true covering. It is possible to be constantly advancing yet spiritually empty. Plans may be sharp, opportunities may increase, and doors may open, but without prayer and intimacy with God, those very blessings can begin to compete with the One who gave them. What begins as purpose can quietly drift into pride when God is no longer at the center of what is being built. Before Noah built a future, he built an altar. That is the order of a godly man. Worship anchors success so it does not become an idol. It reminds a man that everything he has came from God and must remain surrendered to Him. When a man keeps the altar alive, his building stays pure, his heart stays humble, and his life stays aligned. But when the altar is neglected, even good things can take the wrong place. A wise man builds, but a righteous man worships first and everything he builds flows from that sacred place.

Worship after deliverance is a declaration of continued dependence. It is a man standing on dry ground yet lifting his hands as if he were still in the storm, saying, "Lord, I still need You." Too many only cry out when the waters rise, but maturity is revealed when a man keeps seeking God after the danger has passed. He understands that deliverance was not the end of God's involvement, but the evidence of it. His worship is not driven by panic, but by an awareness that the same God who brought him through is the God who must sustain him moving forward. A grounded man knows that calm seasons are not seasons of independence, but opportunities for deeper reliance. Without wisdom, he can drift. Without protection and grace, he is still vulnerable. So he builds a lifestyle of worship, not just a reaction to crisis. He remains anchored in God when the skies are clear, because he understands that true strength is not proven in surviving storms alone, but in staying surrendered when there is no storm at all.

Noah set a standard for what comes after deliverance. Before building shelter, before reclaiming land, before establishing a future, he built an altar. And his sons were watching. They saw a man who understood that survival was not his doing, but God's mercy. They saw gratitude take priority over ambition. His altar spoke, "We are here because of Him, and nothing we build will come before Him." A man's worship still carries that same power today. What he honors, his family will notice. What he prioritizes, his household will feel. When a man stops to give God thanks and to build spiritual altars in his life, he is shaping the hearts of those who follow him. His gratitude becomes their understanding. His reverence becomes their reference point. Noah didn't just build an altar - he built a legacy of total dependence on God. And every man who chooses worship over pride, and gratitude over self-sufficiency, is preaching the same message to his family, "We don't move forward without God."

Every man is building something, whether he realizes it or not. With every decision, every habit, every response under pressure, he is laying bricks that shape a name, a legacy, a home, and a future. The real question is not whether a man is building, but who sits at the center of what he is building. A life constructed without God may look impressive on the outside, but it lacks the weight of eternity. When a man builds without worship, success can quietly turn into pride, progress can drift into self-reliance, and achievement can pull him away from the very foundation that sustains him. But when a man builds from the altar, everything changes. Worship becomes the starting point, not the afterthought. It anchors his identity, purifies his motives, and keeps his heart aligned even as his influence grows. The altar reminds him that he is not the source - only a steward. From that place of reverence, his work carries purpose, his leadership carries humility, and his legacy carries the presence of God.

The altar is where a man lays down more than sacrifices - he lays down himself. It is the place where pride is confronted and stripped of its voice, where entitlement is humbled, and where the illusion of self-sufficiency is broken. At the altar, a man stops rehearsing his accomplishments and starts remembering his dependence. What once sounded like, "Look what I have done," is replaced with a deeper revelation, "Look what the Lord has done." Worship realigns the heart, restoring God to His rightful throne and placing man back in his rightful posture - submitted, grateful, and aware of the source of every blessing. A worshiping man is not weak; he is rightly ordered. He understands that strength without submission is not power - it is a danger waiting to unfold. True strength is forged in surrender, where authority is governed by humility and confidence is anchored in God. At the altar, a man learns that his greatest victories are not won by force, but by yielding to the One who fights for him.

Noah did not wait until the earth was fully restored or life made comfortable again before he turned his heart toward God. He stepped into a broken, unfamiliar world and chose worship first. That decision speaks volumes. A godly man understands that worship is not something reserved for when everything is finally in place - it is what invites God into the process of rebuilding. When a new season begins, uncertainty often lingers, but worship anchors the soul before stability ever arrives. It declares, "God, You brought me through, and I trust You to lead me forward." That kind of posture sets the tone for everything that follows. Too many men delay their devotion, convincing themselves they will worship once life feels settled, organized, and secure. But that mindset builds life on fragile ground. Worship is not the reward for having it all together - it is the foundation for starting over. The altar should never be an afterthought tucked behind accomplishments; it must be the first stone laid in any new chapter.

There are seasons when God carries a man through what would have destroyed him if left to his own strength. In those moments, it was not his wisdom that preserved him, nor his power that sustained him, but the unseen hand of God guiding, restraining, and keeping him. When he emerges on the other side, still standing and still believing, he must recognize that he is living proof of divine mercy. Survival was not accidental - it was grace. Preservation was not luck - it was the faithfulness of God. But a wise man does not rush forward as if nothing happened. He pauses. He builds an altar in his heart. He remembers the nights God kept him, the doors God closed, the dangers God turned away, and the strength God supplied when he had none left. He honors the Deliverer, not just with words, but with a life that reflects gratitude and reverence. Because when a man forgets what God brought him through, he risks becoming proud; but when he remembers, he stays humble, anchored, and faithful.

An altar is not confined to stone, wood, or a sacred place - it is formed in the unseen decisions of a man's heart. Every time a man chooses prayer over panic, thanksgiving over complaint, obedience over convenience, and repentance over pride, he is building an altar before God. When he pauses to seek God first, giving Him the first word in every decision, he is declaring that his life is not his own. These daily acts rise like a fragrant offering, establishing a life that is centered not on self, but on surrender. A man builds an altar when he refuses to let success elevate him above humility, remembering that every victory is a gift of grace. He builds it when he serves without applause, gives without recognition, and worships without condition. His altar is revealed in the posture of his heart when he says, "Lord, all that I am and all that I have is Yours." This is the altar God honors - not one made by hands, but one built by a life fully yielded, where devotion is not an event, but a continual offering.

God was never meant to be an afterthought to a man's success; He is meant to be the foundation of it. When a man builds the altar first - when he chooses worship, reverence, and communion with God before he ever lays a brick of his own ambition - he establishes something far greater than an empire. Worship before achievement keeps his heart anchored, gratitude before expansion keeps his spirit humble, and surrender before strategy ensures that his plans are guided by the hand of God. A man who honors God at the beginning carries that awareness into every season that follows. When success comes, he remembers who gave it. When pressure comes, he knows where to turn. And when the journey stretches longer than expected, he is sustained by more than his own strength. Starting with God protects a man from losing himself in the very things he once prayed for. It guards him in the middle, where many forget, and it prepares him for the end, where only what was built with God truly remains.

Noah's altar rose from the ground as a silent but powerful testimony that the flood did not wash away his faith - it revealed it. The waters had receded, the ark had rested, and the storm that once threatened his life had finally passed, yet his first instinct was not to build, plant, or pursue comfort - it was to worship. That is the mark of a godly man. When everything around him had been shaken, his devotion remained unmovable. The storm may have tested him, but it did not define him - his worship did. A godly man does not reserve his praise for moments of desperation; he offers it as a continual sacrifice. His worship is not seasonal, rising and falling with circumstances, nor is his reverence temporary, fading once relief comes. Instead, his life becomes an altar - steady, visible, and surrendered. When a man truly walks with God, every victory and every answered prayer becomes fuel for greater worship. He does not forget who brought him through - he builds an altar to remember.

A godly man remembers the nights when strength failed, the moments when only mercy held him together, and the unseen hand that carried him through. Like Noah stepping onto dry ground, he chooses worship over self-recognition. He builds an altar, not to mark his endurance, but to honor God's faithfulness. His first response is not pride - it is surrender. This kind of man lives with a holy awareness that every victory is a witness. He does not rush to build his own name, platform, or empire, because he knows that what he builds first sets the tone for everything that follows. Worship becomes his foundation. Gratitude becomes his posture. Obedience becomes his path. He understands that altars keep the heart aligned, reminding him that success without God leads to pride, but success rooted in worship produces legacy. May every man who survives the storm carry this wisdom: build an altar before you build anything else and let your life forever testify of the God who brought you through.

| 23 |

"A MAN WHO OFFERS SACRIFICE"

When Noah stepped out of the ark, he stepped into a world that had been washed clean by judgment and mercy, a fresh beginning shaped by the hand of God. The silence of that new earth must have been overwhelming - no crowds, no cities, no familiar life as he once knew it. Yet in that moment, Noah understood something that many miss: before rebuilding his life, he honored the One who preserved it. He did not rush to secure comfort or establish control; he paused to give God what was rightfully His. The altar he built was more than a structure - it was a declaration that God was still first, still worthy, and still the center of his existence even after the storm had passed. In the same way, when God brings you through seasons of trial, transition, or even correction, your first response matters. It is easy to focus on recovery, on what's next, or on restoring what was lost - but a righteous heart turns first to worship. Gratitude becomes the foundation for everything that follows.

That one act reveals the heart of a righteous man. Noah did not step off the ark celebrating his own endurance or wisdom - he stepped off in reverence. In a world that had been judged and wiped clean, Noah recognized that he was standing only because of the mercy of God. His first response was to honor the One who carried him through what no man could survive on his own. That posture reveals that when a man truly knows God has spared him, gratitude becomes his first language. A righteous man does not move on casually from what God has brought him through. He marks the moment. He gives honor. He remembers. Noah's response teaches that true righteousness is not just about obedience in the storm, but worship after it. When a man understands that every rescue, every breakthrough, and every preserved breath is a gift from God, he will not live carelessly - he will live sacrificially. That one act of worship becomes a testimony: this man knows who kept him, and he will never take it lightly.

Gen. 8:20 says that Noah "took of every clean beast, and of every clean fowl, and offered burnt offerings on the altar." Noah did not give God leftovers. He offered what was clean, valuable, and acceptable. This reveals the heart of a righteous man. He took what carried value and offered it to God. This was not convenience; it was costly devotion. True worship is never about giving God what remains after we have satisfied ourselves - it is about bringing Him what is first, what is best, and what is worthy. Noah's sacrifice teaches us that a righteous man recognizes that everything he has comes from God, and the proper response is to return to Him an offering that reflects gratitude, reverence, and honor. God is not honored by what costs us nothing; He is moved by what requires surrender. This kind of sacrifice shifts the atmosphere of a life, a home, and a generation. It declares that God is not secondary, but supreme so we must offer Him what is clean, what is costly, and what truly reflects the weight of His worth.

Worship costs something. Any man can speak praise when the sun is shining and life is smooth, but real worship is revealed when obedience is required, when sacrifice is inconvenient, and when surrender stretches the soul. True worship is giving God your time when you feel busy, your obedience when you feel resistant, your resources when it requires trust, and your heart when it would be easier to hold back. Worship becomes real when it moves beyond words and becomes an offering. A man who truly worships understands that

God is worthy of more than moments - He is worthy of everything. Real worship lays down pride, releases control, and chooses surrender even when it costs reputation, comfort, or control. It is in that place of costly honor that transformation happens. When a man gives God his first and best - not his leftovers - he aligns his life with heaven. That kind of worship rises as a pleasing sacrifice, declaring not just with words, but with action, "God, You are worthy of it all."

Noah had just stepped out of a world that had been washed clean by judgment, yet his first instinct was not to celebrate survival - it was to honor God. He did not allow the relief of dry ground to replace the reverence he carried through the storm. Many men are quick to cry out when the waters rise, when fear grips their soul and control slips from their hands. But when the storm passes and stability returns, their hunger for God fades just as quickly as their desperation once burned. Noah shows us a different spirit. He was a man who understood that God was not just his refuge in trouble, but his Lord in victory. Deliverance did not distract him; it deepened his devotion. This is the mark of a mature man of God: he remembers God not only in crisis, but in calm. If a man only seeks God in the storm, he will drift in the sunshine. But if he anchors his heart in gratitude and worship after deliverance, he will walk in lasting alignment with God. The ground may be dry, but the fire on the altar must still burn.

A righteous man understands that mercy is never something to take lightly. When God extends grace, when He delivers, preserves, and restores, the first response is not self-congratulation but sacred reverence. He does not rush to tell his story before he first honors the Author of it. He recognizes that every breath after the storm, every step after the fall, is a gift that came from the hand of God. So he pauses, lifts his heart, and gives worship. Giving honor to God becomes the natural overflow of a soul that knows it did not save itself. He knows that if God had not intervened, there would be nothing to build upon. So he acknowledges the One who kept him when he should have been lost, who showed mercy when judgment was deserved. This posture keeps his heart aligned and his future blessed, because he never forgets the foundation of his life is not his strength, but God's mercy. And when worship comes first, everything that follows stands on holy ground.

Sacrifice reveals gratitude. It is the quiet but powerful declaration of a heart that understands its own limitations and God's unlimited grace. When a man offers something back to the Lord - his time, his resources, his praise - he is not trying to repay God, for that is impossible. Instead, he is acknowledging that every breath he breathes was given, every door that opened was ordained, every victory was carried on the strength of God's hand. Sacrifice becomes a language of humility, where pride is laid down and thanksgiving rises up. A grateful man does not cling tightly to what he has, because he knows it was never his to begin with. He gives freely because he remembers the pit he was brought out of, the mercy that met him in his weakness, and the grace that covered his failures. Sacrifice is the evidence of a life that sees God in every detail and refuses to take His goodness for granted. When a man lives this way, his offering becomes more than an act; it becomes a testimony to the goodness of God.

Sacrifice reveals reverence because it acknowledges who God truly is. Noah did not step off the ark and move on with life as usual - he paused, he built, and he offered. His actions recognized the holiness, power, and sovereignty of the Lord, and his sacrifice became an expression of deep honor. A man who fears the Lord carries this same posture. He does not treat sacred moments lightly, nor does he reduce worship to convenience. Instead, he approaches God with intentionality, understanding that reverence is not just a feeling - it is demonstrated through what he is willing to give. When a man truly reveres God, it shapes how he lives, speaks, and worships. He guards his heart against casualness in holy things and refuses to let familiarity breed dishonor. Sacrifice becomes more than an act - it becomes a declaration that God is worthy of his best, not his leftovers. This kind of reverence positions a man to walk in alignment with God's presence, because honor always draws him closer.

Sacrifice is never just about what is placed on the altar - it is about what is released from the heart. When Noah lifted those offerings before God, he was not merely presenting animals; he was presenting ownership. In that moment, he surrendered control, laying down every right to claim anything as his own. The ark was behind him, the flood was over, and a new beginning stretched before him. True sacrifice declares, "Lord, it all belongs to You." It is the quiet but powerful acknowledgment that our lives are not self-built or self-sustained but divinely given and divinely governed. Noah's sacrifice rose as a testimony that his family and the entire new world ahead were safely entrusted to God's hands. In the same way, when we offer our lives fully to the Lord, sacrifice becomes more than an act - it becomes a posture. It reveals a heart that no longer clings, but releases; a life that no longer grasps, but yields. And in that surrender, we find not loss, but alignment with the will and favor of God.

Every man needs an altar in his life - not necessarily one built with stone, but one established in the heart. It is the place he returns to daily, where he meets God in prayer, aligns himself through obedience, and humbles himself in repentance. This altar is where he lays down his pride, releases selfish ambition, confronts his fears, and surrenders every hidden bitterness. In that sacred space, he stops striving to be seen by others and begins to be shaped by God. A man without an altar will eventually be ruled by whatever he refuses to surrender. But a man who builds his life around that place of dedication becomes anchored, steady, and transformed. The altar is where strength is forged - not through control, but through surrender. It is where God refines character, restores vision, and renews purpose. When a man consistently returns to that place, he doesn't just encounter God -

he carries His presence into every area of his life. And from that place he lives with a power that cannot be shaken.

When Noah stepped onto unfamiliar ground after the flood, he did not demand a blueprint for the future before building an altar. He understood that worship is not the result of certainty, but the expression of trust. True faith does not say, "I will honor God when I understand everything," but rather, "I will honor God because He is worthy, even when I understand nothing." Sacrifice becomes the language of a heart that believes God is still in control, even when the landscape has completely changed. Faith that honors God kneels before answers arrive. It gives before outcomes are secured. Noah's offering rose to heaven not because he had everything figured out, but because he recognized the hand of God in his deliverance. A righteous man does the same - he responds to God with gratitude, obedience, and surrender before the details unfold. In doing so, he declares that God's character is more trustworthy than his circumstances, and that obedience is greater than explanation.

There is power in giving God the first and the best after deliverance because it realigns a man's heart at the very moment he is most vulnerable to pride. When the storm has passed there is a subtle temptation to quietly take credit, to believe that survival was due to one's own strength, wisdom, or endurance. But the man who pauses in that moment and gives God his first and best offering is making a bold declaration, "I did not bring myself out - God did." In honoring God first, he keeps his heart anchored in truth rather than drifting into self-exaltation. This kind of giving reminds a man that he is not the source of his own preservation, strength, wisdom, or success, but a recipient of divine mercy and grace. Every victory, every escape, every open door traces back to the hand of God. When a man consistently gives God the first and best, he stays humble, grateful, and dependent. He refuses to build altars to himself and instead builds them to the One who carried him through.

Some men want blessing without surrender, favor without obedience, and deliverance without devotion but that is not the pattern of a man who truly walks with God. The life of Noah reminds us that salvation is not the end of the story; it is the beginning of a response. After being preserved through judgment, Noah did not first build a house or plant a vineyard - he built an altar. His first act after deliverance was worship. A man who has been rescued by God should be moved to honor God, not casually, but sacrificially. True worship requires laying something down, giving God the first and the best, and acknowledging that everything we have is because of Him. The modern temptation is to seek His benefits without bowing to His authority. But Noah shows us a better way. His sacrifice rose as a pleasing aroma because it came from a heart of reverence, gratitude, and surrender. A real man of God understands that devotion is not proven in what he receives, but in what he willingly gives back.

The sacrifice pleased the Lord because it came from a heart that remembered, not a life that forgot. Gen. 8:21 tells us that "the Lord smelled a sweet savor," meaning the offering rose before Him as something deeply acceptable. It wasn't the aroma of the sacrifice itself that pleased God - it was the posture behind it. A man who understands grace responds with gratitude, and true gratitude always expresses itself through sacrifice. God is still moved by what rises from a surrendered heart whether it's obedience when it's hard, worship when no one is watching, or giving when it stretches you. The "sweet savor" is not about ritual; it is about relationship. It is the fragrance of a man who says, "Lord, everything I have is because of You, and everything I am belongs to You." When you live that way, your life becomes pleasing to God not because of perfection, but because of devotion. And just as with Noah, when God is pleased, He responds with blessings that extend far beyond the moment of sacrifice.

A man's worship has the power to reach beyond the surface and touch the very heart of God. When it flows from humility, it acknowledges that God alone is worthy; when it rises from gratitude, it remembers His goodness; and when it is anchored in obedience, it proves that love for God is genuine. This kind of worship is not about performance, repetition, or outward display - it is about a surrendered heart. It is the quiet reverence of a man who knows he is nothing without God yet deeply loved by Him. In that posture, worship becomes real, alive, and deeply personal. When a man lives this way, his worship becomes a sweet fragrance before the Lord - pleasing, sincere, and powerful. True worship is carried in how a man walks, speaks, and serves. It is proven in the unseen moments where obedience costs something. And it is there, in that authentic devotion, that God is moved - not by perfection, but by a heart fully given to Him.

Giving God honor is not confined to a moment in a sanctuary - it is revealed in the life a man lives once he walks back into the world God just brought him through. True honor shows up in the decisions he makes when no one is watching, in the restraint of his words when he could speak harshly, and in the integrity of his actions when compromise would be easier. A man who truly honors God does not leave his worship at the altar; he carries it into his home, his work, and every relationship. His life becomes a living testimony that God's hand was not only powerful enough to deliver him, but worthy enough to be obeyed afterward. This kind of honor is revealed in his generosity, giving back to God from a heart of gratitude, not obligation. It is evident in his leadership, guiding others with humility, strength, and reverence for the One who leads him. And perhaps most powerfully, it is proven in his private devotion, where no applause exists and no recognition is given. That is where true honor is forged.

Noah's altar teaches every man that deliverance demands a response. When God brings you through the flood - through the storm, the loss, the uncertainty - you are not meant to simply move on as if nothing happened. Survival is not the finish line; worship is. Noah stepped off the ark into a new beginning, but before he built anything for himself, he built an altar for God. That moment declares that a righteous man does not forget who carried him. He pauses, reflects, and gives honor where it is due. Gratitude becomes his first act, not an afterthought. When God opens a door, heals a situation, or brings you out of what should have taken you under, don't rush into the next chapter without acknowledging Him. Stop, remember, worship, and offer Him something that costs you - your time, your praise, your obedience, your surrender. The altar is where pride dies and reverence is restored. It is where you recognize that you didn't make it by your own strength.

A man who offers sacrifice is a man who understands honor. He recognizes that God is not to be approached casually, but reverently with a heart that is willing to give, not just receive. He does not offer what is leftover, convenient, or costless; he brings his first, his best, and what carries weight in his life. In doing so, he declares that God is worthy above all else. Honor is not just something he speaks; it is something he lives out through intentional sacrifice. His life itself becomes an altar. Every act of obedience, every moment of surrender, and every expression of gratitude rises before God as worship. He understands that true sacrifice goes beyond the physical - it touches the inner man, where pride is laid down, control is released, and self is crucified. Through this, his life tells a powerful story: that God alone holds the highest place in his heart. His sacrifice becomes his testimony, revealing to the world that the Lord is not only good, but worthy of everything.

| 24 |

"A MAN WHO RECEIVES COVENANT"

Noah had walked through devastation that few could comprehend - a world undone, familiar voices silenced, and the weight of starting again resting on his shoulders. Yet Noah remained anchored in obedience when nothing around him made sense. And when the waters finally receded, he did not step into a world of answers, but into a moment of divine encounter. It was there, on the other side of judgment and survival, that God met him - not with more burden, but with covenant. This reveals that God does not abandon a man in the storm, and He does not forget him after it. He waits on the other side with purpose, promise, and presence. Noah's faithfulness positioned him to receive something eternal in the midst of a temporary world. Where there had been chaos, God established order. Where there had been loss, God spoke promise. And where there had been fear, God gave assurance that He would never again destroy the earth in that way and gave a rainbow as a sign of that promise.

A man who receives covenant understands that his life is not held together by chance, luck, or human strength, but by the unshakable faithfulness of God. Because of this, the covenant man walks with a quiet confidence in the One who holds all things together. When storms rise and uncertainty presses in, he does not crumble, because he knows his life is secured by divine promise, not human performance. This understanding reshapes how he lives, leads, and endures. He does not chase validation from the world, because he already stands accepted within God's covenant. He does not panic in adversity, because he knows God's faithfulness is not seasonal - it is constant. A covenant man carries a deep assurance that what God has spoken over his life will come to pass, and that every step he takes is under divine covering. Therefore, he lives with purpose, walks in obedience, and stands firm in trials, knowing that the same God who established the covenant will also sustain him to the very end.

When God spoke to Noah after the flood, He was not simply issuing commands for survival - He was revealing His heart through covenant. In a world that had just witnessed judgment, God responded with mercy and assurance. He anchored Noah not in fear of what had been, but in the promise of what would never be again. This covenant declared that even after devastation, God is still a promise-maker, still a restorer, and still committed to His creation. This covenant extended beyond Noah to his family and every living creature, showing that God's promises are expansive and generational. God was establishing a divine covering, a relationship rooted in commitment rather than condition. For a man of faith, this means his identity is no longer shaped by past storms, but by present promises. This gives him the assurance that God's word will stand long after the waters have receded. When a man receives covenant, he learns to build his life not on what he sees, but on what God has spoken.

This truth reveals the heart of God in its fullness: He is not limited to judgment, though He is perfectly just. His judgments are righteous, but they are never detached from His love. Even when God corrects, He does so with the intention of restoring, not destroying. His mercy steps in where judgment could have consumed, offering grace to the repentant and hope to the broken. His correction is not rejection; it is an invitation to return, to be made whole again, and to walk in right relationship with Him. God always demonstrates an unwavering commitment to His people. He is a covenant-keeping God who does not change His mind or withdraw His promises based on human failure. Where man is inconsistent, God remains faithful. He restores what was lost, rebuilds what was broken, and renews what seemed beyond repair. His mercy rewrites endings, and His commitment secures our future. In Him, we find not only forgiveness for yesterday, but strength and assurance for tomorrow.

A righteous man must come to understand that storms do not cancel what God has spoken - they often confirm it. When the winds rise and the waters deepen, it can feel as though everything God promised is being swept away. Yet, the storm is not sent to erase the word of God, but to test a man's confidence in it. Faith that only stands in calm weather is unproven, but faith that holds on in the storm becomes anchored in something eternal. There are moments when the storm itself becomes the very place where God reveals His covenant more clearly. It is in the chaos that God draws nearer, speaks louder, and makes His faithfulness undeniable. The rain may fall, and the floodwaters may rise, but when they begin to recede, the man of God sees what he could not see before - a clearer sign of God's hand, a deeper assurance of His word, and a stronger understanding of His covenant. What once felt like destruction becomes revelation. The storm did not cancel the promise; it unveiled it.

Covenant means that God binds Himself to His own word. When God makes a promise, He is not hoping it will come to pass; He is declaring what will come to pass. His power ensures He can do it, His character ensures He will not lie, and His authority ensures nothing can stand in His way. What God has spoken over your life is backed by the full weight of who He is. Because of this, covenant calls a man to trust beyond what he can see. There will be moments when circumstances seem to contradict the promise, but covenant truth does not shift with conditions. God does not revise His word to fit the moment; He fulfills it in His time. This means your responsibility is not to force the outcome, but to remain faithful to the promise. When you stand on what God has said, you are standing on something eternal. Covenant gives you confidence to endure, clarity to walk forward, and assurance that what God started, He is fully able and fully committed to complete.

Before Noah ever stepped into a new world, God had already spoken promise over his life. The covenant came not as a reward, but as a declaration. It was God who established, God who initiated, and God who guaranteed. This reminds us that a man's relationship with God is never built on what he can achieve, but on what he is willing to receive. Grace reaches where striving cannot. When a man understands that covenant begins with God, it humbles him and anchors him. Noah walked in righteousness, but even his righteousness did not produce the covenant - God's grace did. That means the promises over a man's life are not sustained by his perfection, but by God's faithfulness. The same God who initiates covenant also sustains it. A man who receives covenant learns to live not in pressure, but in promise; not trying to earn God's hand but trusting it. And from that place, obedience flows not as a way to gain favor, but as a response to the grace that was already given.

A man who receives covenant is no longer an orphan trying to prove his worth, nor a wanderer drifting without direction. The covenant places him within the care, authority, and covering of God Himself. Where others see uncertainty, he sees promise. Where others feel abandoned, he knows he is claimed. His life is not defined by what he lacks, but by Who he belongs to. The covenant gives him a name, a place, and a purpose that cannot be shaken by circumstances. Because he belongs to God, he does not live as a victim of what happens to him, but as a steward of what God has spoken over him. He walks with the assurance that God's hand is upon his life, guiding, correcting, and sustaining him. Even in seasons of silence, he is not forgotten. Even in moments of delay, he is not denied. A man who receives covenant lives with quiet confidence, knowing that his future is not left to chance, but secured by the faithfulness of the God who called him His own.

Covenant gives a man identity because it anchors him in a voice greater than his own. When God speaks over a man, defining his purpose, calling, and future, that man is no longer left to wander in confusion or shape himself by the opinions of others. He knows who he is because he knows who has spoken. The noise of the world grows quieter when the certainty of God's word grows louder. A covenant man stands firm, not because life is easy, but because his foundation is unshakable. He carries within him the assurance that his life has been named, claimed, and ordered by God. When challenges come, he does not question his worth, because his identity was never self-created. When doors close, he does not lose himself, because his purpose was never dependent on circumstances. He lives from a place of being chosen, spoken over, and set apart. In covenant, a man finds rest from the exhausting pursuit of validation, because he is already validated by the One who cannot lie.

When God establishes covenant with a man, He entrusts him with purpose, identity, and divine representation. Noah was not saved from the flood just to survive; he was preserved to stand as a witness of God's righteousness in a world washed clean. The waters did not just carry him away from judgment - they carried him into assignment. Covenant marked Noah as a man who would walk differently, lead intentionally, and live with the awareness that his life now spoke on behalf of God. In the same way, every man who enters covenant with God must understand that preservation comes with expectation. Covenant gives a man responsibility to build what honors God, to lead his household in truth, and to walk in obedience even when the world around him has forgotten its way. Just as Noah stepped into a renewed earth with a divine mandate, a covenant man steps into every season knowing his life carries weight, meaning, and a sacred responsibility to represent God faithfully.

Every promise from God carries divine intention, direction, and purpose. His promises are assignments wrapped in grace, calling a man to rise into who he was created to be. A promise shapes decisions, refines character, and demands growth. The man who understands this does not treat God's word as a passive blessing, but as an active calling that requires his whole heart. A man cannot claim covenant while refusing obedience, because covenant is not built on words alone - it is sustained by surrender. God's promises are sure, but they are partnered with responsibility. To walk in covenant is to walk in agreement with God's ways, even when they challenge comfort or confront personal will. Obedience is the evidence that a man truly believes what God has spoken. Without it, promises remain distant rather than manifested. But when a man aligns his life with God's instruction, he steps into the fullness of where promise and purpose meet, and where covenant becomes a living reality.

To live under covenant is to walk with a deep reverence for the God who has bound Himself to you in promise. It is to recognize that your life is no longer casual or self-directed, but sacred and set apart. A man who lives under covenant does not take God's mercy lightly; he remembers, he honors, and he gives thanks, knowing that every breath and every blessing is tied to a faithful God who never breaks His word. Faithfulness, then, becomes the natural response to covenant. It is the steady decision to align your life with God's truth, even when no one is watching and when the path is difficult. A faithful man does not drift from what God has spoken; he builds his life upon it. In reverence he bows, in gratitude he worships, and in faithfulness he endures. And as he walks this way, his life becomes a testimony that God's covenant is not merely a declaration, but a living reality that is guiding him, preserving him, and anchoring his future in unshakable hope.

When life feels uncertain, covenant becomes the anchor that steadies a man's soul. After the flood, the world Noah stepped into was unfamiliar - stripped, quiet, and forever changed. Yet in the midst of that uncertainty, he did not stand on what he saw; he stood on what God said. The covenant God established was not based on the stability of the earth, but on the unchanging nature of His word. Where everything else had been shaken, God's promise remained firm. A man who understands covenant does not panic when life shifts; he remembers what God has declared. Noah could look at the empty landscape and still walk with confidence, knowing that God's word would outlast every storm. In the same way, when uncertainty surrounds you, covenant calls you back to trust. It reminds you that your future is not held together by what you can control, but by what God has already secured. God has not changed, His promises still stand, and what He has spoken over your life will come to pass.

A man needs that kind of anchor. Without God's promises, he becomes vulnerable to every shifting wind that comes his way. Fear speaks loudly when there is no promise to silence it. Pressure feels overwhelming when there is no word from God to stand on. Disappointment begins to define him, and confusion clouds his direction. A man without an anchor drifts but when a man lays hold of God's promises, something within him becomes steady. Even when storms rise, he is not easily shaken because his confidence is not rooted in circumstances, but in the unchanging Word of God. God's promises remind him that what God has spoken will not fail, even when everything around him feels uncertain. When disappointment whispers that it's over, the promise declares that God is still working. This is the anchor that holds a man steady in every season. A man who lives anchored in that truth becomes unmovable, because he is no longer governed by what he sees, but by what God has said.

When a man stands on covenant, he plants his life on something unshakable. Covenant is not built on how a man feels, but on what God has declared. It anchors him when feelings betray him, steadies him when life becomes uncertain, and gives him direction when voices around him grow loud and conflicting. A man rooted in covenant does not live reactionary; he lives anchored. He does not move because of pressure - he moves because of promise. This kind of man carries a quiet strength. When others are shaken, he stands. When others retreat, he holds his ground. Not because he is untouched by struggle, but because he is secured by something greater than it. Covenant gives him identity when the world tries to redefine him, responsibility when others abandon their post, and assurance that what God has spoken will not fail. A man standing on covenant is not easily moved, because he knows he is standing on the very word and faithfulness of God and that foundation cannot be broken.

God's promises anchor a man when life tries to drift him into fear, doubt, and uncertainty. When storms rise and everything familiar begins to shake, it is not his strength that holds him steady, but the unchanging word of God spoken over his life. A promise from God reaches beyond present circumstances and ties a man's heart to what cannot be moved. In seasons where the winds are loud and the waves are high the promise reminds him that he is not at the mercy of the storm but secured by the voice of God. These promises become the foundation upon which a man builds his future. They remind him that what God has spoken is greater than what life has shaken. Even when delays come, the promise stands as a declaration that God's purpose has not been canceled. A man who holds onto God's promises walks forward with quiet confidence, knowing that his tomorrow is not defined by yesterday's damage but by God's faithful word.

A covenant man understands that his life is not his own, but one entrusted to him by God. Because of this, he refuses to live carelessly with his thoughts, his words, or his actions. There is a sacred awareness within him - a steady conviction that he has been called out of darkness into purpose. He knows he is covered by God's grace, guided by God's hand, and sustained by God's faithfulness. Even in moments of uncertainty, he does not crumble, because his confidence is anchored in covenant, not circumstance. This kind of man walks differently. He carries himself with quiet authority, knowing he has been commissioned for something greater than himself. His decisions are shaped by purpose, and his steps are ordered with intention. His life becomes a testimony that when a man knows he is called, covered, and commissioned, he doesn't live loosely - he lives deliberately, faithfully, and with unwavering confidence in the One who made the covenant with him.

The man who receives covenant does not walk as one guessing his way through life - he walks with assurance anchored in the unchanging nature of God. When storms rise and circumstances shift, he is not moved by what he sees, but by what God has spoken. Covenant reminds him that he is not alone, not forgotten, and not subject to chance; he is held by a faithful God whose word cannot fail. While others are shaken by uncertainty, he stands firm, because his confidence is rooted in divine promise, not human outcome. This assurance gives him a steady forward motion. He does not retreat when tested, nor does he lose heart in delay, because he knows that God's promises are not bound by time or circumstance. The covenant speaks louder than the storm, declaring that what God has established will endure beyond every trial. So he walks on with quiet strength, unwavering faith, and settled peace knowing that the God who made the promise will also bring it to pass.

| 25 |

"A MAN WHO STARTS AGAIN"

Noah stepped out of the ark into a changed earth, carrying the weight of what had been lost and the memory of what had been endured. The ground beneath him was a testimony of judgment and mercy intertwined. When a man finds himself standing in the aftermath of loss, what feels like emptiness is often the soil where God plants the next assignment. A righteous man must learn that God's voice does not fade just because the storm has passed. In the quiet after devastation, direction still comes. God blessed Noah and gave him a command, reminding him that his life still carried purpose beyond the pain. The future is not constructed from what was lost, but from what God has spoken next. If God preserved you, it is because He intends to use you. The same hand that brought you through will guide you forward. Stand firm in that place of new beginning, for it is not the end of your story - it is the proving ground of your faith.

Genesis 9:1 says, "And God blessed Noah and his sons, and said unto them, Be fruitful, and multiply, and replenish the earth." Before God gave Noah another assignment, He gave him a blessing. A man can start again when he knows the hand of God is still upon him. The blessing was evidence that Noah was still chosen, still covered, and still capable. Only after the blessing did God say, "Be fruitful, and multiply, and replenish the earth." The assignment followed the assurance. God was showing Noah and every man after him that your future is not rooted in what you lost, but in what God has spoken over you. Starting again is not a sign of weakness; it is a testimony of divine continuity. The same God who sustained you before the flood is the God who commissions you after it. When a man embraces the blessing of God, he no longer fears beginning again for he understands that every new beginning carries the authority, provision, and purpose of heaven behind it.

Noah had survived the flood, but survival was not the end of his story - it was the beginning of a new assignment. The ark preserved Noah, but it did not define his purpose; it simply carried him to the place where purpose would be revealed. God did not bring him through judgment just to stand still on dry ground. He brought him through so he could step forward into calling, into responsibility, and into a future that still required faith, obedience, and leadership. When God speaks blessing over a man, He is also entrusting him with continuation, with rebuilding, and with influence beyond himself. Noah had to leave what saved him in order to walk into what God had spoken over him. In the same way, a man must understand that surviving the storm is not the goal - moving forward in obedience is. What carried you through yesterday cannot contain your tomorrow. God brings a man through the flood not just to preserve his life, but to position him to build, lead, and multiply according to His purpose.

A righteous man understands that loss is real, and he does not pretend otherwise. He feels the weight of what is gone and the ache of what cannot be restored by his own strength. Yet he refuses to build his life around the ruins. Faith teaches him that grief has a place, but it does not have permission to take the throne. He honors what was, while still lifting his eyes toward what God is calling him to do next. In this, he proves that his strength is not rooted in circumstances, but in obedience. To begin again is the quiet decision to rise when everything in him wants to stay down. It is the willingness to pick up purpose in the middle of pain and walk forward without having all the answers.

A righteous man knows that God does not withdraw assignment because of loss; if anything, He reaffirms it. What was taken may have changed him, but it has not disqualified him. Faith anchors him in this truth: that God can still build, still bless, and still move through a man who chooses to step forward again.

Noah stood in a world that no longer existed yet heaven did not go silent. God spoke again, not about what had been, but about what must still become. The revelation every man must come to grips with is devastation does not cancel divine assignment. When everything around you looks stripped down and emptied out, it is not proof that your purpose has died - it is often the very place where God begins to redefine it. The flood may have erased the past, but it also cleared the ground for a future that only obedience could build. A man of God must learn to hear destiny in the aftermath. Where others see endings, he discerns instruction. Noah teaches us that survival is not the finish line - it's the doorway to renewed responsibility. God will place vision on soil that looks barren and call it fruitful before it ever produces. The true mark of manhood is not just enduring the storm, but rising afterward with ears open, heart aligned, and hands ready to build again.

The flood altered everything Noah could see, but it did not alter what God had spoken. When Noah stepped onto dry ground, he stepped into a world that looked empty but heaven still saw it as full of potential. God's command to be fruitful was not postponed because of devastation; it was reaffirmed in the middle of it. What looks like an ending to man is often just a reset point in the hands of God. A man of faith must learn to hear God's expectation above the noise of what has been lost. Noah could have focused on what was gone, but instead he responded to what was commanded. In the same way, faith refuses to stay buried in the aftermath. It rises to rebuild, to plant again, and to believe again. God can command fruitfulness even after devastation because He is the source of life itself. When a man aligns himself with that truth, he becomes a vessel through which God restores, multiplies, and advances His purpose, no matter what the storm has taken.

Starting again requires courage. It takes courage to build after losing, to plant after weeping, and to believe after everything around you has shifted. This is not the courage of certainty, but the courage of obedience. It is the strength to move forward when your hands still remember what they lost and your heart still feels the weight of what once was. Like Noah stepping out onto a cleansed but unfamiliar earth, courage is choosing to trust God when there is no visible evidence, only His word. It is waking up each day and saying, "I will begin again," not because it is easy, but because God has spoken. Noah did not have a blueprint for the world ahead - only a promise and a command. Yet he moved forward, planting, building, and believing that what God declared would come to pass. Starting again is not about recovering what was lost - it is about stepping into what God is creating next. It is a decision to trust God more than your fears and to walk forward into a future He has already prepared.

Before Noah was ever told to multiply, to rebuild, or to step into the weight of a new beginning, God released favor over his life. Divine assignment is never meant to be carried by human strength alone. What God commands, He first empowers. What He requires, He first supplies. Noah stood in a world washed clean, facing a future that had to be rebuilt from nothing, yet he was not sent forward empty-handed. The blessing of God went before him ensuring that the task ahead would not crush him but be sustained by grace. When a man is called to begin again he must understand that the call itself carries provision. You are not restarting in your own ability; you are stepping forward under divine empowerment. The same God who speaks the assignment also breathes life into it. So when God says "begin again," He is not asking for human effort alone - He is inviting you to walk in a strength that comes from Him, a blessing that makes the impossible not only possible, but fruitful.

A man must not confuse a hard season with a finished life. Storms have a way of making everything feel final but God does not measure your future by your present pain. What feels like an ending is often just a transition under divine direction. Noah stepped off the ark into a world that looked nothing like the one he had known, yet it was not the end of his story - it was the beginning of a new assignment. The rain had stopped, but God's purpose had not. In the same way, the chapters that close in your life clear the ground for what God is about to build next. What ended behind Noah did not cancel what God intended ahead of him. The flood buried the past, but it also made room for what God would do next. The same God who carried you through the storm is the One who will commission you after it. Do not settle in the mindset of "it's over" when heaven is declaring "begin again." The door that closed was not your destiny - it was simply the passage that led you into it.

Though Noah endured the terror of the flood, the loss, and the isolation, God did not call him to relive the storm - He called him to rebuild after it. The danger is not just in the storm itself, but in allowing the memory of it to shape every step forward. When a man clings too tightly to what almost destroyed him, he can unknowingly limit what God is trying to create through him. God's voice always points forward. Noah stepped off the ark into a new assignment, a new blessing, and a new responsibility. In the same way, a man must release the identity of "what I went through" and embrace the calling of "what I am sent to do." Trauma may be part of his story, but it is not the title of his life - commission is. When God speaks, He does not speak to the broken version of a man, but to the builder, the leader, and the carrier of promise within him. A man who answers that call refuses to be shaped by fear or memory alone; he chooses to be shaped by purpose, obedience, and the future God has placed in his hands.

When God told Noah to replenish the earth, it was more than a command to multiply - it was a call to restore what had been broken. The flood had wiped away corruption, but it also left behind emptiness, silence, and the weight of starting again. In that moment, God entrusted Noah with more than survival; He entrusted him with the future. Restoration always begins with a man who is willing to obey God beyond convenience. Noah had already proven his heart when he built the ark under pressure, ridicule, and uncertainty. Now, God places in his hands the sacred responsibility of rebuilding life, order, and purpose. Restoration is never random - it is assigned to those who have walked faithfully through the storm. This word also speaks of responsibility and rebuilding. God did not choose a man at random; He chose a man who had already demonstrated obedience when it was difficult, lonely, and costly. The same obedience that carried Noah through judgment would now carry him into restoration.

When Noah stepped off the ark, he carried more than his own second chance; he carried the future of generations yet unborn. His obedience to God in a season when no one else understood became the foundation upon which his sons would build their lives. What looked like a personal act of faith was actually a generational turning point. A man who walks with God does not walk alone - his decisions echo into the lives of his children, shaping their direction, their understanding of God, and their capacity to trust Him. When a man starts again with God, he must recognize that his renewed obedience becomes a pathway others can follow. His faith becomes a testimony his family can stand on. Just as Noah's righteousness preserved and positioned his household for a future, so every man who returns to God creates a ripple effect beyond himself. The courage to begin again is not just an act of humility; it is an act of leadership, declaring that what God rebuilds in one life can become a blessing for many.

There are moments in life when everything familiar has been stripped away, and the future seems uncertain and unformed. Yet it is often in these very moments that God begins His greatest work of rebuilding. Obedience in uncertainty becomes the seed of restoration, and what feels like an ending is often the foundation of a new beginning shaped by God's hand. A man who walks with God learns that purpose is not sustained by comfort but by trust. When he chooses to move forward in faith, even when he does not fully understand the path, he becomes a vessel through which God can rebuild what was lost and establish what has never existed before. One obedient step can shift generations, because God's power is not multiplied by numbers but released through surrender. When a man yields himself fully, heaven responds, and through his obedience, God begins to write a future that carries His promise, His purpose, and His glory.

When the floodwaters receded, the world Noah stepped into was not the one he once knew. Everything had changed, yet Noah did not withdraw, complain, or cling to what was lost. Instead, he adjusted his steps to God's voice, built again, and walked forward in faith. A righteous man understands that when God allows the landscape to change, it is not an invitation to quit, but a call to trust Him at a deeper level. A new world will always demand renewed faith. Noah could have retired in spirit after surviving the storm, but righteousness does not settle into survival - it presses into purpose. God gave him a fresh commission because heaven never calls a faithful man to stand still when there is still ground to take. In every season of change, the righteous man keeps moving, keeps building, and keeps walking with God. He does not allow unfamiliar territory to weaken his resolve, because he knows that the same God who sustained him in the old world is the One who will establish him in the new.

Every man will face seasons where he must begin again - after failure that humbled him, after loss that emptied him, after disappointment that tested his expectations, or after unexpected change that disrupted everything familiar. These moments are not signs that God has abandoned the man; they are often evidence that God is still working on him. The ground may feel unfamiliar, the path unclear, and the future uncertain, but the call of God does not disappear in transition. A man of faith understands that beginning again is not starting from nothing - it is starting from experience, from lessons learned, and from a deeper awareness of his need for God. The true question in these seasons is not whether circumstances have changed, but whether the man still has an ear to hear. When everything shifts, the voice of God becomes more vital than ever. The man who can still hear God in the middle of change is the man who will not only recover but he will also be repositioned for what God intends next.

A man who starts again must learn the sacred discipline of release. Just as Noah could not live in the ark forever, a man cannot cling to past seasons when God has already opened a new door. The ark was necessary for survival, but it was not designed for fruitfulness. When God calls a man forward, He is not asking him to forget what He has done, but to trust Him enough to step into what He is doing now. Holding onto yesterday too tightly will make a man miss the ground God has prepared for him today. The same God who said "enter" will also say "come out," and both commands require faith. A man who refuses to release the past will struggle to receive the future. The soil of a new season cannot be cultivated while standing inside an old refuge. What once covered him must now be left behind so that something new can grow through him. A man who starts again understands that God's faithfulness is just as present in the new beginning as He was in the place of preservation.

As long as God is still speaking, your story is not finished. The waters may have been deep, the loss may have been real, and the season may have tested everything you thought you knew but God's voice is the evidence of a future still unfolding. The same God who carried Noah through the flood did not leave him drifting in survival mode; He called him forward into purpose. When God speaks after the storm, it is the reminder that new beginnings are not built on what was lost, but on what God is now saying. Noah stepped onto dry ground not as a man who merely survived, but as a man recommissioned. In the same way, God preserves you to rebuild, to lead, and to establish what comes next. The blessing of God is not only seen in deliverance, but in the assignment that follows it. Every man must learn that when God brings you out, He is also calling you up. And if He is still speaking over your life, then new beginnings are not only possible - they are also already in motion.

A man who starts again is not pretending the storm never happened. Instead, he stands in the aftermath with a deeper understanding of God's faithfulness. Where others see ruin, he sees a place where God can speak again. He knows that the storm may have taken much, but it did not take the promise, and it did not silence the voice of God over his life. With God's blessing, a righteous man rises not by his own strength, but by obedience to a renewed call. He receives fresh direction in the very place where everything once fell apart, and he begins again with clarity and conviction. His steps are no longer driven by fear of what was lost, but by faith in what God is rebuilding. Through simple, steady obedience, he becomes a vessel through which restoration flows - not just for himself, but for others. The storm does not have the final word; God does. And when God speaks, a faithful man answers, rebuilds, and walks forward into a future that is being made new.

| **26** |

"A MAN ENTRUSTED WITH THE EARTH"

After the flood, Noah stepped into a world made clean, but not a world made effortless. The waters had receded, yet the weight of responsibility remained. When God blessed Noah and his sons, it was not a passive favor - it was a calling. Blessing in the hands of a righteous man is never without direction; it carries the expectation of stewardship. Noah was entrusted again with life, with family, and with the order of creation. In that moment, he was not just a survivor of judgment - he became a guardian of what God had preserved. The same God who shut the door of the ark now opened the door to responsibility, reminding Noah that grace does not remove duty; it refines it. So it is with every man God blesses. Favor is not freedom from accountability, but an invitation into it. A washed world still requires clean hands. A new beginning still demands obedience. God gives increase, but He also gives instruction so that what is given is not lost again.

Noah had survived judgment, but survival was not the end of his assignment - it was the beginning of it. God did not preserve him simply to exist, but to rebuild, to reestablish, and to carry forward what had been entrusted to him. When the waters receded, responsibility rose. In the same way, a man who has been brought through seasons of testing must understand that deliverance is not the finish line - it

228

is a commissioning. What God brings you out of, He also brings you into. God placed the future back into Noah's hands, and with it came the weight of stewardship. True manhood is revealed not just in enduring storms, but in what a man builds afterward. It is in how he leads, how he plants, how he governs what God has restored. A righteous man understands that preservation is proof of trust. God kept him because God intends to use him. And when a man embraces that truth, he does not waste what was saved; he cultivates it, multiplies it, and honors the God who placed it back into his hands.

A godly man must recognize that deliverance is never an ending - it is a beginning. When God brings a man out of trouble, He is not simply rescuing him for comfort but restoring him for purpose. The floodwaters recede, the prison doors open, the battle ends but then comes the call. Deliverance is God's way of saying, "Now you are ready." The same hand that pulled you out is the hand that now points you forward. A man who understands this does not waste his freedom; he honors it by stepping into the assignment God has prepared for him on the other side of his trial. Too often, men rejoice in being delivered but shrink from the responsibility that follows. Yet true godliness embraces both - the rescue and the requirement. What God has brought you through has shaped you, strengthened you, and proven you trustworthy. Your survival was not accidental; it was intentional. A godly man does not ask, "Why did I go through this?" but rather, "What has this prepared me to do?"

Noah stepped out of the ark not just as a survivor, but as a steward of a renewed world. God was beginning again through him. This reveals something powerful about divine trust: God entrusts new beginnings to men who have proven faithful in hidden seasons. Noah had obeyed when no one understood, built when no one believed, and endured when no one else remained. Now the same obedience that preserved life would be required to guide it. The earth may have been washed, but it still needed leadership shaped by reverence, wisdom rooted in God, and a heart aligned with His voice. This is the essence of godly manhood - understanding that every blessing carries responsibility. Noah's assignment reminds us that after every storm, God is looking for a man who will walk carefully, lead faithfully, and honor Him deeply. Noah was not just called to live in the new world - he was called to lead it rightly.

In Genesis, when God told Noah and his sons to be fruitful and multiply, He was not merely restoring population - He was reestablishing purpose. The earth had just been cleansed by judgment, and now God was entrusting man with a fresh beginning. This command carried the weight of divine intention: to fill the earth not just with people, but with lives that reflected His order, His righteousness, and His design. Fruitfulness was meant to flow from obedience, and multiplication was meant to spread what was aligned with God, not what had previously corrupted the earth. This speaks deeply to manhood today. To be fruitful is not just to produce, but to produce what honors God. To multiply is not just to expand influence, but to expand godly influence within family, within leadership, and within the world. A righteous man understands that he is called to rebuild what has been broken, to restore what has been lost, and to establish God's order wherever he has been given ground.

When God places favor, provision, or opportunity into a man's hands, He is also entrusting him with purpose. A man who understands this does not become passive in his blessing; he becomes intentional. He seeks God for direction, stewarding what he has with wisdom, humility, and reverence. True manhood recognizes that every blessing carries an assignment, and every gift calls for obedience. A man who receives from God must also respond to God with action, alignment, and accountability. It is not enough to be favored - he must be faithful. He must lead his household, guard what has been entrusted to him, and walk in obedience even when it is difficult. Blessing without response leads to complacency, but blessing with response produces legacy. When a man answers God with his life, he transforms what he has been given into something that honors God and impacts others. This is the mark of a mature man - not just that he is blessed, but that he knows how to carry the blessing well.

Godly manhood is revealed in how a man handles life - his own and the lives entrusted to him. When a man understands that life belongs to God, he recognizes that every breath he takes and every relationship he holds carries divine weight. This kind of man does not live recklessly or selfishly, because he knows he is accountable to the One who gave life. He leads his home, treats others, and makes decisions with the awareness that life is holy, and it must be handled with honor. A godly man also values others deeply because he understands that every person bears the image of God. He does not measure people by status, usefulness, or opinion, but by the divine imprint placed upon them. This produces compassion, restraint, and responsibility in his actions. He refuses to harm what God has created and instead becomes a protector, a builder, and a life-giver. His words bring encouragement, his actions preserve dignity, and his leadership reflects the heart of God.

Noah stepped into a new world after the flood with fresh authority, but God immediately reminded him that human life was sacred. In that moment, heaven set a boundary around power: authority does not elevate a man above life - it binds him to honor it. True authority is not proven by control, but by restraint; not by what a man can take, but by what he chooses to protect. Life is not ours to misuse, but to steward with reverence. When a man understands the sacredness of life, he speaks more carefully, acts more justly, and walks more humbly before God. Authority that is not rooted in reverence becomes dangerous, but authority surrendered to God becomes a covering for others. The man who fears God will not treat people as disposable because he sees them through heaven's eyes. In a world that often handles life lightly, the righteous man stands apart, honoring what God has declared sacred, and using every ounce of his authority to protect, preserve, and give life rather than diminish it.

A righteous man understands that strength is not given for dominance, but for stewardship. He does not weaponize his authority to control or crush; instead, he uses it to cover, to defend, and to preserve. Where others may use power to take, a righteous man uses strength to protect what God has declared valuable. He recognizes that true masculinity is not proven by how much he can overpower, but by how faithfully he can guard what heaven has entrusted to him. There is a discipline in restraint that only a godly man carries. He has the ability to tear down but chooses to build up. He could speak harshly but instead speaks life. This is the mark of righteousness - that his strength is governed by reverence for God's heart. He knows that to misuse his strength is to betray his assignment. So he stands as a protector, not a destroyer, understanding that everything God values must be handled with care, defended with courage, and preserved with unwavering faithfulness.

Godly manhood is a calling that reaches beyond the man into everything entrusted to him. When God spoke to Noah after the flood, the command was not given to him alone but included his sons, revealing that true responsibility carries generational weight. A godly man understands that his obedience, faith, and character are not isolated acts; they are seeds sown into the lives of those who come after him. Stewardship of family means more than provision - it means spiritual leadership, setting a standard, and cultivating an environment where faith can grow. What a man builds in his lifetime becomes the foundation his children must stand upon. He does not live casually, because he knows others are following his example. Instead, he embraces responsibility with reverence, guiding his household with wisdom, humility, and faith. His life becomes a living testimony that stewardship is not just about managing what is in his hands but preparing those who will carry it after him.

A man must learn to see beyond the boundaries of his own life. His choices are not isolated moments - they are seeds planted in the soil of generations. What he builds becomes a foundation others will stand upon. What he teaches becomes the voice that echoes in the minds of those who follow. What he protects defines what is preserved, and what he honors reveals what will be valued long after he is gone. A man who lives only for himself builds something that dies with him, but a man who lives with vision builds something that outlives him. True manhood carries the weight of legacy. It understands that every act of integrity strengthens the future, and every compromise weakens it. The way a man leads his family, conducts his life, and walks with God shapes the direction of those who come after him. When a man chooses righteousness, he is establishing a path for tomorrow. A wise man lives with eternity in mind, knowing that his life is not just being lived - it is being followed.

God did not merely preserve Noah; He positioned him. The animals that surrounded him, the ground beneath his feet, and the generations yet to be born were all placed within his care. This was not ownership, but stewardship. Creation itself had been reset, and Noah became the first man to walk in that renewed order. His responsibility reached beyond survival; it extended into preservation, cultivation, and reverence for what God had restored. In Noah, we see that a righteous man is not only saved from judgment but entrusted with purpose after it. This moment reveals that true manhood holds the future in its hands. Noah's obedience secured more than his own deliverance; it safeguarded life itself. Mankind's future was not left to chance but anchored in the faithfulness of one man who walked with God. In the same way, every man called by God must recognize that his life influences more than he sees. What he builds, protects, and nurtures today becomes the foundation for tomorrow.

A man who walks rightly before God recognizes that his life, his family, his resources, and even his opportunities are divine deposits, not personal possessions. This understanding produces humility, because he knows he is accountable to the One who gave it. It shapes his decisions, because he manages not for self-glory, but for God's purpose. When a man remembers that he is a steward, he handles what he has with care, reverence, and intentionality, knowing that one day he will give an account. Ownership breeds control, pride, and independence from God, but stewardship produces obedience, gratitude, and faithfulness. A faithful man does not grasp what he has as if it belongs to him; instead, he releases it in alignment with God's will. He leads his household not as a tyrant, but as one under authority. He uses his strength not to dominate, but to serve. True manhood is revealed in how well a man manages what is not his, while honoring the One to whom it all belongs.

A man who walks in true authority understands that it was placed in his hands by God. Because of this, he carries it with reverence, humility, and awareness. He does not use authority to dominate, but to serve; not to elevate himself, but to fulfill divine purpose. Reverence keeps a man grounded, reminding him that he is accountable to the One who gave him influence. The higher the authority, the deeper the responsibility to reflect God's character in how it is exercised. But when a man forgets where his authority came from, something dangerous begins to grow within him. He starts to see himself as the source instead of the steward. Pride replaces humility, control replaces care, and power becomes a tool for self rather than service. This is where authority becomes destructive - when it is no longer governed by reverence for God. A man disconnected from the source of his authority will misuse it, but a man who remains in awe of God will handle it with wisdom, restraint, and righteousness.

God gives men strength to stand, influence to shape lives, leadership to guide others, and provision to sustain what has been entrusted to them. Strength is meant to protect, not dominate. Influence is meant to uplift, not control. Leadership is meant to serve, not exalt self. Provision is meant to steward, not hoard. When a man walks in the fear of the Lord, he recognizes that nothing he has is truly his own, that it is all entrusted to him for a higher purpose. Without reverence, however, those same gifts can become dangerous. Authority, when disconnected from the fear of the Lord, easily turns into pride, and pride blinds a man to his dependence on God. What was meant to build can begin to tear down. What was meant to lead can begin to control. But the man who fears the Lord remains grounded, humble, and accountable. He governs his strength with restraint, his influence with wisdom, his leadership with humility, and his provision with generosity.

Noah stepped into a cleansed world not just as a survivor, but as a steward. The same God who preserved him through judgment now entrusted him with responsibility in a renewed creation. When God places His favor on a man, He is not lowering the standard, He is raising the expectation. The ground beneath Noah's feet was a gift, but it also became an assignment. Every promise carried a responsibility to walk upright, to lead his household well, and to honor the God who had delivered him. God's favor is not permission to drift into carelessness, but a call to walk with greater intentionality and reverence. What God gives must be governed with wisdom, guarded with discipline, and surrendered daily in obedience. A faithful man understands that grace empowers him to rise to the responsibility, not escape it. When he embraces this truth, he does not take God's blessings lightly - he carries them with humility, knowing that what was given in favor must be sustained through faithfulness.

A righteous man understands that what God places in his hands is not casual- it is sacred. His family is not merely his responsibility, but a trust; his work is not just labor, but an assignment; his influence is not accidental, but intentional. Every decision he makes plants seeds that will grow into consequences. He recognizes that obedience is not selective, but complete. He does not separate the spiritual from the practical, because he knows that God is present in both. What he does in private shapes what he becomes in public, and how he leads at home echoes into every other area of his life. Because of this, a righteous man walks carefully, not in fear, but in reverence. He seeks God before he speaks, listens before he acts, and submits before he assumes. His life becomes a vessel through which God's order, peace, and purpose flow. In honoring what God has placed in his hands, he proves himself trustworthy for even greater things, knowing that true strength is not in control, but in surrender.

A man entrusted with the earth must carry his life with holy seriousness, for what he holds is not his own, but a sacred trust placed into his hands by God. Blessing is not permission to drift into ease, but a calling to walk with awareness, discipline, and reverence. Every provision, every opportunity, and every sphere of influence is a responsibility wrapped in grace. To walk in blessing while embracing stewardship is to live with the constant awareness that God still watches. Not with condemnation, but with expectation. Heaven observes how a man handles his family, his words, his resources, and his authority. A righteous man does not take lightly what God has placed in his care; he guards it, grows it, and governs it with humility. He knows that blessing and accountability walk together, and because of this, he chooses faithfulness in both the seen and unseen moments, honoring God not only for what he has been given, but in how he manages it.

| **27** |

"A MAN WHO MUST GUARD HIS WEAKNESS"

Noah stands as a powerful witness that a man can walk with God in a corrupt world and still find grace. He obeyed when others mocked, built when others doubted, and trusted when there was no visible sign of rain. His life declares that righteousness is not perfection, but alignment with God in the midst of darkness. Noah had just walked through a victory that few men will ever understand yet the same man who endured the storm faced a different kind of battle after the victory. Genesis 9 reveals that the greatest danger is not always the storm outside, but the unguarded moment within. After the ark, after the promise, after survival Noah let his guard down. Noah had just come through one of the greatest victories in human history. He had built the ark, endured the flood, protected his household, and stepped into a new world under the blessing of God. But after the flood, in a quiet moment, he planted a vineyard, drank of the wine, became drunken, and was uncovered in his tent.

Noah obeyed God when no one else would, endured a storm that wiped away a generation, and carried his family into a new beginning under divine favor. But victory does not eliminate vulnerability - it often exposes it. What the flood could not destroy, an unguarded moment threatened to dishonor. This reminds us that the greatest dangers in a man's life are not always found in the battle, but in the quiet

237

places after it. A godly man must learn that consistency in character matters more than moments of triumph. Noah was righteous, but he was still human, and humanity must always be governed by watchfulness. The same discipline that carried him through the storm was required to sustain him after it. When a man stops guarding his heart, even briefly, he opens the door to compromise. The calling of a man of God is to remain faithful when no battle is being fought, to stay covered when no one is watching, and to honor God not only in the storm, but also in the silence that follows.

A man is often shaped in the storm, but he is revealed after the storm. It is in the pressure, the fear, and the uncertainty that he clings tightly to God, stands firm in conviction, and walks carefully in obedience. Yet when the storm passes and the ground feels steady again, a different kind of test begins. Victory can quietly invite complacency. The urgency that once drove prayer can fade, and the vigilance that guarded his heart can weaken. What once required dependence can begin to feel like personal strength. In this way, the absence of battle can become more dangerous than the battle itself. The same man who stood unshaken in crisis must learn to remain watchful in comfort. A godly man does not lay down his discipline when the threat is gone; he strengthens it. He understands that his greatest failures may not come when he is under attack, but when he assumes the war is over. True strength is not only enduring hardship but also stewarding victory with humility and awareness.

Noah's failure did not erase his righteousness; it revealed the reality that even a man who walks closely with God still carries human vulnerability. His life reminds us that righteousness is not the absence of weakness, but the presence of a heart that has chosen God again and again. A godly man is not defined by perfection, but by the steady pursuit of obedience even after moments of failure. What Noah built before God stood firm, not because he never faltered, but because his life had already been anchored in faith. His stumble did not cancel his calling; it simply exposed the places where vigilance was still required. Every man must understand that faithfulness must be renewed daily, and strength must be guarded intentionally. The areas where a man is most vulnerable are often the ones he assumes are secure. Complacency is the quiet doorway through which weakness enters. A wise man builds watchfulness into his life, knowing that what he does not guard can be compromised.

Great men do not usually fall in the spotlight of open rebellion - they fall in the shadows of private carelessness. The danger is not always a loud departure from righteousness, but a quiet drifting when vigilance is relaxed. It is in the moments when discipline is set aside, when restraint is loosened, and when the soul assumes it is strong enough to stand without watchfulness. A man who has walked faithfully for years can still stumble if he forgets that strength is not self-sustained but God-dependent. The greatest victories can create the illusion that the battle is over, when in truth, the need for guarding the heart has only deepened. A wise man understands that consistency in righteousness requires constant awareness. He does not trust his past victories to secure his present integrity. Instead, he keeps his spirit alert, his desires submitted, and his heart anchored in reverence toward God. He knows that the enemy of his soul often waits not for moments of weakness, but for moments of ease.

Every man has places where his judgment dulls, where his guard slips, and where his spirit becomes exposed. It may be pride that blinds him, fatigue that weakens him, temptation that entices him, or past wounds that quietly influence his decisions. A wise man does not ignore these places or excuse them - he studies them. He pays attention to patterns, moments, and environments where he is most vulnerable. Self-awareness becomes a form of protection, because what a man can name, he can guard against. What he refuses to acknowledge will eventually master him. Wisdom, then, is not found in pretending to be unbreakable, but in building boundaries where weakness has been revealed. A man who understands himself sets limits before failure ever has a chance to take root. He orders his life in such a way that his weak places are not constantly tested but carefully guarded. He invites accountability, leans on discipline, and remains watchful even in seasons of strength.

Noah's uncovered condition reveals a quiet but serious truth: a man can walk with God in great moments and still fall in unguarded ones. What began as something natural - planting, harvesting, and partaking - became a place of exposure because it was not governed by restraint. There was nothing inherently evil in the act itself, but without self-control, it crossed a boundary and left him uncovered. This is the subtle danger every godly man must recognize: not everything that is permissible is safe when it is allowed to rule the heart. When natural desires are left unchecked, they can slowly erode spiritual awareness until what once strengthened a man now weakens him. A godly man must therefore live with discernment, not just avoidance. The issue is not always what a man does, but whether what he does begins to master him. Anything that dulls his sensitivity to God, lowers his guard, or exposes his spirit must be brought under discipline. Strength is not proven by indulgence, but by restraint.

The enemy is not always looking for you in the heat of battle - he often waits for the quiet moments that follow. He watches for when your guard is lowered, when relief replaces vigilance, when success whispers that you can finally rest your discipline. It is when you are tired from the fight, satisfied with the victory, or alone without accountability that subtle compromises begin to creep in. What you resisted under pressure can become what you entertain in comfort if your spirit is no longer watchful. Many men do not fall because they lacked strength in the conflict, but because they neglected wisdom after it. Victory can be just as dangerous as struggle if it leads to carelessness. When the pressure lifts, discipline must remain. When the storm passes, watchfulness must stay in place. A godly man does not only prepare for the fight - he prepares for the moments after it. He builds habits that remain steady in both adversity and ease, knowing that spiritual consistency is what guards his life.

After God lifts a man, he must bow lower. After God blesses him, he must walk more carefully. After God uses him, he must guard his spirit more closely than before. Victory is not the moment to loosen discipline; it is the moment to deepen it. Many men stand strong in the storm but stumble in the calm, because they mistake relief for release. The man who survives the flood must still guard himself in the tent. Private moments reveal what public victories can conceal. It is not the crowd, the battle, or the pressure that often brings a man down - it is the quiet place where he assumes he no longer has to watch. Humility must follow him where applause cannot. Sobriety must remain when urgency fades. Watchfulness must continue when no one is looking. A godly man understands that the same God who preserved him through judgment expects him to govern himself in peace. If he does not guard his heart after the victory, he may lose in a moment what took a lifetime of faith to build.

A man may begin with fire in his heart and clarity in his vision, but if he does not remain watchful, what was once strong can slowly weaken in unseen places. The danger is not always in open rebellion, but in quiet neglect. It is in the small compromises, the unguarded thoughts, and the habits that drift without correction. To continue well, a man must keep his heart with diligence, examine his ways, and stay anchored in the fear of the Lord. Victory in one season does not guarantee strength in the next. Righteousness must be maintained with intention, humility, and daily surrender. He guards his appetites so they do not rule him, disciplines his habits so they do not weaken him, and submits himself continually to God so pride does not deceive him. Watchfulness is the quiet strength of a man who refuses to drift, who refuses to grow careless, and who chooses daily to walk upright before God. To finish well, he must live alert, stay submitted, and remain faithful in the places no one else sees.

Noah's life stands as a sobering reminder that yesterday's obedience does not excuse today's neglect. A man may have walked with God when others turned away, built what others mocked, and led his family through storms that destroyed everything else but none of that removes his present responsibility. Spiritual history is not a shield against future failure. The same man who found grace in the eyes of God still had to guard his heart, his habits, and his private life. Victory in one season does not cancel the need for vigilance in the next. Every man must understand that discipline is not a one-time decision but a daily commitment. It is not enough to lead publicly; a man must also govern himself privately. The strength that carried him through past trials must be maintained through present watchfulness. A man who does not stay anchored in God can drift proving that true righteousness is not proven in a single act of obedience, but in a life that remains surrendered, watchful, and disciplined before God.

The private life of a man is never truly private in its impact. What happens behind closed doors eventually presses outward. A man may believe his hidden struggles, compromises, or indulgences are contained, but they shape his spirit, influence his decisions, and alter the atmosphere of his home. What is cultivated in the "tent" becomes the seedbed for what grows in the family. Integrity in secret strengthens a household, but weakness left unchecked quietly erodes trust, stability, and spiritual covering. A man's life is interconnected, and his choices are rarely isolated. When weakness is ignored instead of guarded, it begins to ripple outward affecting his leadership, his relationships, and those who look to him for strength and direction. What he allows in private will eventually reveal itself in public. That is why vigilance is not optional for a godly man; it is essential. A man who guards his inner life protects not only himself, but everyone connected to him.

Humility is not just for the storm - it is for the silence that follows it. A man who walks humbly understands that his greatest danger is not always in the flood, but in the quiet days after, when vigilance fades and self-reliance begins to whisper. He does not place too much confidence in his own strength, because he has learned that yesterday's obedience does not guarantee today's protection. He remembers that it was God who carried him through the storm, and it must be God who keeps him steady when the waters have receded. So he stays low before the Lord, aware that even in peace, he still needs grace. A humble man continues to pray not only when the winds are strong, but when the air is still. He knows that the same God who delivered him in crisis is the One who must sustain him in normalcy. So he keeps his heart aligned, his spirit dependent, and his posture surrendered. Because true strength is not found in standing tall on one's own—it is found in staying bowed before God, in every season.

A man does not wait for the storm to start building walls - he prepares long before the winds ever rise. He sets boundaries when his mind is clear, not when his emotions are pulling him in every direction. He chooses what he will not touch, not because he is weak, but because he understands his humanity. He decides where he will not go, not out of fear, but out of wisdom. Discipline is not restriction - it is protection. It is the guardrail that keeps a man from drifting into places he never intended to be. A man who walks with God also chooses the voices that are allowed to speak into his life. He surrounds himself with truth, accountability, and correction, because he knows isolation is dangerous ground. He does not entertain everything that comes before his eyes or ears, because he understands that what he allows in will eventually shape what comes out. These safeguards are not built in a moment of crisis - they are established in seasons of clarity and strengthened through consistency.

A man who knows where he is vulnerable is not living in fear; he is living in truth. He does not wait until temptation rises to decide his response - he has already settled it in his heart. He builds walls where others leave doors open, not because he doubts his calling, but because he honors it. Wisdom teaches him that even great men fall when they ignore small compromises, and so he guards his eyes, his thoughts, his time, and his associations with intentional care. The man who sets boundaries is not fragile - he is fortified. He understands that carelessness carries a cost that is often paid in regret, broken trust, and lost purpose. Strength is not proven by how much he can handle, but by what he refuses to entertain. He chooses discipline over desire, conviction over convenience, and obedience over impulse. In doing so, he preserves not only his integrity but his future. A guarded life is not a restricted life - it is a protected one, positioned for lasting impact and sustained by the quiet power of wisdom.

Every man has a private place where no audience applauds, no pressure demands performance, and no eyes measure his actions. It is there, in the quiet and unseen moments, that true discipline is revealed. When a man is alone, tired, and comfortable, he is stripped of pretense and left with nothing but his character. The world may celebrate his public strength, but heaven examines his private life. What he entertains in secret, what he tolerates in stillness, and what he chooses when no one is watching are the true indicators of who he is becoming. A man who governs himself in the hidden places builds a life that cannot be shaken in the open. Godly manhood is not proven on platforms but in private surrender. It is forged in the decisions made when it would be easiest to compromise, when discipline feels inconvenient, and when no consequence seems immediate. In those moments, a man either strengthens his spirit or weakens his foundation.

Noah's failure stands in scripture not to diminish his righteousness, but to remind every man that no life of obedience removes the need for vigilance. God did not hide Noah's weakness, but revealed it, so future generations would not walk blindly in their own strength. A man may build faithfully for years, but if he ceases to guard his heart, a single unguarded moment can uncover what took a lifetime to establish. God preserved Noah's story so that men would not only fear failure but prepare against it. The righteous man does not trust in his past obedience; he remains alert, humble, and dependent on God in every season. He sets watch over his desires, his decisions, and his private moments, knowing that integrity is not proven once, but protected daily. Noah's fall is not just a record of weakness - it is a call to awareness. It teaches that the man who continues to walk closely with God after the storm is the man who remains covered, steady, and trustworthy when the next test comes.

A man who guards his weakness understands how easily the heart can drift and how subtly pride can rise. So he walks carefully, not in fear, but in awareness. He watches his steps, measures his thoughts, and keeps his spirit anchored in prayer. He knows that the very areas where he feels strongest are often the places he must remain most alert, because dependence on God is not a one-time decision but a daily posture. He recognizes that the same grace that carried him through the storm is the grace that must sustain him after it. Many men endure the flood, but stumble in the quiet that follows because they lower their guard. But a wise man stays low before God even when he stands tall before others. He understands that without God, he is just as vulnerable after the victory as he was in the battle. So he remains dependent, humble, and watchful, knowing that grace is not just what saves him in crisis, but what keeps him steady in calm seasons.

28

"A MAN WHOSE LEGACY AFFECTS HIS SONS"

Noah survived the flood, but survival was only the beginning of a deeper responsibility. When the waters receded and the ark rested, God had preserved more than Noah's life; He had preserved his influence. A man can come through storms, overcome trials, and endure seasons that would have destroyed others, yet still be called to something greater on the other side. Noah stepped into a cleansed world, but he also stepped into a calling to lead, to guide, and to establish righteousness in a new generation. Survival proves God's grace, but what a man does afterward reveals his stewardship of that grace. After the flood, Noah still had a household watching him, sons learning from him, and a future being shaped by his choices. A man must understand that his private decisions echo into the lives of those connected to him. The same hands that built the ark now had to build a legacy. His words, his discipline, and his devotion would either strengthen or weaken what God had preserved.

A man may stand strong while the storm is raging, holding tightly to God as the winds howl and the waters rise. In those moments, his faith is sharp, his prayers are constant, and his dependence on God is undeniable. But when the storm passes and the waters recede, a different kind of test begins. The urgency fades, the pressure lifts, and the discipline that once came naturally must now be chosen intentionally. It is often in the quiet seasons that a man lets his guard down, not realizing that spiritual drift can begin where vigilance ends. A wise man understands that what happens after the storm can shape his legacy just as much as what happened during it. He does not trade devotion for comfort or allow ease to weaken his convictions. Instead, he builds on what the storm produced in him - greater faith, deeper humility, and stronger dependence on God. He remains anchored, knowing that calm seasons are not a time to coast, but a time to guard, grow, and prepare.

Noah's life stands as a powerful reminder that a man's influence does not end with his public obedience - it continues into his private moments. After the flood, the same man who built an ark in faith found himself uncovered in a moment of weakness, and what should have remained private became exposed within his household. In that instant, his personal lapse did not stay contained; it touched his sons and shaped their responses. One chose honor, another chose dishonor, and the ripple effects moved beyond the moment into generational consequences. This reveals a sobering truth: a man's private life is never truly isolated, because those closest to him are watching, learning, and being formed by what they see. A righteous man must therefore guard not only his public walk with God but also his unseen life. Integrity behind closed doors strengthens a household, while compromise quietly weakens its foundation. What a father permits in private can become what his children struggle with in public.

A man often believes that what he does in private stays contained, hidden from the eyes of others and separated from the rest of his life. But the truth is, what is cultivated in secret never remains isolated. It grows and eventually reveals itself. The attitudes he nurtures, the habits he permits, and the compromises he justifies begin to seep into his character. And character is not something that can be confined; it speaks through his words, his reactions, and his decisions. In time, what was once hidden begins to influence the atmosphere of his home, the tone of his leadership, and the direction of his life. This is why a man must guard his private life with the same intensity that he guards his public reputation. His children may not see everything he does, but they will feel the impact of who he becomes. A wise man understands that integrity is not proven in the spotlight, but in the quiet places where choices are made alone.

A father's strength flows outward into the lives of his sons. When a man walks in integrity, discipline, and reverence for God, he lays down a path his sons can follow with confidence. His faith becomes their foundation, his consistency becomes their stability, and his character becomes a living blueprint for manhood. Sons often learn not only what a father teaches, but what he tolerates, what he avoids, and what he fails to confront. Sons inherit more than a name - they inherit patterns, examples, wounds, and warnings. What is not healed in one generation often reappears in the next, unless a man chooses to break the cycle through surrender and obedience to God. Yet even in this, there is hope. A son is not bound to repeat every failure he witnessed; he can learn from both the strength and the weakness of his father. Where there was righteousness, he can build further. Where there was failure, he can choose restoration. In this way, a man passes on something stronger to those who come after him.

Ham saw his father's shame and chose exposure instead of covering. In a moment that revealed more about his own heart than his father's condition, he allowed dishonor to rise where humility should have stood. But Shem and Japheth responded differently - they walked in backward, refusing to let their eyes feast on failure, and covered their father with honor. This reveals a powerful truth: a man is not defined solely by what he sees, but by how he chooses to respond to it. Every son must make a decision - will he expose weakness or cover it with wisdom? Honor does not mean agreement with failure, but it does mean choosing a higher way in how you handle it. A man who walks in honor understands that how he responds to imperfection will shape his own future, his own household, and his own legacy. You cannot always choose what you see in your father, but you can always choose what kind of man you become because of it.

A man must come to grips with the reality that his greatest influence is not displayed on the stage of his public victories, but in the quiet, unguarded moments of his life. His children are not only observing what he achieves, but how he responds when things do not go his way. They are watching how he carries disappointment - whether he becomes bitter or remains steady. They are learning from how he handles weakness - whether he hides it in pride or humbles himself with honesty. In his moments of rest, they see whether he trusts God enough to be still, and in his success, they discern whether he walks in gratitude or drifts into self-exaltation. Every response is a lesson, every reaction a blueprint being etched into the next generation. His life becomes a living testimony that strength is not the absence of struggle, but the presence of God in it. A man who walks this way builds a legacy that will echo in the hearts and character of his children long after his victories have faded from memory.

Noah had been a righteous man, a man who walked with God when the world around him was corrupt and violent. His obedience preserved his family, and his faith carried him through the storm. Yet righteousness in one season does not guarantee strength in the next. A man cannot live today on yesterday's victories. The disciplines that carried a man through one battle must be maintained, guarded, and strengthened for the next. There is no season where vigilance is no longer needed. The heart must still be watched, the mind still renewed, and the flesh still brought under submission. The enemy often waits not for the moment of weakness during the storm, but for the quiet after the victory. Therefore, a wise man does not trust in what he has been but remains committed to what he must continue to become. He understands that faithfulness is daily, discipline is ongoing, and a life that honors God is built not just in great moments, but in consistent, careful steps with Him.

This is a warning to every man: do not let yesterday's obedience make you careless today. Victory can be dangerous if it leads to complacency. The same discipline that carried you through yesterday's battle must remain intact today, because the enemy does not retreat simply because you once stood strong. A man who relaxes his guard after a victory often opens the door to a fall he never saw coming. Obedience is a lifestyle. It must be renewed daily, guarded intentionally, and walked out with humility before God. Great victories demand greater awareness, deeper humility, and stronger boundaries. The moment a man begins to rely on what he has done instead of staying anchored in who God is becomes vulnerable. A wise man understands that every day requires fresh surrender, fresh discipline, and fresh dependence on God. He does not coast on past success - he builds on it with continued obedience, knowing that finishing well matters more than starting strong.

A man's legacy is not forged only in the visible arenas where others can witness his strength, but in the quiet, hidden places where no applause is given and no recognition is offered. The choices he makes in private and the standards he refuses to lower become the foundation of the life he is building. Integrity in the unseen becomes strength in the seen. What a man consistently practices in secret will eventually manifest in the open, shaping not only his reputation, but the spiritual weight of his legacy. God measures a man not by the noise of public moments, but by the faithfulness of his private walk. A man who honors God in silence, who resists temptation when it would be easy to give in, and who chooses righteousness without recognition is building something eternal. In time, the unseen seeds of obedience and character will bear fruit that impacts generations. For it is in the hidden places that God forms the kind of man whose life will speak long after his voice is gone.

Sons are always learning, even when no words are spoken. A father may preach truth with conviction, but what he allows to live in his home will often speak louder than anything he says. They watch how he handles pressure, how he speaks when he is frustrated, what he laughs at, what he tolerates, and what he refuses. They study his tone, his habits, his reactions, and his appetites. A man may declare righteousness, but if he permits compromise, his sons will learn that standard instead. What a father consistently allows becomes the unspoken permission his children carry into their own lives. Yet there is also grace in this reality, because sons do not only learn from perfection - they learn from repentance. When a father humbles himself, corrects his course, and returns to what is right, he teaches something just as powerful as discipline: he teaches how to recover. They learn what truly matters by what he prioritizes, and they learn the heart of God by watching how their father responds when he falls short.

A father does not need perfection to leave a godly legacy - he needs awareness. Every choice, every reaction, every quiet moment is shaping something in the hearts of his children. They are reading his life more than listening to his words. When he shows integrity in private, patience under pressure, and faith in uncertainty, he is preaching sermons without ever opening his mouth. Even his failures, when met with humility and repentance, become powerful lessons. A man who admits when he is wrong teaches his children what strength truly looks like. Legacy is not built on flawless performance; it is built on consistent direction. A father who turns his heart toward God, even after stumbling, leaves behind a pattern worth following. His life becomes a compass, not because it never wavered, but because it always found its way back to truth. Children do not need a father who never falls. They need one who shows them how to rise with grace, how to walk in humility, and how to depend on God.

A righteous man lives with eternity in his decisions and legacy in his vision. He understands that every word spoken, every habit formed, and every boundary set becomes a seed planted in the soil of his children's lives. His life becomes a blueprint, not just a moment. He realizes that character is inherited through example, and that what he tolerates today may become what his children struggle to overcome tomorrow. Because of this he disciplines himself not only for personal growth, but for generational stability. He chooses integrity when compromise would be easier, faith when doubt would be natural, and obedience when rebellion would be unnoticed. He sees beyond his own lifetime and understands that righteousness is not just about being right with God today, but about leaving a path that leads his children toward God tomorrow. His life declares, without words, "Follow me as I follow the Lord," and in doing so, he builds a legacy that speaks long after he is gone.

A man does not live for appetite alone. He refuses to be governed by impulse, craving, or momentary desire, because he understands that unchecked appetite can lead him where purpose never intended him to go. Instead, he disciplines himself knowing that every decision carries weight beyond the present moment. He lives with an awareness that his life is not just his own, but a testimony being written daily before those who are watching. He understands that his choices are seeds, and seeds never remain alone - they multiply. What he plants today will one day rise in the lives of his family. If he sows integrity, they will reap stability. If he sows compromise, they will inherit confusion. This awareness causes him to pause, to consider, to choose differently. He is not just thinking about today - he is thinking generations ahead. Because a wise man knows that legacy is not built in grand moments, but in daily decisions, quietly sown into the soil of his household, where time and truth will reveal the harvest.

Noah's life reveals that a man can walk in great obedience before God in public and still need vigilance in his private life. He built the ark when no one else believed, stood righteous in a corrupt generation, and became a vessel through which God preserved humanity. Yet after the flood, within the quiet walls of his own household, a moment of uncovered weakness brought disorder to his family. This reminds us that spiritual victories do not excuse us from personal discipline. The same man who hears God's voice in the storm must still exercise wisdom in the stillness of home. God never intended for a man's public anointing to replace his private accountability. The ark may have survived the flood, but the home still required covering. True righteousness is not only proven in what a man builds for God, but in what he preserves within his own walls. A wise man understands that his greatest legacy is not just what he accomplishes before men, but what he cultivates and protects among those who call him father.

Every man must come to a place where he invites God into the hidden places of his life, asking not only for strength to stand, but for integrity to remain consistent. When a man walks uprightly before God, he builds a foundation of clarity, conviction, and stability that his sons can stand on. But when compromise enters in, it sends mixed signals, creating confusion where there should be confidence, and uncertainty where there should be direction. A godly man understands that his example will either reinforce truth or weaken it in the next generation. He does not strive for perfection, but to be quick to repent, quick to correct, and committed to living what he believes. When a man asks God to order his steps, his life becomes a testimony that strengthens his sons, giving them a clear picture of what it means to walk with God in both word and deed. His consistency becomes their compass, his obedience becomes their courage, and his faithfulness becomes their inheritance.

When a man falls, the fall itself is not the final testimony - his response is. A man who humbles himself before God begins to write a different ending than the failure itself suggested. Repentance is not weakness; it is a heart that still fears God enough to return. In that moment, a man teaches his sons that righteousness is not the absence of failure, but the presence of a heart that refuses to stay down. He shows them that God honors the man who gets up and realigns his life with truth. Sons are always watching and when they see humility instead of hardness, repentance instead of denial, and renewed obedience instead of compromise, they learn how to walk forward with wisdom. They learn that failure does not have to define them, and that the fear of God leads a man back onto the right path. A father who rises rightly after falling leaves his sons a pattern for restoration, a reverence for God's ways, and the understanding that even in weakness, a man can choose to finish strong.

A man whose legacy affects his sons must live with holy seriousness, recognizing that his life is constantly preaching a message louder than his words. Every decision he makes, every boundary he keeps or breaks, every act of obedience or compromise becomes a visible pattern laid before those who follow him. His life is a seed being sown into the soil of the next generation. What he tolerates, his sons may embrace. What he honors, they will learn to pursue. Therefore, he must walk before God with reverence, understanding that even in unseen moments, he is shaping the future of his household. Such a man does not live casually, but intentionally. He understands that legacy is built in daily choices, in quiet disciplines, in private integrity, and in public faithfulness. Long after his voice grows silent, the echo of his life will remain either as a foundation that strengthens his sons or a fracture they must struggle to repair. So he seeks God not only for himself, but for those who will rise behind him.

29

"A MAN REMEMBERED BY GOD"

God remembered Noah. In the middle of a flooded world, when every familiar landmark was buried beneath judgment, Noah was not forgotten. The ark may have been surrounded by water, silence, and waiting, but heaven still knew exactly where he was. Noah was not drifting aimlessly; he was being carried by the unseen hand of a faithful God who never loses sight of the obedient. To be remembered by God is greater than to be recognized by men. God does not forget the man who walks with Him, even when that walk leads into long seasons of waiting. In your own moments of silence, when answers seem distant and movement feels slow, take heart - God knows exactly where you are. The same God who remembered Noah will move in His perfect time, shifting winds, opening doors, and bringing you into a place of renewal. A righteous man can rest, not in what he sees, but in the unshakable faithfulness of the God who never forgets.

To be remembered by God is one of the greatest honors a man can carry, because it means his life has not been lived in vain before heaven. Men may forget your labor, overlook your obedience, and fail to honor your sacrifice, but God never loses sight of the man who walks with Him. Every quiet act of righteousness, every hidden sacrifice, and every moment of integrity is recorded before Him. What is unseen by people is never unseen by God. When God remembers a man, He moves on his behalf with purpose and power. Just as God remembered Noah and caused the waters to recede, He knows exactly when to step into your situation and bring change. A man who is remembered by God can rest, even in seasons of silence, knowing that heaven has not forgotten him. In due time, God will respond, reward, and reveal His faithfulness. To live for God's remembrance rather than man's recognition is to anchor your life in something eternal, unshakable, and sure.

Noah's obedience was not validated by what he could see, but by the word he had received. While the skies were still clear and the ground was still dry, he labored in faith, building something that made no sense to those around him. The sound of his hammer echoed against the laughter of skeptics, yet he did not slow down. He understood that obedience to God will often look strange before it looks wise. Faith builds before evidence appears. Faith prepares in the silence before the storm. Noah trusted God enough to act on a warning that had no visible confirmation, and in doing so, he aligned himself with a future only God could see. There is a kind of obedience that requires a man to stand alone, to move forward when no one else understands, and to remain committed when there is no applause. Noah teaches us that true faith does not wait for proof - it responds to God's voice. While others ignored the warning, he prepared. While others lived casually, he lived intentionally.

After the storm had done its work and the ark was no longer being built but simply carried, Noah entered a deeper dimension of faith. Before, faith was active, visible, and measurable - cutting wood, gathering animals, obeying specific instructions. But now, faith became stillness. It became waiting in the unknown, trusting that the same God who gave the command would also determine the timing of release. There were no new instructions, no visible signs of progress - only the sound of water and the passing of time. In that season, Noah had to learn that obedience does not always look like movement;

sometimes it looks like remaining where God has placed you until He speaks again. There are seasons in a man's life when the greatest act of faith is not doing more, but trusting deeper. When the door is shut by God's hand, and the outside world is beyond your control, you are invited into a place of surrender. It is there that patience is forged, and confidence in God's faithfulness is refined.

Genesis 8:1 declares, "And God remembered Noah," not as a sign of forgetfulness, but as a moment of divine movement. When scripture says God remembered, it reveals that He turned His full, faithful attention toward Noah with intention to act. While the waters still covered the earth and the ark floated in what seemed like an endless season, God was preparing a shift. The same God who led Noah into the ark had not abandoned him in it. His remembrance was active, deliberate, and perfectly timed. What looked like delay to Noah was actually divine orchestration. This truth anchors every man who walks by faith. There are seasons when obedience places you in waiting, when you cannot see what God is doing next. But "God remembered" means He is working even when you cannot feel it. His attention brings transition, His faithfulness brings movement, and His timing brings fulfillment. You are not forgotten - you are being prepared for what comes next.

A man remembered by God is never abandoned, even when everything around him suggests otherwise. There are seasons where he feels hidden from view, where his obedience seems unnoticed and his prayers seem unanswered. He may walk through delays that test his patience, or confinement that challenges his faith, yet none of these conditions remove him from the awareness of heaven. God does not lose sight of the man who trusts Him. Even in silence, God is working; even in stillness, God is moving. What feels like distance is often divine positioning, and what feels like delay is often divine timing unfolding. Though he may be surrounded by circumstances beyond his control, he is never beyond God's reach. The same God who remembers knows how to sustain, preserve, and deliver. A remembered man is a kept man. His life is held in the hands of a faithful God who does not forget covenant, does not overlook obedience, and does not abandon His own.

Being celebrated by men is a fleeting moment, a passing echo that fades with time. Applause rises quickly, but it also dies quickly. Recognition can place a man on a pedestal today and forget him tomorrow. The same voices that cheer can grow silent, and the same crowds that praise can turn their attention elsewhere. Human approval is unstable because it is rooted in perception, emotion, and circumstance. But when God remembers a man, everything changes. When God remembered Noah, the waters began to recede, and purpose began to unfold. When God remembers a man, heaven responds with intention, timing, and power. There is no fading in God's remembrance, no shifting in His faithfulness. A man remembered by God does not need the noise of human praise, because he walks in the quiet assurance that the Creator sees him, knows him, and acts on his behalf. What God establishes cannot be undone, and what He remembers carries eternal weight.

Noah did not need applause while he was building the ark; he needed obedience while the skies were still clear. What preserved Noah was not popularity, but the faithfulness of God. There will be seasons where obedience looks like isolation and faithfulness looks like foolishness. But survival in the flood was never tied to the crowd's agreement - it was anchored in God's covenant. When the rain began to fall, it was not the opinions of men that held the ark together, but the hand of God that sealed it. A man who walks with God must shift his desire from being recognized by people to being remembered by God. When God remembers a man, He moves on his behalf, sustains him through impossible circumstances, and fulfills every promise tied to his obedience. Noah was not celebrated while he labored, but he was preserved when it mattered most. The goal is not to be known by the crowd, but to be known by God. For when God remembers a man, that man will stand when everything else is swept away.

God does not forget the man who obeys Him. In a world that often overlooks quiet faithfulness, heaven keeps perfect record. Every act of obedience carries eternal weight. The prayers whispered in private, the sacrifices made without recognition, and the choices to walk in righteousness when compromise would be easier are all seen by the Lord. What may feel unnoticed on earth is honored in heaven. God's memory is not like man's; He does not lose sight of the faithful, nor does He dismiss the cost of obedience. Every step of faith matters. When a man chooses integrity over convenience, truth over acceptance, and holiness over comfort, he is building something that God Himself acknowledges. Though the reward may not come immediately, it is never withheld. The Lord sees, the Lord remembers, and in due time, the Lord responds. A man who walks with God can rest in this assurance: nothing done in obedience is ever wasted, and no faithful life is ever forgotten.

There are seasons when a man walks in quiet obedience and begins to wonder if it carries any weight. He may labor in faithfulness without applause, choose restraint when no one is watching, pray when answers seem delayed, and lead when no one affirms his direction. Yet the life of faith has never been sustained by visibility, but by trust. A man must remember that what is done before God is never wasted, even when it is hidden from men. God sees what others miss. He notices the discipline no one applauds, the integrity that goes unrewarded, the prayers whispered in secret, and the endurance carried without complaint. Heaven keeps record of what earth overlooks. The man who remains faithful in unseen places is building something eternal, something God Himself honors. In due time, what was hidden will be revealed, and what was sown in quiet obedience will bear undeniable fruit. A righteous man does not measure his life by who sees him, but by the One who never takes His eyes off him.

Noah's righteousness did not shield him from the storm - it positioned him within the care of God when the storm came. Righteousness is not an escape from hardship; it is an alignment with God that ensures His covering in the midst of it. The ark was not built to avoid the storm, but to survive it, and every act of obedience Noah walked in became a plank of preservation beneath his feet. God's faithfulness does not always keep the waters from rising, but it guarantees that they will not have the final say over the man who belongs to Him. When others were overtaken, Noah was sustained. When chaos filled the earth, he rested in divine assurance. This is the confidence of a righteous man - not that life will be free from storms, but that God will be present, attentive, and committed through every wave. A man who walks with God can endure what others cannot, because he is not preserved by circumstance, but by the unchanging faithfulness of God.

A righteous man can rest in God's faithfulness because his confidence is not rooted in his own understanding, but in God's unchanging character. He does not need to have every answer, see every outcome, or make sense of every delay. His rest is not the absence of questions - it is the presence of trust. While the world labors under the pressure of needing control, the righteous man releases that burden into the hands of a faithful God. He knows that the same God who called him, led him, and sustained him will not abandon him in the unknown. Rest, then, is not passivity - it is surrender anchored in assurance. It is the quiet strength of a man who knows he is remembered by God even when he feels forgotten by circumstances. When the waters are still high and the ark has not yet settled, he remains steady because his hope is not in what he sees, but in who God is. The righteous man rests not because everything is clear, but because God is faithful and that is enough.

The ark was not Noah's idea - it was God's provision, designed long before the first drop of rain ever fell. God was not scrambling to rescue Noah in the middle of the flood - He had already made a way of preservation in advance. This is the nature of God's faithfulness: He prepares what we will need before we even recognize the danger. When God speaks, His instruction is never empty; it carries within it the blueprint for our survival. In the same way, every instruction God gives is tied to His desire to preserve what belongs to Him. What may feel inconvenient, restrictive, or even confusing in the moment is often the very structure that will sustain you later. Obedience builds arks in dry seasons - quiet, unseen preparations that become life-saving vessels in times of crisis. A man who walks with God learns to trust that divine instruction is not about limitation, but about protection. When the floods of life rise, he does not panic, because he is already positioned inside what God told him to build.

There is a deep and steady comfort in knowing that God sees the man who keeps building when others stop believing - when the crowd has walked away, when encouragement has dried up, when the outcome is still unseen. Like Noah, who labored in obedience before there was any sign of rain, that man is not forgotten. Every act of faithfulness and every unseen sacrifice is recorded before God. What others overlook, God honors. What others dismiss, God remembers. God also remembers the man who stands as a covering over his household, who chooses responsibility over convenience and obedience over popularity. That kind of man may not always be celebrated in the moment, but he is deeply known in heaven. And when God remembers a man, it is active, intentional, and powerful. His remembrance brings provision, protection, and fulfillment of promise. The man who walks with God can rest knowing he is never overlooked, never forgotten, and never alone.

Noah's life reveals that faithfulness does not always lead to applause - it often leads to isolation. While the world continued in corruption, Noah walked with God in quiet obedience, separated not by accident but by divine design. God will often remove a man from noise and even from familiar relationships so that his heart can remain anchored in righteousness without compromise. There are seasons when God will shut the door, not to confine a man, but to preserve him. What feels like being cut off is often God cutting away what cannot go where He is taking you. Noah's time in the ark was a season of waiting, trusting, and enduring without visible evidence of what was ahead. Yet every moment inside was proof that God remembers, God sustains, and God fulfills His word. A faithful man must learn that if God has you set apart, it is not because He has rejected you - it is because He is preparing to bring you out at the right time, into a promise that only faithfulness could inherit.

When the time was right, God caused the waters to decrease. The same God who shut him in the ark was the very One who brought him out into a new beginning. There are seasons when God closes doors, limits movement, and calls a man to wait. In those moments, it can feel confining, even uncertain, but what God seals, He seals with purpose. And when His appointed time arrives, no barrier can hold back what He has ordained to be released. A man remembered by God does not have to force doors open or manipulate outcomes. He learns to trust the rhythm of God's timing. He understands that obedience positions him, but God's faithfulness moves him. Just as the waters receded at the command of heaven, so too will obstacles, delays, and confinements give way when God speaks. The man who trusts this rests in quiet confidence, knowing that the God who brought him in will surely bring him out and when He does, it will be at the perfect moment, with clarity, purpose, and undeniable direction.

When God remembered Noah, it was not merely a reflection on what had been, but a declaration of what was about to begin. The waters that once covered the earth began to recede, not by chance, but by divine command. In the same way, when God remembers a man, He begins to move circumstances, shift seasons, and open what has been shut. His remembrance brings renewal. It signals that the trial had a purpose, the waiting had meaning, and the preservation was not the end of the story. Noah did not step out of the ark into the same world he once knew; he stepped into a cleansed place with a fresh assignment. What looked like an ending becomes a beginning, and what felt like isolation becomes preparation. When God remembers you, He doesn't just bring you out - He sends you forward. He places new ground beneath your feet, new responsibility in your hands, and new purpose in your spirit. God's remembrance is the bridge between what was and what will be.

A man remembered by God learns to stand firm when everything around him feels uncertain. He is not shaken by silence, delay, or opposition, because his confidence is not rooted in what he sees but in who God is. This kind of man can wait patiently without losing heart, because he understands that divine timing is never late. He rests securely, not in circumstances, but in the unchanging faithfulness of God, knowing that what God has spoken will surely come to pass. No flood can sweep away what God has preserved and no place of waiting can cancel what God has purposed. Even in hidden seasons, God is working beneath the surface, aligning moments, shaping character, and preparing fulfillment. A man remembered by God does not need to force doors open or fight for validation, because God Himself becomes his defender and his reward. And when the time comes, what God has remembered will manifest with power, proving that His faithfulness alone was always enough.

| 30 |

"BECOMING A NOAH MAN"

Jesus warned that the last days would mirror the days of Noah. People were fully engaged in life yet completely disconnected from the reality of God's timing. They were not watching, not discerning, not preparing. Their hands were full, but their hearts were empty of urgency. They mistook delay for denial, and routine for safety, not realizing that judgment was drawing near while they carried on as if it never would. A man of God in these days must not fall into that same sleep. He must live with spiritual awareness while others live distracted. He must build like Noah built - with obedience, reverence, and a clear understanding that what God has spoken will surely come to pass. While the world laughs, he listens. While others drift, he discerns. His life becomes a testimony that awareness matters more than activity. He walks with God in a time when many ignore Him, and he prepares his household not just for today, but for what is coming. In a blind generation, he chooses to see.

Noah lived in a generation where darkness was normal, compromise was common, and reverence for God had nearly disappeared. Yet he refused to let the condition of the world become the condition of his heart. While others drifted further from God, Noah drew closer. Long before the ark was built, a man was being built - one who chose obedience over convenience and devotion over distraction. True manhood begins in that same place today, not in the approval of others, but in a personal, unwavering commitment to walk with God when no one else does. Righteous manhood is not defined by how a man performs in public, but by who he becomes in private. Noah proved that a man can live clean in a corrupt culture, faithful in a faithless time, and obedient in a disobedient world. Every man must make that same choice: to walk with God regardless of who walks away. That is where legacy begins - with a man who refuses to let darkness define him, because he has already decided that God will.

A Noah man discerns the darkness of his generation without allowing it to dim the light within him. He understands that the times may be evil, but his assignment is still holy, and heaven has not revised its standards to match the culture. While others justify compromise because "everyone is doing it," he remembers that righteousness has always been a personal commitment before God. Like Noah, he walks with God in a world that walks away, proving that holiness is still possible when a man chooses alignment over acceptance. He does not lower his standard to survive the times - he raises his obedience to meet God's call within him. His life becomes living evidence that integrity can endure pressure, that purity can outlast perversion, and that faithfulness can stand when everything else falls. He becomes proof that a man can remain righteous even when unrighteousness surrounds him, and in doing so, he doesn't just preserve himself - he creates a path for others to follow.

Hebrews 11:7 reveals that Noah was "moved with fear," but this was not a paralyzing fear - it was a reverent response to the voice of God. It stirred him to action. While the world around him lived unconcerned, Noah picked up tools and began to build something that had never been seen before. A Noah man does not wait for confirmation from people, applause from crowds, or comfort in circumstances. When God speaks, he moves. His faith steps out of the invisible and takes shape in obedience, even when it looks foolish to others. A Noah man understands that real faith always constructs something.

It builds an ark in the middle of dry ground and prepares for what has not yet happened. Every act of obedience becomes another board in the ark, another step toward preservation, purpose, and promise. Faith that does not move the hands is incomplete, but faith that obeys becomes a refuge not only for the man himself, but for those connected to him.

Noah did not wait for clouds to gather before he started building. There was no rain, no visible threat, no evidence that judgment was coming, yet he committed himself fully to obedience. While others lived casually and dismissed the warning, Noah labored in faith, day after day, shaping something that only made sense through trust in God. Righteous manhood is revealed in that kind of obedience - the willingness to stand apart, to endure misunderstanding, and to act decisively on what God has said rather than what circumstances suggest. This is the strength of a man who walks with God: he does not require visible proof to remain faithful. He builds when it looks unnecessary, prepares when others are careless, and obeys when obedience feels costly or even foolish. Faith like this anchors a man's life in something deeper than public opinion or present reality. It forms a man who leads his household, guards his calling, and honors God long before the storm ever arrives.

A Noah man is not governed by the noise of the crowd, but by the voice of God. While others demand explanations, he walks in obedience. While others mock what they cannot understand, he continues building what God has commanded. He knows that when God has spoken, clarity does not always come to those watching - it comes to the one who is listening. And so he moves forward, not because it makes sense to everyone else, but because it is right before God. He endures misunderstanding without becoming bitter, rejection without losing focus, and questions without wavering in faith. A Noah man is anchored in something deeper than public opinion - he is anchored in the Lord. He understands that obedience often isolates before it elevates, and faithfulness may look like foolishness before it becomes testimony. But he keeps building, keeps trusting, and keeps walking, knowing that in the end, it is not the crowd that validates him - it is God who called him.

In dark times, when confusion is loud and compromise is convenient, the voice of God still calls for men who will walk differently. A man who walks with God develops a steady spirit in an unstable world. He does not panic when others panic, nor does he bend when others bow. While others are reacting, he is listening. While others are drifting, he is anchored. These are the men who carry light into dark places simply because they refuse to let go of God's hand. Families are strengthened, and communities are stabilized, by men who live this way. A man who hears God can lead his home with clarity when everything around him is uncertain. Discipline shapes his daily walk, and integrity guards his decisions. He does not yield to pressure, because he has already settled in his heart who he belongs to. In every generation, God looks for men who will stand when it is easier to sit, who will speak truth when it is safer to stay silent, and who will remain faithful when others fall away.

A Noah man understands that building is a calling. Long before the first drop of rain fell, Noah was already at work, shaping a future no one else could yet see. In the same way, a man of God builds faith in his home through consistent prayer, steady example, and unwavering trust in God's Word. He establishes order in his life by aligning his priorities with heaven, refusing to let chaos rule his decisions. He develops discipline in his spirit, choosing obedience when it is hard and consistency when it is inconvenient. Every quiet act of faithfulness becomes another beam in the ark he is constructing, strong enough to carry those entrusted to him. He does not wait for the storm to reveal his weakness; he prepares so the storm will reveal his strength. While others delay, distract, or deny what is coming, a Noah man moves with urgency and purpose. He builds protection around his family, his mind, and his calling, guarding what God has placed in his hands.

A Noah man does not shrink back when truth becomes uncomfortable. Just as Noah preached righteousness in a generation that refused to listen, so a man of God today understands that silence can be a form of compromise. He does not speak to condemn, but to awaken. His words are not driven by pride or anger, but by a deep burden for souls and a reverence for God's voice. With humility, he refuses to dilute truth to gain acceptance. He knows that real love does not hide truth - it reveals it, even when it is costly. His life reinforces his message. A Noah man does not only warn with his lips, but with his obedience. Every choice he makes becomes a visible testimony that judgment is real, grace is available, and obedience still matters. While others dismiss the warnings, he continues to build, to walk with God, and to stand firm in righteousness. In doing so, he becomes a signpost to his generation - proof that God still speaks, still saves, and still honors those who take Him at His word.

A Noah man leads with intentionality, not passivity. He understands that drift is the silent destroyer of households, and he refuses to let his family be carried by the currents of culture, fear, or compromise. Instead, he sets direction by aligning his life with God's voice. Like Noah building the ark in obedience to what he had never seen, this man moves with conviction before results are visible. His leadership becomes a covering formed not by control, but by consistency, prayer, and example. He brings his household into alignment with obedience, knowing that what he builds in private will preserve them in public. He also knows that true leadership is not domination, but responsibility before God. A Noah man does not rule with force; he carries the weight of accountability. He answers for the atmosphere of his home, the values that are lived out, and the spiritual direction being set. He stands as both a protector and a guide, willing to go first in obedience and endure misunderstanding if necessary.

A Noah man protects with intention and conviction. He understands that the floodwaters of corruption, confusion, temptation, and unbelief are always rising, always pressing, always looking for an open door. He does not live casually with what he allows into his home through conversations, influences, media, or relationships. He discerns what belongs and what does not. Just as Noah built the ark according to God's instruction and sealed it against the waters, a righteous man establishes boundaries that guard the spiritual atmosphere of his household. He knows that protection is having the wisdom to recognize that what enters the house today can shape the destiny of his family tomorrow. A Noah man also protects by presence and example. He does not send his family into safety - he leads them into it. His life becomes the covering, his obedience becomes the shield, and his faith becomes the anchor when storms rise.

A Noah man worships. When the waters recede and the storm has passed, his first instinct is not to celebrate himself, but to honor God. In Gen. 8:20, Noah steps onto dry ground and builds an altar - not a house, not a tower, but a place of sacrifice. This reveals the posture of a righteous man: he remembers who carried him when he could not carry himself. A Noah man understands that deliverance is not the end of the story - it is an invitation to worship. His gratitude becomes visible, his honor intentional, and his devotion unmistakable. Righteous men do not forget God after God brings them through. They do not allow comfort to erase dependence or blessings to replace reverence. A Noah man knows that the same God who shut him in is the God who brought him out, and both moments deserve worship. He refuses to become casual with what once required desperate faith. Instead, he establishes altars in his life so that every new beginning is marked by remembrance.

A Noah man obeys even when the path is unclear and the outcome is unseen. He does not wait for full understanding before he moves - he moves because God has spoken. While others demand explanations, he responds with action. His obedience is not built on comfort or popularity, but on trust. Every step he takes in alignment with God becomes a testimony that faith is alive within him. Where others hesitate, he builds. Where others doubt, he moves forward. His life declares that obedience is greater than explanation, and surrender is greater than certainty. A Noah man would rather stand alone with God than blend in with a crowd moving in the wrong direction. He understands that obedience may cost him approval, relationships, and comfort - but disobedience costs far more. In the quiet places where no one else sees, he chooses righteousness. In the moments where compromise would be easier, he chooses truth. His obedience becomes the evidence that his faith is real, not just spoken.

The making of a righteous man does not begin with perfection - it begins with surrender. It begins with a single, decisive "yes" to God, often spoken in moments of uncertainty, when the path ahead is unclear and the cost is not fully known. That yes may call him to step away from what is familiar, to separate from voices and environments that pull him away from God's will. It may require laying down personal desires, ambitions, and comforts in exchange for obedience. It demands patience when promises seem delayed, and endurance when obedience feels heavy. Yet in that yes, heaven takes notice. God is not looking for a flawless man, but for a willing one - a man who will align his heart with divine instruction no matter the cost. That one yes carries more power than he realizes. It becomes a covering over his household, a shield that preserves his family in times of trouble. It sets a standard that shapes the hearts of those who follow after him, creating a ripple effect that extends beyond his lifetime.

Noah's righteousness did not make him passive - it made him prepared. While the world around him drifted deeper into corruption and indifference, Noah stood anchored in obedience. Righteousness gave him the strength to act when others ignored the warning, to build when there was no visible sign of rain, and to trust when obedience looked foolish. True righteousness is not a retreat from responsibility; it is a readiness to respond to God with unwavering conviction. It is strength under submission - choosing God's way over comfort, over opinion, and over the pressure to conform. In a collapsing world, righteousness becomes a man's stability. It produces faithfulness when everything around him is falling apart. It empowers him to lead, to protect, and to persevere when others quit. Noah did not survive because he was passive - he survived because he was prepared. And that preparation was born from a life surrendered to God.

While others drift through life consumed by what is temporary, a Noah man lives with his spirit alert, discerning the times and recognizing the voice of God when it speaks. He walks with God in quiet obedience, allowing divine insight to shape his decisions. He sees beyond what is visible and understands that what God reveals carries greater weight than what the world celebrates. His life becomes a testimony that spiritual vision is not reserved for the extraordinary, but for the man willing to stay awake when others turn away. To become this kind of man requires courage and commitment. It means preparing for what God has shown you, even when no one else understands the urgency. Like Noah building the ark under clear skies, a righteous man moves by faith, not by popular opinion. He invests his time, energy, and obedience into what will matter when everything else fades. While others are entertained by the moment, he is anchored in eternity.

In the last days, when confusion rises and darkness seems to press in from every side, God is not searching for perfect men - He is searching for obedient men. Men who will build what He commands, even when it makes no sense to others. Men who will speak what He says, even when their voice shakes and the crowd resists. Men who will protect what He has entrusted to them with unwavering resolve. These are the men who stand like Noah, building in faith before the rain ever falls, anchored not in what they see, but in what God has spoken. The measure of a man is found in his response to divine instruction. A true man of God does not retreat when the storm comes - he endures it, leads through it, and when it passes, he worships because he knows who carried him through. These are the men heaven recognizes: builders in secret, voices of truth, guardians of what is sacred, and worshipers in every season. The last days will reveal the men who chose to shine.

A Noah man is formed in quiet, costly obedience. When God spoke to Noah, there was no evidence in the sky to confirm the coming flood - only a word that demanded faith. Yet Noah chose obedience over opinion. He built when it looked foolish, he listened when others mocked, and he followed when it would have been easier to blend in. A man becomes trustworthy to God when he responds with a consistent "yes," even when that yes isolates him. Obedience shapes his character, aligns his heart, and establishes a foundation that cannot be shaken by culture, pressure, or fear. When a man walks with God, builds according to God's instruction, and refuses to compromise, he becomes a refuge in chaotic times. He doesn't panic when the storm comes, because he prepared in obedience before the rain ever fell. This is the kind of man who leads others into safety - not by force, but by example because his life proves that when God can trust a man, that man becomes a shelter in the storm.

SUMMARY

Noah's life reminds us that one righteous man can make a difference in an unrighteous generation. He did not change the world by becoming like the world. He changed the future by obeying God when the world refused to listen. His faith was not passive. His righteousness was not hidden. His obedience was visible, costly, and consistent.

The making of a Noah man begins with grace, but it is revealed through obedience. A righteous man hears God and moves. He believes what others mock. He builds what others do not understand. He leads his family with conviction. He prepares before the storm. He trusts God when the waters rise. He worships when the ground is dry again. And even after failure, he reminds us that righteous men must keep guarding their hearts, their homes, and their legacy.

This generation still needs Noah men. Men who will walk with God when others walk away. Men who will build by faith before the rain begins. Men who will protect their families from the flood of compromise. Men who will stand for righteousness when wickedness becomes normal. Men who will worship after deliverance and begin again with humility.

A Noah man is not perfect, but he is surrendered. He is not popular, but he is faithful. He is not controlled by culture but led by God. He understands that storms do not destroy what obedience has prepared. He knows that when God gives the command, faith must pick up the hammer and start building.

In the end, Noah's greatest testimony was not merely that he survived the flood. It was that he walked with God before the flood ever came. That is the foundation of righteous manhood. That is the strength every man must recover. That is the call of this book. Become a man who walks with God. Become a man who obeys when others laugh. Become a man who builds what heaven commands. Become The Noah Man.